ENDORSEMENTS

Hope. Saving grace. The beauty of redemption and its life-altering effects are set out in Redemption Inc. When you yearn to be a helper but do not know what to do, there is our Beautiful Hope when you think a situation is too tough.

—Marion R. Syversen
Founder & President
Norumbega Financial

Dr. Bucci paints a compelling vision of his road to recovery—how to enter it, travel it, and who will travel it with you—until you reach your destination, a place of purpose, peace, and joy. Share his vision, and the journey becomes better for everyone.

—Mike Klausmeier
Founder & Principal Engineer
Redox Resource Engineering

In an increasingly throw-away world that often discards people when they fail, Dr. Bucci's work is a ray of hope and encouragement for leaders working through complex and possible life-altering situations with those in their charge. A must-read for leaders that genuinely care for their employees.

— Dr. Wendel Weaver
Dean, Chesapeake Energy School of Business Professor
Oklahoma Wesleyan University

Failure is not the end, and Dr. Bucci masterfully goes through the restoration process to complete redemption. This book addresses the damaged, wounded, and cast aside to seek to restore them to fulfilling God's plan for their life. Failure is a learning opportunity and a building block for future success, and this book will take you on the journey to total redemption.

—Jeffrey Ganthner, DSL, AIA
Vice President & General Manager
Mid-Atlantic Region, Burns & McDonnell

Redemption is a concept desperately needed in an increasingly polarized world where people celebrate the fall of their opponents, and the goal too often is to cancel someone rather than see them flourish. Dr. Bucci's work, therefore, is a breath of fresh air, as it focuses on how to restore people—even if that journey is long and hard. Furthermore, as Bucci notes, there is great beauty in a restored life.

—Dr. Josh McMullen
Dean, College of Arts & Sciences
Regent University

Before reading Redemption Inc., I thought I understood redemption as; the act of redeeming or atoning for a fault or mistake. Dr. Joseph Bucci draws us in more profoundly by telling the stories of real people living through real crises. Dr. Bucci takes us on a journey showing what biblical redemption looks like in the lives of ordinary people who miss the mark. My perspective has been wonderfully enhanced and enriched.

—Mark Lawrence
Director of Campus Ministries
Regent University

Redemption Inc. is a compelling compilation of extraordinary stories that remind us that the work of redemption and restoration does not end when we leave the church building or our church circles. This work is an insightful prompt that our own experience of the biblical principle of restoration in our personal lives can and should be applied in varied and practical ways in our vocational lives.

—Jonathan Capeci, MBA
Executive Director
Petra Community Housing

Dr. Bucci conveys the message of hope for many who believe that we serve the God of the second chance. The examples he uses deeply strike the redemptive work that Christ has done in each of us who believe in the salvation of that lost. Having worked with Joe at Geneva, I saw a man who loved the Lord and loved people, and he gave many students a second chance while modeling the heart of a Christian to his peers. Jesus calls us to redeem our world for Him, and this book is an excellent reflection of the power of the Holy Spirit in the lives of many.

—Geno DeMarco
Head Football Coach
Assistant Professor of Business, Geneva College

Through the lives of real people, Dr. Bucci walks us through their pain, brokenness, and the hope of redemption. In reading through each chapter, I could see a mosaic. Each story, each life, represents people we possibly meet every day. Individuals who have made decisions or by no fault of their own; their lives, families, and careers are shattered. Unfortunately, for many, that is how the story ends. Throughout Redemption, Inc., Dr. Bucci reveals the powerful potential of God's grace in redeeming broken, shattered lives. Redemption, Inc. will inspire everyone to be intentional in any way they can to help pick up the broken pieces, and although painful, a mosaic of God's grace, with time, will appear.

—Dr. John O. McCloud
Senior Pastor
Grace River Church

This book introduces an important topic that has long been avoided or ignored in organizational life. In an era when many organizations prefer to "play it safe" and avoid risks, a few find the practical, philosophical, and spiritual motivation to offer second chances to those who have paid the price to experience freedom, sobriety, or personal redemption. This is their story. This is MY story. I am who I am today because of people like those described in this timely book who believe in healing and restoration. My friend Joe Bucci has done us all a favor in providing a thoroughly-researched yet practical guidebook for leaders, employers, and board members worldwide. Redemption Inc. is a must-reading for anybody committed to building resilient, powerful teams and organizations.

—Andy Wood, Ph.D.
Chairman and President
LifeVesting International

A fresh perspective shift permits those who want to apply biblical truths to how they approach business—for both employee and employer.

In a pivotal time in history where the Christian professional must refocus on the Great Commission, Redemption, INC. offers its readers a lively discussion on avoiding personal burnout while establishing a culture of forgiveness rooted in patient mentorship and grace-filled guidance.

A relevant, updated conversation with timeless truth to fill the need for a successful business—personnel relationships. The new standard for Christians on people strategies in the workplace. Through relatable stories, this book gifts its readers hope that they too can witness a miraculous turnaround of someone in a professional setting. It is a simple yet forgotten formula for business: personalized patience paired with a concrete, specific call to action leading to changed lives & mutual blessings.

The advantage every business can feel good about ethically and professionally. The Lord is the only one that will increase profits, protect owner assets and simultaneously advance the Kingdom of God. A brilliant lesson for a growth mindset for the Christian professional through a culmination of success. This author offers the truth that this strategy can offer every occupation and industry the hope and joyful peace that rests in a Divine promise—where God reigns and mutual blessings are guaranteed.

Reedption Inc is a new, relevant solution to yesterday, today, and tomorrow's burnout problem in the Christian business heart & office building. This is a business opportunity every industry will not want to miss. This is the business secret every Christian cannot afford to forget. What I love about this book is its vast range of examples. It offers a relatable story for everyone, interacting with every population and situation. The best part is how the author unifies all by offering the same strategy, revealing its Divine truth. The revolutionary business strategy will see lasting change in every culture and every occupation.

—Louisa Brizendine Curry
Author
#Love Warrior: Admire Him; Adore Her

Joseph Bucci, educator and pastor, and leader, is just Joe. Joe, who loves Jesus. Joe is a consummate professional with a kind and gentle servant's heart, always looking for better ways to help his students and those in our businessmen and pastors' bible study or his church do better.

His latest book Redemption Inc is a marvelous study to help us do better. It is a treatise and a roadmap for coming back from a wide array of destructive behaviors and life hazards; centered around the one true Way, Jesus Christ. And additionally about how businesses can be intimately involved in redemption. Who does not need a way back?

I have my own story of destructive behavior and finding a way back through Jesus, but my friend, Johnny's story, is much more exciting and seemingly impossible. Johnny shot his wife when he caught her cheating on him—fast forward to several years of prison, redemption, struggling to survive because of his new faith in prison. I came to meet Johnny when he was in a halfway house working in the company's warehouse for which I was the new controller.

God used Johnny to be my mentor in the new faith I discovered. Johnny is a black man who shot his wife, and I was wearing 3-piece suits. We were worlds apart on the outside but true brothers on the inside. Johnny exemplified 24/7 Christianity for me. I saw redemption in action daily, in our company, through this ex-convict and his impact on my life and family and many others in our work environment who found the redemptive work of Jesus.

All this was going on while our company had the highest return on investment in our industry. Johnny went on to marry and become a pastor.

I believe in redemption through business because I have seen it through Johnny and many others over time. I believe in Joe, and I believe his book can significantly impact those who need redemption and those who would like to see this happening in their business life.

—Thomas R. Noon
President
C Level Services & Catalyst Cohorts

REDEMPTION INC.

REDEMPTION INC.

From Failure To Forgiveness—From Forgiveness To Freedom—From Freedom To Fulfillment

Why Offering Second Chances Makes Good Business Sense

DR. JOSEPH J. BUCCI

KINGDOM BUSINESS
PRESS
Norfolk • Virginia

Redemption Inc. | Why Offering Second Changes Makes Good Business Sense.

Published by:

Kingdom Business Press | an imprint of New Dominion Press
Norfolk, Virginia 23504
www.NewDominionPress.com

First Edition | First Printing: July 2022

Cover Design by It's a Snapp Designs, Bonnie Snapp Boumt, ItsASnapp@verizon.net
Graphics Design and Typography by Kingdom Business Press

Publisher's Library of Congress Cataloging-in-Publication Data:
(provided by Five Rainbows Cataloging Services)

Names: Bucci, Joseph J., author.

Title: Redemption Inc. : why offering second chances makes good business sense / Joseph J. Bucci.

Description: Norfolk, VA : Kingdom Business Press, 2022. | Includes bibliographical references.

Identifiers: LCCN 2022903337 (print) | ISBN 978-1-7357483-3-7 (paperback) | ISBN 978-1-7357483-4-4 (ebook)

Subjects: LCSH: Business--Religious aspects. | Social responsibility of business. | Success in business. | Work--Psychological aspects. | Spiritual life. | Self-actualization (Psychology) | Biography. | BISAC: BUSINESS & ECONOMICS / Leadership. | BUSINESS & ECONOMICS / Human Resources & Personnel Management. | SELF-HELP / Motivational & Inspirational. | BIOGRAPHY & AUTOBIOGRAPHY / Business.

Classification: LCC HF5387 .B83 2022 (print) | LCC HF5387 (ebook) | DDC 174/.4--dc23.

"E'er since by faith I saw the stream
Thy flowing wounds supply,
Redeeming love has been my theme,
And shall be till I die:
And shall be till I die,
And shall be till I die;
Redeeming love has been my theme,
And shall be till I die."

1772, William Cowper, There is a Fountain

TABLE OF CONTENTS

Appendices

ACKNOWLEDGMENTS

- To Jesus, without whom there would be no redemption.
- To Debi, the love of my life. Thank you for your encouragement and friendship, and for providing the support I needed to see this project through to the end.
- To my beloved children, to whom I am grateful beyond measure, not only for their feedback throughout this project, but also for their testimony of Redemptive Faith which they model so well for the Next Generation.
- To the men and women of the Thursday morning Bible study. You have modeled Redemptive Leadership to me and to so many others. Many of the stories in this book started with you.
- To my friend and publisher Chuck. I told you we'd get it done. It just took 7 years. Thanks for your patience and help.
- To everyone who picks up this book and reads the stories. I was told I needed to cut back on the content. But I couldn't. The stories are so inspiring, and they all need to be told.

INTRODUCTION

Things Are Not Always What They Seem

"Things are not always what they seem; the first appearance deceives many; the intelligence of a few perceives what has been carefully hidden."

— ***Phaedrus***

Abstract: Things are not always what they seem to be. Successful people may not simply be perfect, and many have needed support and help to overcome life-controlling substances. The book begins with the story of an entertainer who needed such help; and the work of redemption and restoration outside of the "altar" experience.

A Funny Guy Changed from the Inside

It is hard for us to imagine that anyone starring as a children's entertainer or coming into our homes with a positive message could have been the complete opposite as a human being growing up. However, that is the story of Tim Allen.

His birth name was Timothy Allen Dick. He grew up in a home where he lost his father to a drunk driving accident at 11 years old. According to Bailey (2017), Tim wondered if he could have done something to prevent his father's death. Could he have prayed more? He wanted answers from God at that minute.

Like many others who lost a loved one in that situation, Allen turned to drugs and alcohol abuse. According to Longeretta (2021), Allen learned to play games with people and told them what they wanted to hear.

Allen lived a double life, pretending to be sincere while abusing alcohol, drugs, and stealing from everyone (Longeretta, 2021). He also became a dealer.

A dramatic turn occurred when drug sniffing dogs caught Allen at the Kalamazoo Battle Creek airport with about 650 grams of cocaine, about a pound and a half. This could have quickly put him in prison for life, and he pled guilty and gave up the names of the other drug dealers in his Network. This lowered his sentence, putting his life in extreme danger (Longeretta, 2021).

In prison, Allen said he learned to live day-by-day and to shut up. He went back and forth between three prisons following his arrest for his protection, and each experience affected him differently. Nevertheless, an overall shame permeated the entire time. There was this sad irony: while Tim was broken-hearted that a drunk driver killed his father, he found himself at the time driving stone-cold drunk from place to place with people in his car. The memory haunted him (Longeretta, 2021).

All of the hardship and tragedy and the shame of the experience drove Tim to fundamental questions about his life and who made him (FaithIt.com, 2016). He talked about seeking the builder who made him, and he wanted to know his purpose. This builder concept became fundamental in his transformational recovery and later life (Bailey, 2017). We know this builder to be God.

It seems that those in the evangelical community would be well-versed in redemption and transformational change based on their understanding of the "born again" experience and the admonition in 2 Corinthians 5:17 (English Standard Version), "Therefore, if anyone is in Christ, the new creation has come: The old has gone, the new is here!" Participants have a front-row seat to some of the most exciting transformational change processes.

One of the significant tenets of Evangelicalism is the belief that lives need to be transformed through a sanctification process, including a "born-again" experience and an ongoing process of discipleship (NAE, n.d.). When speaking of the "born-again" experience of change, many articles reviewed for this book utilized personal anecdotes to describe the change process. Ackers and Preston (1997), in an article describing the impact of religious experiences in the lives of employees in the workplace, move beyond personal anecdotes to more substantial support with data to verify that a transformation does occur in the lives of individuals who express having gone through this born-again experience (Ackers and Preston, 1997). The authors cite Martin (1993) and write that there is little doubt that a religious identification with becoming a new creation can be a significant and life-changing experience (Ackers and Preston, 1997). So much for this spiritual transformation (2 Corinthians 5:17)—we do become new creations.

Most people leaving the altar after praying the sinner's prayer do not recognize that while all things have become new in the spiritual realm (2 Corinthians 5:17), there are still some habit patterns that must be changed and new habit patterns learned to support this transformation. So there is a combination of spiritual renewal, sometimes accompanied by an emotional response, combined with a recognition that something has changed in the relationship between God and man, followed by the admonition that behavioral change needs to occur to complete the transformation (John 8:11; Romans 6:1). There is solid spiritual support in repentance and its related renewal process to build actual behavioral change (Hebrews 4:12), with the Holy Spirit as Advocate and Teacher guiding this process (John 14:26).

What is the value of offering a new life through Christ's redemptive work if not accompanied by a complete change in behavior? It was our sinful state, evidenced by selfish behavior, which required atonement for sin and transformational change. Many pastors describe repentance as a 180-degree change of direction (Giorgio, 2008). The redemptive act of Christ, in taking our place, to pay the penalty for our disobedience to God, creates a response by those undertaking this selfless act, who then acknowledge their sinful state and then receive this new life through a confession of sin and an expressed desire to change their behaviors. Historically, we have called this the "ABCs of Salvation" (LifeWay Church Resources, 1984).

Tim Allen was always a funny guy. At least he thought he was. One of his friends challenged him to see how funny he was. On a dare, a friend challenged him to do a stand-up routine at a club in Detroit (Hiskey, 2010). He did this before prison. Once he got out of prison, at 29 years old and being an ex-con, he had difficulty finding any other work.

So he tried his hand at stand-up comedy again. We all know how this turned out for him.

However, this is not the end of the story. While the story of Allen's transformation as a young man is well-reported, what is less known is the relapse into alcoholism and a DUI which occurred some 22 years ago (Bueno, 2020). In our experience with the church world and change management, there's a thought that change happens and sticks. But that is not often the case. Sometimes those demons continue to reside, and we need help to exercise them thoroughly. Allen told Kelly Clarkson that these things do not happen overnight; it is day-to-day (Bueno, 2020).

While Allen does not mention the program in which he found his deliverance, he had help working through the process of recovery in his second bout with alcoholism. He mentioned in the Clarkson interview that he attended rehab and found help to change his practices to avoid this from occurring again.

So this book is about people needing help, what we are calling a redemptive intervention, in order for them to get their lives back on track or to keep their lives on track. However, there is also another fundamental truth here. Once someone goes through this restorative process, can they find a job? Are they employable? Will some employers be willing to take the risk and offer them second-chance opportunities? This is when the brightness of their lives can shine. The employer may think they are getting a deal—taking a chance on using the talents and abilities of this broken and failed individual—what is there to lose? Not only might they gain help for some project or activity in the short term, but they may find a diamond in the rough and infuse this former addict or criminal with the purpose that, once again, they can support themselves and contribute to society.

Tim Allen is a great man because he recognized his problem and admitted he had an addiction. Nevertheless, if those stand-up comedy episodes were not followed up by someone taking a chance on Tim, he would just be another recovering alcoholic or former prisoner. We know him for who he is today because someone took a chance on his abilities and looked past his failings and shortcomings, prison sentences, and addiction.

A former economic policy adviser for two presidents knows the importance of work and the esteem that comes when someone unemployable can again find work after a redemptive intervention (Lapin, 2020). Larry Kudlow openly discussed his battle with alcohol and drug addiction at a White House event as part of National Recovery month in 2020. Kudlow encouraged others and stayed in touch with those who helped him through this process, even after 25 years. "You can get sober, stay sober, and lead a productive life," Kudlow said (Lapin, 2020). Kudlow also acknowledged that it was by the grace of God that his wife did not leave him while he was going through treatment to get his addiction under control (Lapin, 2020). But Kudlow was transparent about his situation: "I was unemployable" (Lapin, 2020). Today we see him as a television personality and senior economic advisor to the highest levels of government. Kudlow heaped praise on his employer, sticking with him through that difficult time.

Called to Partner in Redemptive Action

Christianity has done as well to promote the dignity of each human being since each human being was created in the image of God, and Jesus Christ died on behalf of each human being. Jesus' service while on earth provided dignity and value to those who felt valueless in society. So while true and lasting transformation occurs through a heart change that only God can provide (Ezekiel 36: 26-27), the Spirit of God calls many men and women into service to assist troubled and failed individuals to find a path to recovery so that they can live a whole and bountiful life available to each person created in the image of God. Redemption has already taken place in the spiritual realm, and transformation and sanctification are part of the ongoing work of God.

This book is about those unheralded souls who may be future comedians and advisors to presidents or simply moms and dads or sons and daughters. They are working to recover from substance abuse or life-controlling situation. Someone in a facility or center or someone who leads an unglamorous 12-step group has committed themselves to help in the restoration process of these precious children of God, built, as Allen says, by a master builder who has a purpose for their lives (Bailey, 2017).

Tim Allen has found his sobriety, and God has blessed him with success, and he has taken his success and paid it forward to help others. The same thing can be said about people like Larry Kudlow and Mike Lindell, presently well-known maker of "My Pillow," a former drug addict whose life has been turned around (Lindell, 2019). Lindell's efforts to achieve sobriety have motivated him to create centers to support those struggling with the same life-controlling substances.

We only see the end-product of the work done by those serving in these restorative programs, the process we are calling here "Redemption, INC." There has been much work done behind the scenes to adjust a tragic course of a person's out-of-control life to one of being a positive contributor. These well-known men mentioned here know the power of redemption and restoration. The journey we begin here describes those dedicated servants in many different settings who are working with troubled, broken, and failed people—people just like us—to offer the hope of change and a vision for a life that now can contribute to society, instead of draining resources and frustrating emotional family members. These precious souls are hoping for a second chance to work and express their gifts and talents in our workplaces.

What is our role in response to these issues? Can we be a part of God's means to accomplish His redemptive plan on earth as it is in heaven (Matthew 6:10 NIV)? A great opportunity awaits us all!

CHAPTER 1
Redemption in the Land of Oz

Stories of Overcoming Failure, Fury, and Fear

Abstract: Did you know that the 'Wizard of Oz' was a redemption story? 'The Wizard of Oz' story serves as a proxy or type for three disparate characters, searching for meaning and needing redemption to fulfill a greater purpose. This opening chapter describes three individuals beset by significant challenges, some of their own making. Their stories are introduced here, while the main focus of this book is further developed, that being the agencies and dedicated personnel that pursue the restoration of individuals defeated by circumstances that have come to a desperate end of the line. Each of these stories and the transformation processes through which they all went will then be delineated later in the book.

Introduction

While a few films were beginning to use colorization effects in the motion picture process during the late 1930s, the Technicolor business itself was suffering from more than two decades of losing money and low demand in the heart of the Depression ("Color in the Movies," 1934). This new technology came to the forefront in 1939 when it was used to make two blockbuster films: *Gone with the Wind* and *The Wizard of Oz* (Cook and Sklar, 2017). *The Wizard of Oz* was the first motion picture to attempt the transition from Black-and-White to Color (Campbell, 2014). What might be perceived as a simple process today was technically challenging in 1939, but to the amazement of all who watched it, this transition was an eye-opening special effect.

The movie *The Wizard of Oz* was based on the successful children's fairy tale series, *The Wonderful Wizard of Oz* by L. Frank Baum. Baum published the original children's novel in 1900 and followed up with 13 more books based in the Land of Oz.

According to Zipes, a strong theme of redemption flows through many American fairy tales of the nineteenth and early twentieth centuries (Zipes, 2007). Zipes' examination of the original Oz story reveals that the three characters that Dorothy meets and seeks to help on her way to the Emerald City—the Scarecrow, the Tin Woodsman, and the Cowardly Lion—all have within them the potential that they perceive to be lacking. By their intervention in helping an exasperated Dorothy achieve something beyond herself, these talents are redemptively cultivated and brought to the forefront (Zipes, 2007). How ironic that the use of Technicolor in making this film was one of the keys to the redemption of this business model and the flourishing of the budding color motion picture industry (Cook and Sklar, 2017).

The Wizard of Oz story is very familiar to those growing up in the Baby Boomer generation. While Dorothy seems to be the one in particular who needs to find her way back home to Kansas, on her journey, she inspired three other significant characters who found a higher purpose in serving her.

The Scarecrow sensed no value in his contribution, but is freed by Dorothy from his lofty perch in a vain attempt to scare off birds seeking to eat the crops. He desired a brain to put his life to better use. The Tin Woodsman (also known as the Tin Man) was left out in the rain and rusted up. He had a responsibility to complete tasks but without any sensitivity manually. Like the ax he carried, he was only but a tool in the hands of others—he desired a heart. Dorothy releases him from his frozen state with a can of oil, and he sets about help Dorothy find her way home. The Cowardly Lion was the opposite of how lions are perceived in the wild—ferocious and respected because of their great prowess. Sensing nothing of his proud heritage, he cowered at danger. He desired the courage of his convictions. He follows Dorothy and her rag-tag band, hopeful that this Wizard could give him the courage he lacked.

However, the more significant cause of defending Dorothy on her journey to reach home raised his sights to see that he could be more than he had believed in the past. All three successfully helped defeat the Wicked Witch attacks and facilitated the return of Dorothy to Kansas. In Baum's original story, each one has a vital leadership role in the Land of Oz.

Three Unique Paths to Full Restoration and Usefulness

In this opening chapter, these three disparate characters, searching for meaning and needing redemption to fulfill a greater purpose, serve as types describing three individuals beset by significant challenges, some of their own making. Here is a brief look at three of God's precious children, seeking to serve Him with their whole hearts, looking for a way out of crushing personal failure. Each vignette is summarized here in this chapter; later on in the book, more detail is given about each individual's unique paths to complete restoration.

The first is a ministry leader, unaware of the significance of his influence and the ease in which some innocent teasing might lead to presumptions that his personal needs were not being met. He ended up nearly ruining his family until he became mindful of precisely what had happened. Through a restoration process, he was able to recover not only his family but also his ministry. The second was a soldier who became apathetic to the point of rebellion, where he lost his heart and his desire to serve his country and became destructive and self-serving. Only through the intervention of senior military officers and his internment in a "last-chance" program instituted by volunteer leaders in this branch of the service was he able to find a heart to serve others. Furthermore, the third character finally lost any sense of self-worth and was crushed by a domineering spouse. By God's grace, this one found the courage to leave that circumstance—but needed a redemptive intervention to find purpose and escape beyond her role in bondage.

What do a failed pastor, a rebellious sailor, and an abused wife have in common with the Wizard of Oz? What might they even have in common? These individuals failed to fulfill their perceived role's expectations and were drowning in self-loathing and despair. Apart from a redemptive intervention, each of these people and hundreds like them would go on to destroy the hope of their families, friends, loved ones, and even themselves. But social institutions with compassionate people, many of whom themselves had overcome similar destructive behaviors, stood in the gap to restore the potential of these unique souls, enabling those most deeply hurt by life's circumstances to find hope again.

This book describes these three and other precious individuals, damaged by their own or others' selfish choices. Without some redemptive intervention, they would live only partial lives, some with bitterness and some with contempt for themselves and "the system" that abandoned them.

Here we will meet three people who went through three separate restorative programs. Each of the programs they journeyed through was designed uniquely for the individual in their respective situation. We use The Wizard of Oz as a metaphor for their healing journeys.

In this book, these individuals and several others will describe their journeys from hopefulness through despair and then the restoration process and its effects on their present lives. First, we will briefly introduce the genesis of this research and give an overview of three unique redemptive journeys, facilitated by imperfect processes in the hand of a perfect God, where three lives were reclaimed to live and fully function again as they were meant to be.

Some Reflections on the Previous Work

In the first book *Redemptive Leadership* (Bucci, 2016), the focus was on finding redemption in the management literature and then identifying redemptive managerial behaviors most often observed in the successful reinstatement of employees previously terminated for cause. The first book documents the steps taken by managers who acted to offer redemptive opportunities to workers who were terminated for cause. Examples from the popular culture were also given, offering encouragement to other managers that they might consider following these steps to act redemptively within their organizations. The first book not only told the stories of individuals given second-chance opportunities but organizations that were active in offering second chances. The first book provides catalogs and examples of this effort to offer reinstatement and redemption to a formerly successful employee terminated for cause. It also shows that other talented people, tainted by mistakes and failures, can be restored to contribute to an organization effectively.

In this follow-up work, we will describe organizations and individuals committed to restoring individual lives. The new book details the redemption and reinstatement of people who were previously overcome by life-controlling problems or abused by circumstances that nearly destroyed them. These people have value and are created in the image of God. As image-bearer, we have much to offer to our culture. God designed humankind to serve and contribute to society and live lives that would glorify Him (Isaiah 43:6-7; Mark 3:2-6). However, circumstances and bad choices nearly crippled some of us, and many people of worth need a guide and a redemptive hand to offer hope.

The organizations described in the book have demonstrated a successful approach to restoring and redeeming hundreds of individuals bound in anger and despair. With the approval of recent legislation offering second chances to former convicts (The White House, Office of the Press Secretary, 2019), for-profit businesses and non-profit organizations across the spectrum should be more actively seeking to recruit and hire these potential employees with "success stories."

In the search for more signs of "Redemptive Leadership," we had discovered more writing on this topic than was previously available when the first book was written (Powers, 2019; and others). Nevertheless, this follow-up book focuses on the agencies and dedicated personnel that pursue the restoration of individuals defeated by circumstances that have come to a desperate end of the line. We will briefly use the "Wizard of Oz" motif to highlight three persons needing a redemptive intervention. Each of these stories and the transformation process through which they went will be delineated later in the book.

Redemption from Failure

It is interesting to consider the fallen pastor as a type of Scarecrow in this analogy. Pastors regularly warn people about evil influences in their preaching, and birds in scripture are always associated with wicked behavior (Rickenbaugh, 1997). There is also the parallel of a fallen Minister not using their head: an example of an individual with excellent skills but not thinking through the consequences of an action.

Author Thom Rainer previously served as a Dean at The Southern Baptist Theological Seminary (Rainer, 2014) and has met with countless clergy and church staff regarding the issues of clergy burnout and ministry failure (Rainer, 2014). Rainer describes some mindless choices that should serve as warning signs or mileposts on the road to this failure and destruction. These warning signs include private counseling sessions, which become a place to complain to a friendly audience, and an attraction is built. Then some coworkers begin to confide in each other on a profound level. There is that member of the congregation or ministry who makes us feel good about ourselves while dealing with stress at home. There are too many pastors or church workers who have no accountability systems, and then those who travel much and spend too much time away from family or too much time with members of the opposite sex.

The conversation that seems to come up most often, according to Rainer (2014), starts with the words, "I never thought this would happen to me" (Rainer, 2014). As it is, Pastoral Ministry is a challenging environment. Those who go into it thinking they have it all figured out are often the ones who find that they are not prepared to handle the stress and then find an escape in the arms of someone with whom they are not married.

However, we are not just describing failure from misplaced intimate relationships. There is a growing trend that denominations face from the failures and abandonment in pastoral ministry. According to the book *Fail* (Briggs, 2014), some 1500 pastors per month abandon their pasture vocation either because of burnout or contention in their congregations (Briggs, 2014). Even more striking, according to an older article in *Leadership Journal* (Reed, 2006), 19,200 pastors are asked to leave their ministries each year; no one knows how many of these are due to moral lapses (Reed, 2006).

The problems with the pastoral ministry are compounded by unique pressures faced. While both of the above statistics are particularly devastating, there does not seem to be a clear path on how to stem the tide or help those forced to leave. The Reed article in Leadership Journal (2006) provides good details on many different denominational approaches. Nevertheless, there does not appear to be one unified approach taken in addressing this issue. According to Reed, in 2006, while some denominations had developed at least a cursory approach to address the restoration of failed pastors, there were still many denominations and most independent churches with no plan (Reed, 2006).

One fallen minister looking for restoration to an active ministry role described the process: "Basically, we were told that I would be out of ministry for two years," the young man said. "We would be required to move away from our former church to attend a church in our denomination, and I would meet with the pastor of that church. However, I would not be able to do any ministry during that time. After two years, the denomination would meet to reconsider my appointment. Beyond that, there was no meaningful 'process.' The denominational supervisors did not want to hear from me until my two-year sentence was over. I was mostly on my own to figure it out" (Reed, 2006).

Redemption from Fury

Here our second individual demonstrates a good head for numbers and a strong interest in serving. However, like the Tin Woodsman, his heart was missing in action. He made a series of poor decisions, and the consequences he suffered unmasked a root of bitterness in his heart which grew into a furious rage.

He was promised that after boot camp and some specialized training, he would be able to get on a track where he could pursue Special Operations training. An elite assignment, the best of the best. He was looking at an assignment with an explosives ordinance team, a very high honor with much responsibility. Be believed he was capable and was moving along to pursue his dream.

He began to find trouble because it was there waiting for him. He was first given discipline because he violated the rules by bringing a woman on base. The discipline was pretty significant—14 days of restriction—but this violation also prevented him from pursuing Special Operations training.

He was frustrated and angry by the severity of the decision. This one violation stripped him of all the other options. He went from ship-based training in intelligence to being stuck on a destroyer, a lower-level position. He started acting out and violating rules more and more frequently, which finally led to him being "awarded" a 45-day restrictive discipline. When receiving a punishment, you are "awarded" punishment in the Navy. A 45-day restriction is the most that anyone can be awarded without being kicked out of the Navy. Sailors receiving this discipline lose half of their pay.

They live on the ship and cannot go home; they wake up before everyone else, and they have to work later than everyone else. They are assigned work over and above what their regular job would be. This discipline was a little bit of a wake-up call for this young man, and he tried to turn things around. He demonstrated six months of good behavior, trying to earn his good name back.

He again violated rules while riding a motorcycle without the required safety course. Through some carelessness, a police chase ensued, and he crashed the bike and wound up in the hospital. After that, he went to jail for one night. Once the news reached his command, he received another 45 days of restriction, his third offense. He could have been kicked out, but he was not. After the discipline, he tried again to clean up his act. Then he had another major violation. What now?

The Navy had to do something, either kick him out or something else. There was a pause before the final decision was made. In the interim, he considered suicide. He had enlisted as a young man at 19, trying to get away from drugs and other demons in his hometown. He thought the military would help straighten out his life, but he continued to exhibit poor choices and bad behavior. He was afraid to be sent back home. He had gone from being the head of his academic class, leading in Special Ops training, to being considered an outcast and bound tightly in this extreme restriction. He had cemented his reputation as a mess-up, a rule breaker. So what is to happen to him now? Soon the ship's captain will have to decide what to do with this rule-breaker.

Redemption from Fear

Our final vignette considered the life of a confident and self-assured woman crushed by spousal abuse and overwhelmed with fear of reprisal. This character more closely represents the *Cowardly Lion*—bred with the potential to achieve great things, graced by a demeanor of proud elegance—who was now literally trapped in this situation with no apparent means of escape.

There are alarming statistics for domestic abuse in the United States called "intimate partner violence" (IPV) in a report from the Centers for Disease Control and Prevention (Breiding, Chen, and Black, 2014). According to a 2014 report based on 2010 data by the US CDC (Breiding, Chen, and Black, 2014), nearly 1 in 4 US women will be victims of severe violence by an intimate partner in their lifetimes compared to 1 in 7 US men. Another research article collected data from several sources besides the CDC data and reported that worldwide, the lifetime prevalence of intimate partner violence ranged from 19 to 66 percent among women aged 15 to 24, with most of the data sources identified reporting a prevalence above 50 percent (Stockl, March, Pallitto, and Garcia-Moreno, 2014).

From the perspective of outsiders, everything in her family life seemed normal. Her husband had a good job, and she was active in caring for her two children and taking them to school. DeKerseredy and Schwartz (2009) wrote about intimate partner abuse in rural communities, such as this individual, in their groundbreaking research (DeKerseredy and Schwartz, 2009). These authors sought to address the stereotype that such cases are not as prevalent in small rural communities compared in urban areas. The authors suggested that while a woman in a rural community may face less violent crimes at the hands of strangers, the social structure of this same rural community might make her more vulnerable to violence at the hands of a husband or boyfriend (DeKerseredy and Schwartz, 2009).

For our *Cowardly Lion* character, the abuse and darkness kept worsening and would occur more often. A point of choice came: She had been on her own since she was 17, and now she is 31 with two children. After two years of praying and waiting for a chance to make a change, the time to step away from this abusive environment was at hand. Later, she would reflect on all of this abuse and realize that she was the fourth generation of women living through this terror, giving some sense of how challenging it would be to step away from this toxic situation. The real question is, "into what is she stepping?" This close-knit community was all she knew, and they all knew her—or thought they did. How would she be able to get the help she needed?

Each Life Has Purpose Beyond Frustrations of Failure

The tales of these individuals, who represent the Scarecrow, the Tin Man, and the Cowardly Lion, respectively, do not end with their frustration along the road to Oz. In the fairy tale, each individual makes it to Oz and ultimately finds fulfillment through a redemption process. Not simply because they arrived at their destination, but because of their challenges along the way. These individuals each faced what is described by Harv Powers as their "crucible of crisis" moment (Powers, 2018) and, through these crises, were able to use the talents that they had with some coaching and encouragement by Dorothy and the Wizard, to find their place in contributing to Dorothy's ultimate return to Kansas.

Likewise, the people in the stories mentioned above overcame the despair of the situations in which they found themselves. Because of the grace of redemptive interventions by groups committed to the restoration of individuals like them, they found fulfillment and purpose later in their lives. These lives and their purposes were not permanently labeled failures and were not limited or restricted by the wrong choices or the circumstances outside their control.

Each person has a purpose, one of specific design, and a journey of discovery waiting to be unleashed. Each person is created in the image of God, which ascribes their worth, beauty, and value. Thanks to organizations such as those mentioned in these pages, now these people have been given back their lives and purposes and are positively contributing to society. They are also helping to pay it forward and offer similar opportunities to others to pursue their calling. This book was written to tell these stories, but it was also to awaken employers, those with a desire to invest in the restoration of others, and the opportunity to sponsor groups such as the ones in this book. Without outside support, they could not carry on their mission. Without these organizations carrying out their mission, and without partnering employers and those investing their careers in this work, lives such as our Scarecrow, the Tin Man, and the Cowardly Lion would remain lost in the despair of unfulfilled purpose, and redemption would remain a fairy tale.

A "Dorothy" Named Dina

As we sat in a circle, asking for prayer requests, a petite unassuming woman came forward and asked us to pray for her job. It was not that she was losing her job or that her job was not paying her well. She loved her job, but her job was more than she could handle, especially the heartache.

She worked in a probation officer capacity. She recommended young juvenile offenders for opportunities once they had completed their service term. She could see that many of them had great potential, but they lacked the skills to follow through. She helped them with resumes and applications and coached them on job interview skills. Some of these juvenile program graduates went on to find employment opportunities and found terrific success. Even with a checkered past, some trusting employers offered second chances, making all the difference, thanks to Dina's persistence and her unwavering support for her charges. She called them to follow up and marveled at how a job with a purpose had changed their lives. However, some of her former offenders took jobs, but they were terminated after a while when some bad habits returned.

Dina is our Dorothy, and she is on the front line of helping those who have been strongly affected by a broken home or angry fathers and have sought violence or petty crimes to express their feelings of loss. Now, without a job and a cause for which to live, they will become a statistic and go on from Juvenile Detention to more severe crimes. However, Dina is also at risk.

While focusing on Texas probation personnel, one study (Lee, Phelps & Beto, 2009) also notes information they were able to collect from other states. As noted in the study, Florida probation agencies reported a turnover of 30% for their probation staff, and Texas juvenile probation reported close to 20% turnover among the state juvenile probation officers (Lee, Phelps & Beto, 2009). That compares with a 31% turnover for juvenile detention center personnel (Lee, Phelps & Beto, 2009).

While the article addresses some of the rationales behind turnover, the fact is that turnover among this group of front-line transitional restoration personnel is high. According to the study, Probation officers lack solid emotional support and encouragement from their supervisors. They carry with them some aspects of the tragedies, frustrations, and difficulties of the individuals with whom they work. More than one-quarter of this group, when asked, did not want to spend the rest of their careers in their current functions, and a high percentage did not feel a strong sense of belonging to their department—making their jobs even more complex and performing them at a high level almost impossible. This group of critical personnel is on the front line is helping these disaffected juveniles find success as they return to more of a normative experience. What should we expect from those they serve if this group is not healthy?

Another purpose of this book is to acknowledge an appreciation for the sacrifices and services provided by the "Dinas" of this world—those "Dorothys" who work with the Scarecrows and Tin Men and Cowardly Lions with all their warts and stiff joints—that they might be encouraged that the work they are doing was not in vain. This book offers people, like Dina, the hope that some employers will take the opportunity to offer second chances to juvenile offenders. They will offer hope, encouragement, and some "tough love" counseling, and maybe some of these will achieve restoration to a greater purpose.

Some businesses and individuals believe in this cause. They are willing to partner with organizations to complete this circle—that will allow people to find their connections to meaningful jobs and purposes, apart from the hurt and frustrations they have felt. Their stories are told in chapter 14.

CHAPTER 2
The Slough of Despond

Safely Crossing the Slough of Despond

Abstract: Professional ministry to those who are hurting and need a release from sin is arduous work. This leads to incredible stress, burnout, and occasionally an escape from it into the arms of someone with whom they are not married. This act devastates not only this individual and their family; but also a congregation and a movement. However, even with the increasing numbers of pastors failing, few denominations offer a process for restoration—and some do not believe there should be one. Lessons from one pastor's restoration process are under consideration as a follow-up to Chapter 1.

Introduction

The "Slough of Despond" is an illusory deep bog mentioned in John Bunyan's allegory *Pilgrim's Progress*. In the story, the protagonist, Christian, sinks in the bog under the weight of his sin and, as Thomas writes, "the scum and filth of a guilty conscience" (Thomas, 1964).

Thomas (1964), in his paraphrase of *Pilgrim's Progress,* writes, "this Slough is such a place that cannot be mended. It is the low ground where the scum and filth of a guilty conscience, caused by the conviction of sin, continually gather" (Thomas 1964). Interestingly, in Bunyan's first pass at writing this classic tome, the word 'Slough' was not included; instead, it was the 'Slow' of Despond (Offor, editor of *The Works of John Bunyan*, 1853). The slough or bog is a much more appropriate place to consider where one settles in as they dwell on the guilt and self-loathing of their sin. Thomas, in his paraphrase, continues regarding the slough: "As sinners are awakened by the Holy Spirit and see their vile condition, there arise in their souls' many doubts and fears, and many discouraging apprehensions, all of which merge and settle in this place; and that is the reason for this marshy slough" (Thomas, 1964).

It is easy to see this "Slough" place of self-loathing as a reflection of how a church leader feels after admitting to letting down their family and congregations due to sexual sin.

This chapter is the story of one pastor arriving at a place no pastor wants to be—having broken faith with his commission and his spouse by having sexual relations with a church member. He wants to restore his relationship with his wife and recover an opportunity to serve in this pastoral role again. However, he is unsure of the process for restoration, if there even was one in his particular denomination.

We will recount his story here, along with a review of the previous discussion in the first chapter under the representation of the Scarecrow: someone scattering the birds—which in scripture represents evil—but someone not cognizant about how to protect themselves from a calamitous failure. While he has freely shared his story for this work, we will use a pseudonym and call him "Pastor X" (personal communication, September 25, 2020).

Not a Sudden Fall but a Sudden Realization

Our family attended his church. I had heard pieces of the story in the past but did not realize that it was reasonably open for others to know. He had failed, fallen hard from a senior role in a denomination where he was given not only the leadership of one congregation but oversight for several churches in a region.

We will not get into the gory details. It is not about sensationalism, it is about the fact that Pastor X had violated trust. He had sexual relations with someone in his congregation. It was not a one-time mistake of judgment, and it was an ongoing affair that lasted several months. Furthermore, it does not even appear to have happened by accident. There was some attraction back and forth and movement towards this eventual outcome.

He knew that he was in too deep. His heart and conscience were burning. He knew that he had sinned and violated trust. So he must admit his failure. He was in pain; he was hurting. Moreover, now he will hurt the person closest to him—he admits his failure to his wife. She is devastated.

After confessing to his wife, there must be a decision on whom to tell next. This was a very, very painful time for his wife. He wants to comfort her somehow, but others are involved here, and this private sin could soon become scandalous.

So now, what should he do? Whom should he call? From the point when he acknowledged that he sinned and let down his family and his church, Pastor X knew he needed to do something about it. Is there an approach or standard by which this process takes shape? He told me that he must decide. Does he go to his leaders or just move to another church? Could he just move on to another church and not clean up this mess?

According to this pastor (Pastor X, personal communication, September 25, 2020), in the specific denomination in which he held credentials, there was no official restoration program regarding helping pastors deal with an issue and then get back into pastoral ministry. So, unfortunately, with no plan, process, or approach to pursue, Pastor X honestly expressed what often happened: secrets would stay secrets, and leaders would move on or keep running. Issues were left unaddressed, a family left shattered, and congregations left wondering what happened.

Some pastors would move on, hoping that no one heard about it. Unaddressed, there could be a point in time when a congregant comes and says, "Hey, I heard about you in this other church…" similar to another story in a future chapter with someone coming out of a past life in the Adult Film industry and just trying to move on. In that case, it meant changing their name, hiding from the shameful past, and finding a new place where no one knew them to start again if possible (Sheehy, 2011).

In the case of a pastor who commits adultery and tries to move on, Pastor X may not have dealt with the issue or his splintered family. They are on the run and living with that fear. They want to move on and not even confess their failure outside of their family but act as if nothing has happened. However, this meant looking over his shoulder for the rest of his life.

Claiming Responsibility

So after he talks with his wife about all this, he calls his immediate leadership, his ordaining Bishop. The procedure has to be driven by the individual regional leadership because there is no program. He and his wife did not want to live on the run, looking over their shoulders and then trying to defend something down the road, and they wanted to deal with the issue.

The Bishop recommended that he publicly confess this sin before the church, and the Bishop would come there for this meeting. One rule that the denomination does have is that if a pastor confesses his sin before the church, he and his family must leave the church. Pastor X and his wife had already met with the Bishop, and this was a difficult meeting because they were friends. The Bishop and his wife came over and stayed with this couple prior to this disclosure meeting. Also, most of the State Leadership was there at the pastor's church that Sunday. This was a significant denominational church in the area. So all the State Leadership was there. It was another problematic meeting for all involved.

So the day of the reveal occurs. Now things begin to move very fast. Pastor X explained that he had maybe two weeks to move out of the church parsonage when he stepped down from his leadership role in a congregation. While this may differ among congregations and denominations, suddenly, in two weeks, there is no more housing (if you are in a church home), and in two weeks, there is no job either. The church was gracious and gave Pastor X and his family a little bit of severance. He and his family needed support and counseling, so doesn't two weeks' notice seem sudden and harsh?

Nevertheless, it is not a good idea to stay. Next, Pastor X loses his credentials. A great deal of loss. A challenging time. However, there must be a recognition by the perpetrator that this sin is an issue, and it must be addressed. If Pastor X, or any pastor in a similar situation, does not recognize a need he must address, it will never be addressed.

There is a Need, But for What?

Let us step aside and acknowledge the data suggesting this is a significant issue.

SoulShepherding (Gaultiere, 2019) provided several lists of statistical data about pastoral failure. The website lists seven reliable sources from which they collected the data on which their research is drawn (Gaultiere, 2019).

Under the heading, "Pastoral Ministry Stress Statistics," 75% of pastors report being extraordinarily stressed; 90% of pastors feel fatigued or worn out every week. 78% of pastors were forced to resign at least once from a church (63% at least twice from churches). The data stream continues: 80% of pastors surveyed will not be in this professional ministry role ten years from now. 100% of 1050 Reformed and Evangelical pastors reported having a colleague who left the professional ministry because of burnout, church conflict, or moral failure (Gaultiere, 2019).

Under the heading, "Pastors' Emotional Health, Family and Morality," 50% of pastors admit to using pornography; and 37% report inappropriate sexual behavior with someone in the church (Gaultiere, 2019)—more than one-third of the survey group!

One of the sources cited in the *SoulShepherding* data is the 2007 White Paper "Statistics on Pastors" (Krejcir, 2007) from the *Francis A. Schaeffer Institute of Church Leadership Development*. According to this White Paper, 1500 pastors leave the ministry each month due to moral failure, spiritual burnout, or contention in their churches (Krejcir, 2007).

An interesting survey conducted by the LifeWay Research Group (LifeWay, 2019) highlighted statistics regarding pastors' views on moral failure. This survey was a follow-up to a similar survey conducted four years earlier, which identified 1,000 Protestant pastors contacted in the Fall of 2019. The results in data-speak suggest a 95% confidence that the sampling error was less than 3.3%. So what did these pastors say?

27% of those pastors surveyed said that a pastor who commits adultery should withdraw from public ministry permanently. These results indicated a 10% increase from the previous survey only four years earlier (LifeWay, 2019).

The participants in the survey were given the option to choose from the following statements: a pastor who commits adultery does not need to withdraw from professional ministry; withdrawing for 3 or 6 months; withdrawing for at least a year, or two years or five years or ten years; or finally the choice of withdrawing permanently (LifeWay Research, 2019). The overall results demonstrated a lessening of the leniency evidenced in the earlier survey (four years earlier) and a stronger recommendation to remove the pastor. This choice was one of only two options that increased from the previous survey (LifeWay Research, 2019).

However, a higher percentage in this survey—almost one-third of respondents—was not sure about any of these choices (LifeWay Research, 2019). A 20% increase over the survey from four years ago. So while some pastors in this recent survey have hardened their stance about removing their peers permanently from professional ministry for those who commit adultery, a more significant number were not sure (LifeWay Research, 2019).

This survey also considered the responses of different demographic groups in asking the question of withdrawal from professional ministry for a pastor who commits adultery. The survey results suggested that African-American pastors are the least likely to choose that a pastor should withdraw permanently if caught in adultery (LifeWay Research, 2019). Pastors of churches with smaller attendance were more likely to suggest that a pastor withdraw permanently after committing adultery than those who pastor larger churches (LifeWay Research, 2019). Pentecostal ministers were more likely to select that the pastor who commits adultery should withdraw for at least one year—more than one-third of them said that. This could be based on the approach of their denominations in handling these situations. Meanwhile, Methodist pastors were more likely to select that the pastor who commits adultery does not need to withdraw from public ministry (LifeWay Research, 2019).

Lack of Planning

According to Reed (2006), in his research on pastoral paths to restoration (*Restoring Fallen Pastors*, Reed, 2006), many denominations have no straightforward process or path. Perhaps the previous data tells us why: let them get out of professional ministry (LifeWay Research, 2019).

However, these incidents of moral failure among pastors are not new and the numbers are growing. So how could it be that, as Reed (2006) suggests, many denominations and a large number of independent churches have no path or process at all (Reed, 2006)? Would it be wrong to include the thought that we are the people of redemption? At least we say we are for those filthy sinners who walk down our aisles.

Reed opines that while the press has a field day with its coverage of clergy misconduct, there is limited or no planning for handling pastoral moral failure until it happens (as of the writing of his article). However, then it becomes too late (Reed, 2006). How can denominational leadership or congregational elders make well-thought-out decisions when the fire starts? This lack of planning has perhaps led to the wash-out of many from this professional role to which they felt called. Could this lack of process or planning for such issues be one of the reasons that the LifeWay Research survey found that 80% of pastors surveyed will not be in this professional ministry role ten years from now (LifeWay Research, 2019)? As we will read later, and as earlier data suggested, some pastors believe that restoration should not occur for those pastors who have failed in the manner (Hughes and Armstrong, 1995; MacArthur, 2008; Houdmann, 2017).

With no formal denominational process and no real plan, Pastor X, whom we interviewed, told us that in denominational circles, a former pastor could not very well show up at another denominational church and sit on a pew without drawing significant attention as to "Why are you here?" In order to survive and find some source of income, Pastor X and his family ended up moving to Florida, partly because he knew the leaders there and mainly because he could have employment. His father's legacy in the denomination opened doors for opportunities that would not have been available for other unknown pastors. He and his wife worked in a Nursing Home: she kept the books, and he cut the grass, fixed toilets, and did Elvis impersonations for all the guests (Pastor X, personal communication, September 25, 2020).

The Process: Self-Service?

In Pastor X's case, the program that the denominational leadership developed for him and his wife was to participate in and show counseling attendance records for two years; attend and be faithful to a local church, but no preaching for the first two years. In the third year, if this couple had successfully walked through the counseling and been faithful, and if they were moving in a positive direction, there could be some pulpit involvement in that third year if it was available. After the third year, the denominational leadership and the pastor of the church they were attending would evaluate his path. He stated that he was told, "If we believe you have been restored, you can be re-ordained; and if we do not believe you have been restored, or if we have got question marks, we are not promising anything" (Pastor X, personal communication, September 25, 2020). No specifics were given on how anyone might measure or know "if you have been restored."

While there is evidence of some process, cobbled together as it was, Pastor X stated that for the individual minister going through this process (perhaps unique to him), s/he has to be the initiator on everything (Pastor X, personal communication, September 25, 2020). The responsibility for seeing this process through to completion, such as it was, has been given to this fallen pastor. This seems to be the strangest part of the entire story. While it is true that he or she dropped the ball and disregarded the ordination to which s/he had been trusted, how is it that the one who failed carries the responsibility to find restoration?

There was no condemnation, but they told him he messed up and did not honor the calling. So it was really up to him to see this process through. It sounds much like the 3rd step highlighted in the original research on Redemptive Leadership (Bucci, 2016): **Managers created structured agreements with conditional acceptance; they communicated clearly and directly about conditions and consequences.** A little of the "scared straight" approach refers to a program developed by prisoners to scare juvenile offenders out of their current bad habits to keep them from this same prison life (Scared Straight, 1978). But also a seeming lack of oversight by the denominational leadership.

The bottom line in this process, as identified, is that the denominational leadership did not handle anything for this failed pastor. He had to initiate everything. Still, he was fortunate that his wife remained with him and that someone opened their church for them to attend without being insecure. He stated in the interview that "most men would love to go through a process of being restored, with counseling and just with their family, but even in the [professional] ministry, they cannot afford it. That is massive when you lose identity and everything you are and have to live somewhere else in two weeks. Furthermore, some guys work anywhere they can, living in an apartment. Moreover, the marriage does not make it" (Pastor X, personal communication, September 25, 2020).

So for the first year, Pastor X and his family attended counseling: the husband and wife went every week, while the kids attended every other week in the beginning. Then in the second year, the husband and wife attended every other week. The focus here was on restoring the family, and the profession now is secondary. However, no pastor could even conceive of pursuing reinstatement into such a role once again without the spouse's support. Pastor X and his family relocated for work and found a good church with a supportive pastor. But the people in the church were insecure. They began to find details, and they wondered why a former pastor was attending their church. So this is one oddity they faced that was unexpected (Pastor X, personal communication, September 25, 2020).

Then on to the counseling: They found an older retired pastor willing to work with them. In much of the counseling, they earnestly focused on fixing themselves, not just counting the days until it was time to pursue re-ordination. It is unfortunate that this also happens, where the issues are not fully addressed, but the time is put in, and when the time is up, the former pastor moves aggressively back towards the pulpit. Nevertheless, the process remains entirely on this pastor to pursue this reinstatement (Pastor X, personal communication, September 25, 2020).

Trying to Make it Back

After two years, the now-former, Pastor X, submits an appeal. The denominational leaders suggested that he go through his local church pastor while staying connected to the denomination through their State Office. So he contacted the state office and said, "Hey, it has been two years. We have completed the first part of the process. We would like to proceed with the next step of the process" (Pastor X, personal communication, September 25, 2020). He encouraged the denominational leaders to call the local pastor, interview him, and ask him about the process as he had seen it play out.

Pastor X's son was still young enough not to understand why his father was not Pastor X or Reverend X anymore. They would try to explain restoration;

and that the family was in a restoration program. The son somehow got restoration and probation confused because anytime [someone asked] what does your dad do? The son would respond, "Well, he is in a probation program."

Pastor X soon learns that discussions are occurring between the state office, the observing pastor, and the counselor. Things seem to be moving forward, in which Pastor X can now be considered for re-ordination. Former Pastor X is now allowed to be active in some church programs, slowly moving into a leadership role. One fascinating irony: the pastor, whose church Pastor X and his family attended during the restoration process, began acting out and seemed oddly insecure. They later learned that this man was living out the same deceptive scenario Pastor X and his wife had gone through before attending his church.

There was no expectation of a minimum number of sermons to be preached, "and you will be ready" (Pastor X, personal communication, September 25, 2020). Whenever Pastor X would contact the state office, there was a constant reminder that there was no guarantee for reinstatement (re-ordination). Pastor X was earnest that his desire was not to be re-ordained alone but to prove to his wife his commitment to her and their wholeness as a couple; and express to the leaders their desire to move forward positively. More than anything, he wanted his wife to trust him again. Whether the state officials did was another matter.

Firing Squad

So the state officials now set up a meeting at the denomination's headquarters. A board was formed to review Pastor X's counseling portfolio and the host pastor's efforts to walk Pastor X back into a ministry leadership role. Pastor X knew all the board members very well. When he and his wife arrived, about 20 other couples were lining the hallways. It was a curious sight, but they soon realized that they were all there for the same reason. They had all gone through the same breach of trust that he and his wife had. Moreover, they were all waiting to be grilled by the state officials. Pastor X said it felt like death row because no one said anything to anyone. None of them spoke with each other (Pastor X, personal communication, September 25, 2020). The sight of all of these other couples was a complete surprise. There seemed to be no process before, and now it seemed that the impact of failure had affected many other couples, and this scene cried out for thoughtful procedures.

So then they each take their turn, one couple at a time, going in to meet with this board, and they all are getting grilled. It was like a firing squad, except instead of bullets, there were direct and personal questions that assailed them. It was brutal!

Former Pastor X reflected on this part of the process: "I do not think they did it to embarrass us. There are times where [if we had] the wrong attitude, we could feel like, 'man; they are just making us feel bad every step of the way. We were going to [have to] earn this, [and they] want us to feel bad.' I do not think they did it for that purpose. We are already feeling bad, and now we feel bad for all the other couples going through this same thing. Because we know what we have been through and what they have been through. Furthermore, we were unsure if the board members would tell us whether we would be reinstated while we were in this meeting" (Pastor X, personal communication, September 25, 2020). The board does not indicate what they have decided or when they will decide. The entire meeting feels like a punch in the gut.

Pastor X continued to recount what happened during the meeting: "The members of the Board grilled me. I felt like a junior high sixth-grader who had skipped school for a week. And I just sat there and had to take it" (Pastor X, personal communication, September 25, 2020). His wife grabbed his hand because she feared that he might respond in anger and that his most profound feelings might come out. He asked rhetorically, "Haven't we been through enough? However, I just sat there because, in my mind, I was thinking, okay, maybe they are just trying to push my buttons." Again, we recall the "Scared Straight" approach (Scared Straight, 1978).

Next was his wife's turn after the onslaught on Pastor X. The board began questioning her. The focus was not an attack but an inquiry about whether she thought he had changed. The essential question was, "Do you trust him?" It was highly challenging for both of them.

The couple had endured betrayal, complete loss of security, being removed from their home, scrambling to find work, hastily securing a place to live and a way to care for their family, then years of counseling to restore their relationship. They even endured watching the host pastor of the church they chose to attend following the same failed path that had derailed them. They received an invitation to the denominational headquarters for some word on their situation and some hope of a redemptive opportunity. However, instead of offering hope and encouragement, they were hammered with direct uncomfortable questions for about 45 minutes. Furthermore, there is no word about reinstatement.

When the cross-examination was over, they prayed with the board members and then walked back down the hall past those other couples most likely facing a similar fate in just a few minutes. They walked briskly down the hall with their heads down to escape the eyes of those awaiting a similar inquiry, and they did not know what the future held for them (Pastor X, personal communication, September 25, 2020).

Something else that Pastor X discussed, which was not mentioned until now, was a relationship with a mentor who may have helped him in this process. There was a man that Pastor X knew who was a high-ranking individual in the denomination. He had recently moved from a pastoral role to teach at another denominational university, and Pastor X had gotten his Master's Degree through this university. They became familiar as a teacher and a student. This man was still well known and well connected in the denomination. He was one of the voices who strongly advocated for Pastor X to pursue this reinstatement effort. There is no explicit mention of him at any point in the process, but he did check in with Pastor X several times. It is possible that his voice encouraged this Pastor X to move forward and was one of the voices behind the scenes that led to his eventual reinstatement. We may never know.

Finally, after several weeks they received a letter reinstating Pastor X as an ordained minister within the denomination and within the state in which he was living. He had a history of success and then of failure. However, he has been restored, and there is no longer looking over his shoulder.

While this moment was significant, the more notable achievement was the uniting of the family once again. There was still much work to do, but this was a more important outcome. There is also no church to pastor, which raises questions of whether he should remain in the denomination. During this transition, the former restored Pastor X had built relationships with other denominational connections, most notably his mentor at the university. Pastor X would eventually move on from the denomination and return home to the East Coast of the United States. His parents were very sick, and he would remain here to launch a church on his own, with another denomination.

Can the Cat be Put Back in the Bag?

According to one blog with some considerable data support (Blitz, 2014), the famous saying "let the cat out of the bag" refers to someone who has disclosed a secret or revealed previously hidden facts. It may be used to reference someone who speaks too much or 'blabs' secrets (Blitz, 2014). It is said that the humorist Will Rogers was quoted as saying, "Letting the cat out of the bag is a whole lot easier than putting it back in" (Blitz, 2014). That picture may help in this final discussion about whether someone in the role of a pastor, who has built trust and confronted sin with a congregation, would be able to once again "put the cat back in the bag," being capable of returning to a congregation to confront sin, preach about fidelity to the faith, and renew trusted relationships after exposing him or herself and the deep secrets of a compromised life.

While the notable examples of successful restoration are limited, one such case, documented in his book *Rebuilding Your Broken World* (MacDonald, 1990), was the public confession and restoration of Gordon MacDonald, pastor of the largest church in New England at the time and then later the president of InterVarsity Christian Fellowship. MacDonald acknowledged having an affair and confessed it to his wife in the fall of 1986. In early 1987 he confessed to three national evangelical leaders. Later that year, he resigned from InterVarsity because an anonymous letter accused him of adultery. A team of seven men coached and helped him through the 10-month restoration process. The MacDonalds were reinstated as members of Grace Chapel in the fall of 1987 (Holwick, 1997). MacDonald later became a pastor in New York City and then returned to pastor his former church in Massachusetts. About one-quarter of the congregation opposed the action (Miesel, 2005). Because of his background, he was one of the pastors called upon to counsel President Bill Clinton after his affair with Monica Lewinsky (Fisher, 1998).

There are stridently different views about complete pastoral restoration and being able to return to the pulpit.

Houdmann (2017) from the website GotQuestions.org noted the following (author's paraphrase): "Just because we offer forgiveness does not necessarily mean that everything goes back to normal. We may choose to forgive someone who, while driving drunk, wrecked our car. However, there is a difference between forgiving the act of drunk driving and restoring the car to full use, and it may never happen. In many fields, persons accused of a crime may pay for that crime through jail time or probation but then never work in that field again. A person who embezzles bank funds may be forgiven and pay for their crime, but no bank or financial firm handling funds would want to hire them again. A pedophile may be forgiven, but according to the law, would never be allowed to work with children again" (Houdmann, 2017).

How then does this work with fallen pastors? Houdmann suggests that pastors involved in some moral failing can and should be restored to fellowship with God, their families, and fellow believers. However, restoring a church's leadership position is another matter (Houdmann, 2017). Houdmann suggests that the church should pursue a path of restoration to fellowship within that particular fellowship, following the process of church discipline outlined in the denominational structure and scripture–see Matthew 18:15–20 (Houdmann, 2017).

Pastor and author John MacArthur is a little franker regarding this restoration issue: "Where did we get the idea that a year's leave of absence and some counseling can restore integrity to someone who has squandered his reputation and destroyed people's trust? Certainly not from the Bible. Trust forfeited is not so easily regained. Once purity is sacrificed, the ability to lead by example is lost forever. ...What about forgiveness? Shouldn't we be eager to restore our fallen brethren? To fellowship, yes. But not to leadership. It is not an act of love to return a disqualified man to public ministry; it is an act of disobedience" (MacArthur, 2008, p.288).

Hughes and Armstrong (1995) give a substantial justification for not restoring a fallen pastor (Hughes and Armstrong, 1995). The following paragraphs are the author's paraphrases: They write that a fallen minister or leader who confesses sin, seeks the grace of God, and who desires to remain in fellowship with a particular fellowship or denomination should be welcomed and receive grace and forgiveness as any Christian who has fallen and sinned (Hughes and Armstrong, 1995). The fallen pastor would have the opportunity for forgiveness as Jesus commands in Matthew's gospel chapter 18. However, according to these authors, there is a difference between forgiving a fallen church leader by restoring fellowship and then allowing them to hold the pastor's office (Hughes and Armstrong, 1995).

These authors continue (Hughes and Armstrong, 1995), writing that the church should not punish anyone who has repented from their sin—but refusing to put them back into the role of a pastor is not punishment (Hughes and Armstrong, 1995). This act honors Christ's holy standards, articulated by the Apostle Paul for those in senior leadership positions in the church (1 Timothy 3:1-13; also Titus 1:5-16). Because a person has repented and sought restoration does not mean they meet the qualifications for a pastor's office.

Again, according to Hughes and Armstrong (1995), we need to guard the church body against those who have compromised their significant role. So then, their argument takes an interesting turn (Hughes and Armstrong, 1995). While we use Biblical examples of persons restored to leadership roles in justifying pastoral reinstatement, these authors suggest that there are exceptions in the Biblical story (Hughes and Armstrong, 1995). Moses' sin of murder came 40 years prior to the leadership to which God would call him, and he spent much time in isolation in the desert following this serious crime (Hughes and Armstrong, 1995). David's sin with Bathsheba would have brought the death penalty to anyone else. Besides, they argue, David was not in a shepherding role but in a political role as a warrior who could not build the temple of God and who also kept a harem (Hughes and Armstrong, 1995). Peter's sin was serious, and it was a character flaw. However, it was not against a church body, nor did it break trust with a congregation. Peter's sin was not premeditated or repetitive, but it was a spontaneous foolish decision (Hughes and Armstrong, 1995). The reasoning is part of their justification for not condoning pastoral restoration using Biblical models.

A View from the Garden

As someone who believes deeply in redemption and restoration, while the author appreciates the stand of these fellowship leaders (Hughes and Armstrong, 1995), we can and should consider examples of people from the Bible. The Bible is a great book to study about leadership because we see failed, broken, self-directed leaders whom God works through to accomplish His purposes. We are part of the means to His end, and we are humbly grateful for the opportunity.

While Hughes and Armstrong (1995) cited examples of Moses, David, and Peter and justified why these would not be helpful examples for restoration, the author believes the complete opposite. Not all of Moses' actions were influenced by God: for example, killing the Egyptian; also striking the rock instead of speaking to it as God told him to do. Nevertheless, Moses was allowed to lead the people and was described as "God's Servant" and as "faithful in all God's house" (Num. 12:7; Heb. 3:2, 5). While even after some 80 years, he let his anger get the best of him, and because of this, he could not enter the Promised Land. Some believe that there needed to be this transition from Moses, who represented the law, to Joshua, who helped fulfill God's promise—as a type of Jesus (whose original name in Hebrew would be Joshua). His replacement Joshua also had his moments when they did not pray to take Ai and failed. Joshua did not seek the Lord when he made peace with Gibeonite deceivers from a nearby territory who pretended to be from far away (see Joshua chapter 9). However, he learned from this (Joshua 24:15 English Standard Version).

Paul the Apostle's desire to return to Jerusalem despite several prophecies warning him of the consequences was not influenced by God. Paul may have been selfish in wanting to go back when the spirit warned him several times not to go (see Acts chapter 20). He also made a fuss about John Mark after the first mission's journey, and then there was a subsequent breakup with Barnabas on the second mission trip (Acts 15), although later, his heart was softened towards Mark (2 Timothy 4:11). See the final chapter of this book for more on John Mark. Nevertheless, who would ever suggest that this Apostle did not have a pastor's heart and act as such (Philippians 1:8-11).

David was said to be a man after God's heart (1 Samuel 13:14; Acts 13:22). However, he was passionate and self-centered and took advantage of an opportunity with Bathsheba. What Hughes and Armstrong (1995) forget to mention is that after David repented of his sin with Bathsheba, after they lost their first child, the second child they had would become the greatest king of Israel - Solomon. This is an excellent example of second chances and restoration.

Meanwhile, Peter is a terrific example of someone who failed royally several times and was called out by Jesus and by Paul (see Galatians chapter 2). If Peter cannot be an example of a restored faith leader, should we also then remove the two letters from Peter found in the Bible and not take the advice of this fallen, broken, impetuous but insightful servant of God?

There seems to be much more clarity in the message of redemption when it comes from someone who has passed through the Slough of Despond. It is only in our institutional malaise that we would consider the reinstatement of someone with a heart to serve God as a denominational impossibility. We would do well to heed the admonition of the Angelic visitor to virgin Mary, who clearly stated the obvious to the shaken teen when told she would bear a child but not of a man: "For nothing will be impossible with God" (Luke 1:37).

CHAPTER 3
Three Strikes You're In

Abstract: a story about redemption for those in military service who fail. In one specific case, the story of a rebellious sailor is told, and how he was restored from rebellion and jail is described. The Navy offers Correctional Custody Units (CCU) to support the adjudication of minor disciplinary infractions as an alternative to a court-martial with its ensuing stigma.

Introduction

I met this young man on the first day of a course I was teaching. He seemed very respectful, which is the general response of young men and women who have been in the military. A specific discipline goes along with the lifestyle, which is enforced in their chain of command. So it was a great surprise to me when, after discussing some of the research I was doing on redemption, this young man indicated that he wanted to speak with me privately. He shared a tremendous story with me of his restoration, which caused me to wonder about how his life could have gotten so off course in the first place.

He was talented and had a good head for numbers. It was promised that after boot camp and some specialized training, he would be able to get on a track where he could pursue Special Operations training, an elite assignment, the best of the best. He was looking at an assignment with the explosives ordnance team, a very high honor with much responsibility. He believed he was capable and moved along to pursue his dream.

He began to find trouble because it was there waiting for him. He was first given discipline because he violated the rules by bringing a woman on base. The discipline was reasonably significant—14 days of restricted time—but this violation also removed any opportunity for him to pursue Special Operations training.

He was frustrated and angry by the severity of the decision. This one violation stripped him of all the other options. He went from ship-based training in intelligence to being stuck on a destroyer, a lower-level position. He started acting out and violating even rules more and more frequently, which finally led to him being "awarded" a 45-day restrictive discipline. In the Navy service, you are "awarded" punishment when receiving a punishment. A 45-day restrictive discipline is the most discipline you can be assigned without being kicked out of the Navy. Sailors receiving this discipline lose half of their pay. They live on the ship and cannot go home; they wake up before everyone else, and they have to work later than everyone else. These sailors have a uniform inspection first and then another uniform inspection at the end of the day. They are assigned work over and above what their regular job would be. This discipline was a little bit of a wake-up call for this young man, and he tried to turn things around. He demonstrated six months of good behavior, trying to earn his good name back.

He again violated rules while riding a motorcycle without the required safety course. A police chase ensued, and he crashed the bike and wound up in the hospital. After that, he went to jail for one night. Once the news got back to his command, he received another 45 days of restriction again. This was his third offense. Three strikes—now what? He could have been kicked out, but he was not. After the discipline, he tried again to clean up his act. Then another major violation. What now?

Kick Him Out or Kick Him In?

The Navy has to do something, either kick him out or something else. There was a pause before a decision was made. In the interim, he considered suicide. He had enlisted as a young man at 19, trying to get away from drugs and other demons in his hometown. He thought the military would help straighten out his life, but he continued to exhibit poor choices and bad behavior. He was afraid to be sent back home. He had gone from the head of his academic class, leading in Special Ops training—to an outcast and worse in this extreme restriction. He had cemented his reputation as a mess-up, a rule breaker.

He is now brought before the ship's Captain, the worst-case scenario for a young sailor. The Captain asked his command what they thought about this young man. Each of the commanders liked him. When he was not in trouble, he was a hard worker. Nevertheless, yes, he continued to find trouble. Unfortunately, this infraction led to his fourth non-judicial punishment (NJP). The usual protocol is that after 1 or 2 of these NJPs, a sailor is kicked out.

So the Captain asked this young man what he would do if he were the Captain. If he were the Captain, this young man said he would kick this guy out. He was continually disappointing people. So kick him out!

So, upon hearing all of these recommendations, the Captain decided. He decided to assign the young man to 30 days at the Correctional Custody Unit or CCU, a type of military prison. Sailors from different ships are brought there for correction. The same also goes for Army, Marines, and all services.

What is the CCU?

The Navy's Correctional Custody Units (CCU) were introduced to support the adjudication of minor disciplinary infractions as an alternative to a court-martial with its ensuing stigma. This was the fear of our young rule-breaker: to be kicked out of the military and sent home disgraced. These centers were used as a means of re-training and retaining minor offenders. At one point, with military downsizing and a declining CCU population, some significant reductions required closures of the Pacific Fleet CCUs and all but two of the Atlantic Fleet CCUs (Rudolph, Glaser, and Kerce, 1994). This led to a review of the effectiveness of these facilities.

According to Powers (2016), the Navy uses three levels of incarceration, a tier system based on the length of a prisoner's sentence. The aforementioned correctional custody units (CCU) are considered in the first tier for sailors sentenced to up to one year. For longer sentences (up to 10 years), the second tier of correctional facilities is two consolidated brigs. One is located at Marine Corps Air Station Miramar, Calif., and the other at Naval Weapons Station Charleston, S.C.

The final tier of offenders with sentences of more than ten years, who pose a national security risk or are sentenced to death, are sent to the U.S.

Disciplinary Barracks, Ft. Leavenworth, Kansas. Female prisoners are housed in one location no matter the level of offense. Powers noted that the main focus of these facilities is the leadership's efforts at restoration and redemption. Our young rule-breaker knew the reputation of the CCUs. They could make you or break you.

The Correctional Custody Unit (CCU) is a military program designed to rehabilitate first term military personnel with minor infractions of discipline (minor compared to a courts martial) to re-training and increase their chances of being fit again for active duty service. According to the Manual for Administration of Correctional Custody Units (Rudolph, Glaser, & Kerce, 1994), the goal of the CCU is "to correct the attitudes and motivation of enlisted personnel through a regimen of hard work, intensive counseling, physical training, and motivational and attitudinal training conducted in a strict military environment" (Rudolph, Glaser, & Kerce, 1994). In a report for the Navy Personnel Research and Development Center, it was stated that "the majority of sailors re-trained at the Norfolk and Jacksonville CCU facilities over the preceding two years remained on active duty, and a number of the awardees were filling critical roles for the Navy. Many of the awardees subsequently discharged were separated for additional disciplinary infractions. However, nearly 20% of discharged awardees successfully reached the end of their obligated service" (Rudolph, Glaser, & Kerce). "More than 50% of commanding officers indicated that sailors sent to the CCU were better performers and more committed to the organization after re-training than were sailors disciplined by other measures" (Rudolph, Glaser, & Kerce). "The cost-benefit analysis indicated that successful awardees' net value provided to the Navy was substantial" (Rudolph, Glaser, & Kerce).

One senior leader in Naval Corrections was quoted as saying that the decisions on where to house offenders and the entire operation of the facility have one overarching objective: to maximize the potential for offenders to be fully rehabilitated (Powers, 2016). Sailors chosen to be staff members at these facilities are first selected from exceptional sailors in their own right; and then given rigorous training to "fix people with some pretty serious problems," according to one senior facility Director (Powers, 2016).

> "No discipline is enjoyable while it is happening—it is painful! But afterward..."
>
> —***(Hebrews 12:11 NLT)***

As recounted by our young rule-breaker, the objective of the CCU experience is to get "inmates" to decide what they want to do: to stay in the service or to get out? Each inmate has to decide for themselves (Allen, 2003). As much as the experience was described as an effort to "break men down" to get them to face this choice, the inmates are also told that they can leave at any time. Each day is the same. Wake up very early—5 am each day (Allen, 2003). Immediately stretching begins, and yelling at the inmates commences. Exercise and running follow.

The leaders at the CCU used thought replacement techniques. Like military Boot camps, where sailors have to memorize their service creed, the CCU has its creed. Inmates say the creed every morning, followed by exercises and running. Come back and clean their quarters. Lunch. Study military requirements and rules. Memorize the creed. Instructors would randomly "beat" awardees with push-ups and yelling, not physically but emotionally. This is an inmate's experience in the first week. Then it transitions from random physical harassment and yelling to a more relaxed approach. However, the leaders' emphasis is now focused on those who did not break in the first week, punishing only bad behavior with these beat downs. Several stories of men assigned to the CCU and who later made a career in the service described it as a "second chance" (Allen, 2003).

This troubled and violation-prone sailor knew of people who had been sent to CCU because they were a part of this discipline-restricted group. Some had come back from CCU changed for the better. Many he knew had gone to the CCU, experienced a short-lived change, and then fell back into bad behavior and were kicked out.

Within the first week, our young rule-breaker is now broken himself. He saw that he would be drummed out and go back home if he yelled back at the leaders when they yelled at him. There is some incentive here, it seems. Going home and the disgrace of being kicked out of the Navy and then falling back into the same problems was not an acceptable option. Our young rule-breaker saw that he could continue and stay in the Navy if he would align his thoughts and actions to the appropriate behaviors. There is no one to whom the inmates can go in this situation, and they have to decide.

Our former head-of-his-class recruit finally bought into this program. He started leading the crowd. The leaders did not acknowledge this, but he began to change. The leaders start to recognize him by rewarding him for good behavior. In a short time, the leaders in CCU publicly recognized the change. They allowed him to leave the program early. They said no one had ever been given this privilege.

Full Redemption; Turn-around Completed

So in the case of compliance with Navy rules and protocol, the CCU experience helped break the rebellious bent of this young, formerly bitter sailor and changed his perspective on compliance. Through another chance encounter, this young man's life would be spiritually transformed. Our redeemed sailor would remain in the Navy for five more years. Regarding the spiritual change, he would later be baptized in the water by a Navy chaplain lay leader who had also been one of the leaders who spoke up on his behalf to the Captain prior to his assignment to the CCU. Later a new captain would come, who told our young sailor that he had heard about him, yet he believed in second chances. This was a significant window of opportunity for our redeemed sailor.

His new Captain was a man who operated "by the book" and left no room for margin, although he had been the one to assign our sailor to the CCU. The current ship leadership responded to our sailor's changed attitude with skepticism. They gave him his previous responsibilities but no opportunities for advancement. Because he had made it through 30 days at the CCU, they had to take him back, and they could not kick him out. However, the current leadership expected it would not be long until he got in trouble again. So most of these leaders would leave him alone and let him wash out. However, the tour of duty would end for several officers, and so many of the leaders were gone, and a new command was in place. The new command had only heard of his behavior problems.

The new Captain told our redeemed sailor that he could get his rank back if he stayed clean and on track. This Captain had been known to turn entire commands around. He remained true to his word, and our young sailor received his rank back in one year; and the Captain also removed three of the sailor's four non-judicial punishments (NJPs). This was not typical protocol and allowed our young sailor to get an honorable discharge eventually.

Our transformed young sailor received much grace after not being forced out of the Navy when there were several opportunities for his command to do just that. Also, he could have his original rank reinstated when this was not standard protocol. He became a Leadership Studies major in college, where I met him, and the story began.

He believes that management has a responsibility to hold people accountable and not give too much lee-way when a manager sees problems arise. The ability to sternly discipline will also allow leadership to offer grace, thus setting the stage for a redemptive transformation. Spoken by someone who knows.

CHAPTER 4
God's Magnificent Work Complete

Abstract: Recovery for Abused women is highlighted in this chapter. Here is the story of a confident and self-assured woman crushed by spousal abuse and overwhelmed with fear of reprisal who was trapped in this situation with no apparent means of escape. Her story of escape and the process of restoration are highlighted.

God is magnificent; he can never be praised enough.
There are no boundaries to his greatness.

Generation after generation stands in awe of your work;
each one tells stories of your mighty acts.

—***Psalm 145:3-4 MSG***

Introduction

We worked side-by-side on two significant projects, and I greatly respected and admired her strong work ethic. When I needed assistance in arranging for facilities support for a major convention, she was the liaison with whom I needed to work to coordinate adequate coverage. She demonstrated great poise under pressure and the ability to manage large tasks. She was well-respected in the organization and had been recognized on several occasions for her excellent work and professionalism.

A while later, I happened to have the chance to sit in on some graduate-level presentations. That night this same colleague presented a proposal where she advocated for providing services to persons going through the trauma of being involved in spousal abuse. The stories she told seemed so realistic that it appeared she had a real passion for this program and the women and children who were suffering in these situations. One story was incredibly compelling and caused an emotional response from most folks who sat alongside me. Suddenly, she revealed to the class that it was she whom she was speaking, and it was she who had been a victim of just such abuse. The mood in the room immediately changed, from a riveting interest in the story being told, to now great compassion for the storyteller. The intimacy with which she told the stories made sense. This caring and capable woman's ability to recover from such a devastating tragedy was compelling. I was immediately drawn to understand how someone might recover from such a dehumanizing situation.

Intimate Partner Violence Statistics

There are alarming statistics for domestic abuse in the United States called "intimate partner violence" (IPV) in a report from the Centers for Disease Control and Prevention (Breiding, Chen, and Black, 2014). According to a 2014 report based on 2010 data by the US CDC (Breiding, Chen, and Black, 2014), nearly 1 in 4 US women will be victims of severe violence by an intimate partner in their lifetimes compared to 1 in 7 US men. Almost 25% of women suffer this abuse, and here is a survivor hiding in plain sight. Could others in the room be facing the same challenge?

Another research article collected data from several sources besides the CDC data and reported that worldwide, the lifetime prevalence of intimate partner violence ranged from 19 to 66 percent among women aged 15 to 24, with most of the data sources identified reporting a prevalence above 50 percent (Stockl, March, Pallitto, and Garcia-Moreno, 2014). I wanted to know more about how someone survives such horrific treatment and is restored to a position of success, stature, and competence after an abusive situation.

Previous research identified a redemptive approach used by a group of managers who had successfully reinstated employees who had been terminated for cause. The initial study originated in a search for the practice of redemption leading to restoration in the management literature. In this pursuit, consideration was given to those occasions where employees who had previously failed in their work performance in their first effort were given "second chances" through some remedy of reinstatement, whether through the Last Chance agreement, an Employee Assistance Program, or by an arbitrated or mediated settlement.

The managers observed a series of behaviors that appeared reasonably consistent in each of the cases reviewed. Not all of the employees with whom the managers worked remained with the organization after the initial reinstatement period, but many found tremendous success the second time and prospered through this redemptive process. The act of redemption reminds us of Jesus Christ, who, as the perfect sacrifice and substitution for mankind, took our place and redeemed our lives back from the sinful state in which we found ourselves. Could it be that managers in organizations and the systems in organizations replicate a similar redemptive process? Would the successful work of redemption and restoration experienced by individuals who have overcome drug abuse or who have survived and thrived following intimate partner violence mirror a similar approach taken by the managers in the initial research? If this approach differs from the initial research, where are the behaviors the same, and where are the critical differences?

In the previous research, the author acknowledged that many organizations seek to provide restorative or redemptive support for prisoners coming out of prison and seeking to return to the workplace. There are also programs such as Teen Challenge, which provides structure and recovery tools for persons caught up in life-controlling addictive behavior patterns to find restoration and integration back into everyday life. Is there a similar approach that these redemptive agencies take, and are there any similarities to the behaviors demonstrated by managers who successfully reinstated employees who had been terminated for demonstrating aberrant behavior?

Not Able to Clearly See What Was Happening

In a series of interviews, my colleague described her isolation and inability to remove herself thoroughly from the situation (Anonymous IPV Victim, personal communication, July 11, 2017).

From the outside perspective, everything in her family life seemed normal. Her husband had a good job, and she was active in caring for her two children and taking them to school.

DeKerseredy and Schwartz (2009) wrote about intimate partner abuse in rural communities, as my colleague described, in their groundbreaking research (DeKerseredy and Schwartz, 2009). These authors sought to address the stereotype that such cases are not as prevalent in small rural communities compared in urban areas. The authors suggested that while a woman in a rural community may face less violent crimes at the hands of strangers, the social structure of this same rural community might make her more vulnerable to violence at the hands of a husband or boyfriend (DeKerseredy and Schwartz, 2009).

My colleague confessed that until she departed from this abusive situation, she was not fully aware of the extent to which her life was under the authority of the abuser. This is a common theme among those in abusive situations (Sanchez, 2016). It was really through a dream that her eyes were opened to the despair in which she found herself. She believes that the Lord spoke to her heart through this dream two years before the day that she would depart. In the dream, she saw that she was spiritually dying. There was a vision of her death in an auto accident. In the dream, an older man came past and saw her, and he just looked at her. He seemed to view her with pity as one who was lost. Here was the first moment of seeing the reality of her plight: through this dream, God revealed to her that she needed help and that she was in a toxic situation.

She began to understand and accept that she needed to change something. At this point, she only had God's voice to guide her. The more she sought to obey God's voice, the more her husband mocked her.

God did many things in her life to help prepare her for this transition. It seemed in retrospect that there was a two-year time of obedience, acting by faith on the impressions she sensed the Lord was giving her. Some might say she shared simple acts of obedience that led to amazing coincidences. For example, the color choices she painted the rooms in her house before it was sold were odd and not the neutral colors that most people would choose if seeking to sell a house. However, these color choices matched precisely the interests of the buyers. The house sold very quickly in a flat real estate market.

The abuse and darkness kept getting worse and would occur more often. A point of choice came: She had been on her own since she was 17, and now she is 31 with two kids. It seemed that God brought other people into the process to move the process along until the point of departure came. After two years of hearing God's voice and acting in obedience, the time to step away from this abusive environment was at hand. Later, she would reflect on this abuse and realize that she was the fourth generation of women living through this terror. This gives some sense of how difficult it would be to step away from this toxic situation.

Why Won't She Leave?

Crystal Sanchez, a survivor of domestic abuse herself and someone who now coaches and encourages victims, speaks bluntly and directly about the issue of "Why doesn't she leave?" (Sanchez, 2016). The feelings of unworthiness and blame leave the victim unable to see the reality of the abusive situation in such a way to realize though what they are suffering. Victims instead act as if they are "brainwashed;" From there, they must change their belief system and denounce those who might offer help to them to escape the abuse (Sanchez, 2016).

At some point, according to my colleague, in order for the victim to escape, they must submit to and trust someone else and surrender some control by letting someone else in. There is a small picture of things not right (like the dream previously described), but then there is the act of the will to entrust someone else and begin to share the profound truth of this terrible situation.

On one occasion, the pressure of the situation erupted after driving to pick up her children from pre-school. The pressure was so great that my colleague broke down sobbing uncontrollably. A kind administrator who knew the family for many years reached out and just listened as this woman wrestled openly with doubts and issues of faith conflicted by the abusive treatment she was receiving. Hearing the reality of this challenging and unusual relationship for herself made my colleague aware that this behavior was not typical and not something to dismiss submissively. Later, there was an erratic call to her mom, out of the blue, with the pronouncement of her soon departure and greater insight into what was causing her to leave. Nevertheless, she comforted her mom and said that things would be okay.

Planning for Freedom

How does a victim of abuse for six or more years go from this…to the magnificent, poised colleague I work with every day? What does this redemptive process look like? Crystal Sanchez describes a complex process of progressively greater bondage for those within the control of the abusive partner (Sanchez, 2016). There is an assault on their identity, and the establishment of strong guilt feelings effectively controls the abused victim (Sanchez, 2016). The victim is bullied into blaming people that they have trusted, who could be a source of reality which breaks the mind control that is in effect (Sanchez, 2016). So building trust is a critical but complex first step. Moreover, believing the real story is sometimes the most challenging decision.

Victims may share with a loved one out of necessity, but they are not typically going to share all they are dealing with. Family and friends are too close to the situation and personally know the abuser; therefore, they are not safe. However, sharing with an actual neutral person that is not connected to the abuser on a personal or professional level is huge (Anonymous IPV Victim, personal communication, July 11, 2017).

Finally, a woman intimately involved with my colleague's former husband shared the truth of all he was involved in, including several illegal activities. The depth of the illicit activities was frightening and brought everything into focus. While her husband was away that night, she decided that this was the moment to leave. Tonight she would call her mom, and tomorrow she would plan to take the children to school. However, she would instead meet her mom on the way to school, leave her car and flee with her mom and two children and essentially the clothes on their backs, and head to a women's shelter in their community.

My colleague met her mom at Kmart. However, instead of immediately seeking shelter and protection, she headed to the local Sheriff's office. She spent a significant amount of time writing out a statement about all she had seen and heard. Even though law enforcement is aware of much of this, the act of writing down every detail of her life at that moment would do something else.

Victims do not fully understand that this is happening in their lives. So there is great significance to this public step in the restoration process. Here the victim is writing out and owning that this was their life. They are admitting to external people that this is happening. This is the Sheriff's office. This is a surrender of being in denial. The victim chooses to no longer live in denial.

The victim is the only one to decide to walk out, and no one can take that step for her. This was a critical step: she framed the reality of life the way it was and thus the need for change. By writing this all down, it became real to her. Her husband believed that he was untouchable since he was working with attorneys in town. Eventually, he would be arrested for crimes unrelated to the abuse. However, none of this is about the abuser. This is about the victim and their redemption.

The Process of Change: God Inspired and Directed

God said three things to my colleague. These are significant:

1. Leave with nothing, but I will provide. Red Sea—walk out and do not look back.

2. You will know your purpose, and this is not it

3. If you do what I ask you to do, your children will not have this lifestyle.

The next step for her was forsaking everything and driving to a shelter for battered women. This is another significant step of surrender. According to the *National Domestic Violence Hotline* (Buel, 2021), data suggests that it takes a victim seven times to leave before staying away for good (Buel, 2021; LeTrent, 2013). They would finally decide to get out of the abusive situation; but their spirit would be broken and they would return to that abusive situation.

The shelter is just that—a place of protection, structure, and the starting point for regeneration. At least, this is the intention of the shelter. However, each shelter is different. Some of the shelters were helping to get the victims out of their toxic situation. In contrast, others focused on empowering victims by sharing information with the residents to help to educate them. Nevertheless, the shelter essentially serves two purposes: the point of the shelter is to help the victim get out on their own and stand on their own two feet. These are two different functions.

Different shelters are funded differently and operate differently. My colleague moved among several shelters until landing at one location where some stability was established. With this particular shelter, women (and their children, if they have them) are told that they have only six weeks to adjust to living on their own and being able to provide for themselves. Generally, the shelters will adjust their times based on the victims' needs, but this was their stated goal. The shelter is a weigh station, not a final destination. Nevertheless, the shelter is an essential part of the redemptive process. A victim in isolation will remain in the blinded, brainwashed mindset and denounce that there is reason to getaway. The isolation is what strangles the motivation to escape. In order to live, the victim has to make this leap away from the pattern in which they find themselves.

This is what a shelter may provide (some services differ by location and funding):

Each facility is a massive component in the process. Here victims are protected, and there must be a way to ensure the victims that they are safe.

They give victims the information that they are not alone. When a person is being abused, they perceive that it is all their fault and that no one else is dealing with this. This false narrative supports the dread of isolation. They let you know that others may be suffering from this at the shelter. They provide for victims' basic needs, supplies, room, etc.

Initially, the shelter staff tells victims that they cannot call or communicate with anyone on the outside for 72 hours. This is an effort to ensure the victim's success, and that outside person could threaten or induce shame.

After getting adjusted and settled the first night, the abuse victim starts fresh with a caseworker to get their story and remind them that they are not alone.

Victims now adjust to a new living situation. They are away from the abuse, but now they are also in the midst of other people. There is some mutual support, but people act and think differently. So victims must learn right away to make some significant adjustments. Everyone in the shelter must attend a support group of people in their situation. The support group may be off-site.

The shelter may also offer support programs to help educate and empower victims. Victims learn that abusers may look different, but they all operate the same. The staff begins to educate victims about the behaviors of the abusers. The victim is now essentially homeless. So the shelters have a process and show support for the victims by teaching resume writing and basic money management skills. They try to help people shift from their old lives to new careers. The shelter may support the victims by encouraging them to protect themselves and get an attorney. If you were local, they would provide one.

End of the Story?

The victim has come into the shelter, gotten educated, and is starting to settle into a new routine. Her children may be attending a school near the shelter. However, now the victim has to plan to get out and be safe and standing on their own and still deal with this residual impact of the ongoing legal issues. The abuser could run a credit check and try to find the victim to shame them into returning or to harm them. The abusive partner may try to ruin credit so that the victim cannot work or get credit.

After building up the courage to leave an abusive partner, and after years and years of channeling guilt and coping with abuse, suddenly the victim finds themselves free…but not really. The victim has six weeks (the average stay at the shelters in this story is three months)...to adjust to the truth of their abuse, begin to assess the reality of their situation, and scramble to find work and living arrangements. They are adjusting to a new belief system and right-sizing their self-perception, wondering whether they will ever be safe. Will they always be looking over their shoulder?

In scanning websites and resources to seek closure to this story and to identify possible follow-up steps for the redemption of a victim of abuse, several sites were similar to the one noted here (Murphy, 2021). Most of the discussion involves escaping from the abuser and mentions some of the similar steps as referenced by Sanchez (2016). Seeking legal help and protective orders would also seem important (Murphy, 2021), and this process is recommended by and supported by the various shelters. However, frequently abusers are either violent or emotional and are not warded off by threats of protective orders or incarceration. For example, my co-worker's husband often visited and even stalked locations where this victim and her children resided, or the pre-school her children attended. The school's principal had to call the police for the children's safety and the unknown scope of his potential actions.

More research needs to be done on successful programs that help victims of abuse, both men and women, to go beyond the terror of retribution and looking over their shoulder, that they might live in peace and be restored to the unique and beautiful vessels designed by God to mirror His glory and fulfill their potential.

CHAPTER 5

I Was in Prison ... and You Threw Away the Key

Abstract: In the original book, several groups working with ex-convicts were highlighted. Here is an interview with an ex-con who is now a monk, and he describes actual efforts at making the transition from prison to employment and the challenges he faced. He also describes the ineffectiveness of some national groups who are making a name providing services for those in transition and why these programs are not working. Additionally, he touches on some new legislation efforts available to help ex-convicts.

Introduction

There is a phrase of unknown origin, often used by people demanding harsher sentences for violent offenders. The oft-repeated phrase is, "Lock them up and throw away the key." It plays well with the 'If you did the crime, do the time' crowd, and its source is difficult to trace because the phrase has been used relatively frequently in modern cultural references to criminals. One source attributed the quote to the writer John Edgar Wideman, who wrote of mass incarceration as racist and the ghetto as a terrible place to live, where only blacks reside (Wideman, 1995). Before Wideman, there was Jim Maddox, the former Attorney General of Texas (Mattox, 1993). After overseeing three dozen executions in his state, Maddox was quoted as saying the existence of the death penalty did not deter those who murdered other people. This breathed new life into this phrase—also used by Maddox—that "it is cheaper to lock them up and throw away the key" (Mattox, 1993).

However, before Wideman and Mattox, the phrase was used by then-President Ronald Reagan, based on criminal reform he enacted in California and the work that he would do as president. Reagan was quoted as saying: "There is only one way to get real gun control: Disarm the thugs and the criminals, lock them up, and if you do not throw away the key, at least lose it for a long time" (Reagan, 1983). On June 20, 1983, Reagan's speech included the phrase, but he was not the originator, and it just rang true with his audience at that time. This was around the same time that law and order favorability was high. The U.S. Congress and many state legislatures passed "Mandatory Minimum" sentence laws that required judges to give fixed prison terms to those convicted of specific crimes (FAMM, n.d.).

The unofficial source of the phrase, "Lock them up and throw away the key," could be a poem by Arthur Frederick Saunders (1879-1947), which has little to do with prisoners and crime. Saunders' quote goes like this: "My heart to you is given: Oh, do give yours to me; We will lock them up together, and throw away the key." The phrase most likely morphed from the description of the Court of Common Pleas in England, as it was referred to by Sir Edward Coke (1552-1634), the Chief Justice of the King's Bench, as "the lock and key of the common law" (AALS, 1908).

The whole idea of prison as a place not just to lock up prisoners but to seek the restoration and reforming of offenders is a relatively modern concept. Author Pray writes that Americans invented the modern prison system (Pray, 1987). Although there are prisons mentioned in the Bible (for example, Genesis Chapter 38 and Acts Chapter 16), Pray refers to places for reforming criminals by this declaration. These types of prisons were created as a humanitarian effort and launched in Philadelphia in the 1700s, and from there spread to other cities and back to Europe.

There were no efforts to reform offenders, as noted in the Bible, where the penalty for capital punishment was death (Exodus 21:12). Before these newer prison models, the colonists took a similar approach to this Biblical model, which aligned with the British criminal code. This code utilized corporal and capital punishment approaches (Pray, 1987). A condemned man might be executed, while crimes that did not warrant the death penalty were addressed with fines or flogging. These approaches were meant to terrorize offenders and scare the public to avoid such punishment (Pray, 1987). Pray wrote that there came a realization by the public at the end of the 16th century that cruel physical retribution did very little to curb crime (Pray, 1987). Cue the Jim Mattox quote mentioned earlier (Mattox, 1993).

Efforts to Reform

The Pennsylvania Quakers' movement promoted the limiting of the death penalty to extreme crimes, with the formation of prisons to offer more humane treatment of offenders and as places for reforming criminals. However, as Pray writes in his brief history of criminal reforms (Pray, 1987), citizens had lost faith that these prisons - designed to reform criminals—could cure crime (Pray, 1987). According to data published on a website by an organization dedicated to serving incarcerated people (Onesimus Ministries, n.d.), the site quotes statistics saying that only 13 percent of prisoners will have participated in any pre-release program to prepare them for life outside prison. Nearly 25 percent of prisoners will be released with no supervision (Onesimus Ministries, n.d.).

According to Muhlhausen (2018), 83 percent of state prisoners released in 2005 were re-arrested at least once within nine years of their release (Muhlhausen, 2018). However, the data suggest that when former prisoners find employment after prison, it reduces recidivism and returns to crime (Holodny, 2017). In another study (Cove & Bowes, 2015), statewide rates of recidivism surveyed overall ranged from about 31 to 70 percent, while the rates for prisoners placed in jobs shortly after their release ranged from 3.3 to 8 percent (Cove & Bowes, 2015). So there is evidence that the employment of former inmates helps reduce recidivism rates dramatically.

However, according to one survey (Burke, 2005), between 60 to 75% of ex-offenders are jobless up to a year after their release. Other research by the National Institute of Justice (Blumstein and Nakamura, 2009) has shown great reluctance of employers to hire applicants with criminal records. For example, in a study conducted in New York City, having a criminal record reduced the likelihood of a person receiving a return call for an interview or job offer by nearly 50 percent (Blumstein and Nakamura, 2009). According to these same researchers, whether an applicant states upfront that they have committed a crime or the employer determines this through a criminal background check, there is a likelihood that the applicant will not get the job (Blumstein and Nakamura, 2009).

One Man's Path to Serving Others Began in Prison

Tim's story about his life before prison may not start like others who have found themselves incarcerated (Brother Tim, personal communication, May 17, 2019). However, his story is sadly the same for many who get out and seek to change their life's trajectory. Although freed from prison, it seems that the "key" that was thrown away is the key to everyday life for many former inmates. Many former inmates carry the criminal label like the famous character Hester Prynne in Hawthorne's classic fiction, *The Scarlet Letter* (1850). This label restricts job options and can often lead the former inmate back to prison, as the desperation to survive causes a return to crime.

Tim was born into a Roman Catholic family, the oldest boy with seven sisters. His father was Roman Catholic, while his mother was Presbyterian. His father wanted a large family, and his first wife did not. So he divorced his first wife and married Tim's mom. Because of the divorce, his dad was not allowed to receive the Roman Catholic sacraments. Nevertheless, Tim's family pursued a rigorously religious education for him—Tim attended a Roman Catholic grade school and Catholic high school.

Tim wanted to seek some independence and, in his words, "become a real man." So he joined the Navy when he was 18 with his parent's permission. Part of this growth into manhood also included getting married. Tim met a woman much like himself: while they met in church and shared a faith connection, they both were running away from their families. They were married for a short while and had a child. The marriage did not last, and Tim's life began to spin a little out of control. There was his father's death, the birth of a child, and then going through a divorce. This pressure led him to experiment with different faith backgrounds, including becoming a witch and leading a coven.

As much as Tim was rebellious and tried different faith experiences, he did not experiment with any drugs as a young man among his Navy friends. As a young adult, he became familiar with the properties and effects of the assorted types of drugs available. Tim became more of an educator among his friends about the impact of the different types of drugs. For 18 years, he was anti-drug. Nevertheless, at the age of 38, Tim experimented with the drug Ecstasy for the first time. He also began selling a drug that was not classified as illegal. He became part of an effort to offer a place for people to enjoy these non-classified drugs, and he perceived this to be within the law. Around this time was when he got arrested, and to him, it seemed like a technicality: the drug they were selling was not classified as an illegal substance. There were no statutes under which he could be tried in a state case. However, it became a premier federal case under the Federal Analogue Act, which associated the chemical structure of this non-classified substance as substantially similar to the chemical structure of a controlled substance (Brother Tim, personal communication, August 17, 2020).

Most of this background information set the stage for Tim's conviction and sentencing under a federal code, which resulted in his internment into the Federal Prison system. Although he did not think what he had done was illegal, his lawyer told him to plead guilty. As a result of the government's aggressive efforts to enforce this statute and his perceived role as a drug dealer, he received a strict sentence even though Tim was cooperative. This again refers to the aforementioned "Mandatory Minimum" sentence laws requiring judges to give fixed prison terms to those convicted of specific crimes—most often drug offenses (FAMM, n.d.). The laws were written not to reform but to 'lock them up,' and as Reagan suggested, to lose the key for a long time (Reagan, 1983).

What To Do When You Are Away

Since there was no protocol for first-time offenders in the federal system, Tim was sent to prison for seven years, although he was able to have the sentence reduced for cooperation to 36 months. The challenges of being in prison and adjusting to that life were many. According to Tim, when you are in jail, if you do not have family support, you are screwed.

In an article on "Justice Reform" by Clark (2020), a group called the National Lifers of America (NLA) advocates for mutual support and growth in prisons for prisoners; and organizes for social change with the help of people outside of prison. The efforts of the NLA are to drive prison reform by those who themselves are in prison (Clark, 2020).

Some of the leaders of NLA have identified the needs of convicts for skills and life training, especially those spending many years in prison. They have identified the need for training on economic literacy, conflict resolution, recognizing trauma and triggers, connecting with family, and other types of programs. The NLA efforts are mainly confined to the Michigan prison system. The Michigan Department of Corrections offers skill-based classes and rehabilitation programs of this kind. However, according to this article, these courses are only available to people with sentences in the last few years. Even available college classes are prioritized for soon-to-exit convicts because they need to take these courses before leaving prison (Clark, 2020). Parole requirements call for certain classes to be completed before a person can exit prison. So people nearing a Parole Review are given the priority because it gets them out sooner.

According to Couloute (2018), former inmates are often stuck at the lowest rungs of the educational ladder (Couloute, 2018). These inmates hold limited if any educational credentials (like a high school diploma or GED), and inmates rarely get the chance to make up for the educational opportunities they have missed; this severely impacts their chances of re-entry success (Couloute, 2018). While the unemployment rate among former inmates is very high (as high as 27%), those with limited or no formal education encounter an even higher unemployment rate.

Tim was frustrated in his efforts to better himself while in prison. According to the previously mentioned research (Couloute, 2018), in-prison college degree-granting programs are extremely limited for most incarcerated people. Federal grant eligibility was cut off because of the 1994 crime bill. Even with new initiatives and changes in the law, the number of programs available today is far short of the estimated 350 programs active in the early 1990s (Couloute, 2018). There are other limiting features, depending on the type of crime committed. For example, student inmates who have been convicted of a drug offense while previously receiving federal aid are ineligible for federal aid even after serving their sentences. Also, many colleges and universities continue to include questions about criminal history on their applications, which leads to disqualifications (Couloute, 2018).

A Change of Plans

Not allowed to take college classes—he had taken some college courses previously—Tim was directed to participate in a program that allowed him to take other types of correspondence courses. By God's grace, Tim was able to take a course for younger first-time offenders, for which, technically, he did not qualify; he enrolled in a prison program called "BRAVE," which is the Bureau Rehabilitation and Values Enhancement program (BOP, 2016). Participants who take the coursework seriously gain structure and insight into choices made and learn about substance abuse and addiction. The course helped answer many questions for Tim regarding why he was doing the things he did. Tim also completed 132 correspondence Bible courses, learning about different faith groups.

Tim returned to his historic Roman Catholic faith and became more devout—he called it practicing. Tim gathered several Roman Catholic inmates together and requested that one of the Chaplains—a priest—offer communion to the inmates. Surprisingly the chaplain refused because — they were all convicted criminals! Well, of course, they are—and he was their chaplain! Does that make sense? They could not even get this chaplain or another priest to come in and offer them the sacrament of Confession.

During this time in prison, there was one booklet, above them all, that inspired Tim and changed his thinking and his life. That book was entitled *We're All Doing Time: A Guide to Getting Free* (Lozoff, 1985). In this booklet, Lozoff (1985), who did not have a prison background, spoke honestly to his readers and made a significant impact. Many have said that this book changed their lives, and several touching testimonies of the impact of this book were found (Saldana, 2008). Lozoff's booklet also touched Tim while in prison. Tim made prison his monastery for his survival—thoughts he attributed directly to Lozoff (1985). Later on, Lozoff's influence, outside of his writing, would suffer when allegations of abusive conduct through his counseling work were made against the author (Saldana, 2008).

As his life and perspective began to change, Tim also found opportunity through his administrative skills to manage the supply of toilet paper and other essentials for his unit, creating systems that saved the prison money. This allowed him to get a private cell. This opportunity for some isolation while in prison also allowed him to pursue some deeper faith issues and reconsider his upbringing. His success with the procurement systems in prison would unknowingly prepare him for his next step.

Once he was released, Tim used his maturity and superior administrative skills to apply for highly skilled jobs; and in this process, he impressed one particular business. He managed to stand out from among over 300 applicants for the job, yet the company said it could not hire him three times because he was an ex-convict, even though he was the superior candidate. Finally, the business owner took a risk and invested in him.

Chef Jeff and the Power of a Second Chance

Tim's story about life after prison is not only different because he was persistent–but also because someone took a chance on him. His story after incarceration follows a similar arc to that of the celebrity Chef Jeff Henderson (Capretto, 2016).

Jeff Henderson was born in the Watts neighborhood of Los Angeles. Raised by a single mother, lacking positive role models, and struggling to find his own identity (Winfrey, 2007), Jeff met a cousin who was a drug dealer, and he also started selling drugs. He became increasingly successful with his drug distribution business, earning as much as $35,000 a week dealing cocaine in L.A. and then San Diego. Then at 24 years old, police picked up a small-time dealer who led them to Jeff.

Jeff was convicted and sentenced to ten years and seven months in prison. While incarcerated, Jeff learned to read and started to work on his GED. He was transferred to a prison unit reserved for inmates showing signs of rehabilitation. He almost lost that opportunity by neglecting his responsibilities while working on his GED. Nevertheless, the loss of his cleaning job forced him to take a dishwashing job at the prison. This became the path to his ultimate restoration (Bilyeu, 2014). Jeff worked his way up through the prison kitchen jobs until he taught himself how to make different menu items for the inmates (Bilyeu, 2014). This opened up an opportunity to take over a supervisory role at the Culinary Training School for inmates at Maxwell Air Force Base in Alabama.

Once he was released from prison, Jeff's efforts to find employment frustrated, and he came up empty (Capretto, 2016). Jeff took a considerable risk and contacted some of the top black chefs in the country and offered to do anything for them if they would allow him to work in their restaurant (Capretto, 2016). He admitted that he had failed in his life and that he was an ex-convict. Chef Robert Gadsby offered Jeff a low-level job working out of his restaurant in Beverly Hills. Starting as a dishwasher, he moved up and took every opportunity to learn the business. He ultimately became the first African American chef at Caesars Palace in Las Vegas. Jeff was later named Executive Chef at the Bellagio in Las Vegas.

Jeff says that the "power of food" led him to his calling and restoration (Capretto, 2016). However, without Robert Gadsby giving this opportunity to Jeff Henderson, would this have been such a success story? Former inmate, Tim, was also given an opportunity to start over and find redemption. By God's grace, it only took a prison sentence and a little booklet to find it.

Ministry, for Now, Not Later?

The author spoke with a former local prison chaplain who served in a County (City) Correctional Facility. He was the chaplain there for over 21 years. He only got involved in the prison chaplaincy by divine intervention when seeking an internship to complete his Biblical studies degree (Chaplain Dicky Sherrill, personal communication, December 6, 2019). In this local County Jail, the chaplain was placed there by Good News Jail & Prison Ministry (GNJPM), headquartered in Henrico, VA., which is the largest supplier of Chaplains to jails and prisons in the U.S. In addition to providing ministry to the deputies and staff, the chaplain's work is focused on the men and women in prison, providing support through counseling—they call it sharing—and providing faith material distribution, Bible study classes, and some church services. The chaplains build something called a Chaplain Support Team, a network of local parishioners who grade Bible study coursework, help raise support, and provide visitation services.

In the Bible, Jesus adjured His followers not to forget those in prison and teach them as if ministering directly to Him (Matthew 25:43-45). This passage challenges believers in Jesus to connect with their local jail or prison so that we can do as admonished by Jesus. The former chaplain indicated that he made himself available to the men once they were out of prison. However, once the inmates left, he did not hear from them unless they ended up back in prison or unless they followed up with him.

Some volunteers came to the prison to offer Bible studies and to offer the men rides to their probation officer appointments once they were released. Nevertheless, the volunteers quickly retreated when they realized the complexity of the communications needed and all the safety and liability requirements. Some ministries or agencies in the vicinity of the jail have offered sporadic help to inmates, such as housing assistance, local rides, including bus tickets, and bus rides to destinations outside the area. According to the Chaplain, for liability and jail security reasons, this has been something that has been chiefly communicated to volunteers as strictly prohibitive unless it is part of a ministry function that a church or ministry board has endorsed.

In addition to GNJPM, the local Sheriff does not want individual volunteers at the facility to take it upon themselves to offer inmates anything that could be perceived as a potential security breach or as something that could potentially compromise their safety. For example, offering a former inmate something as simple as a ride usually required contacting someone in the jail's release department to confirm the inmate's identity, the intention to transport the individual to a particular destination, and an approximate time for a return call to verify that the mission was completed safely (Chaplain Dicky Sherrill, personal communication, December 6, 2019).

One volunteer to another local prison facility, who spoke anonymously, acknowledged the restrictive nature of providing support to former inmates. He said that often these policies were not followed and that volunteers who had become familiar with certain prisoners would secretly provide phone numbers for those prisoners so they could offer to connect them with churches, and other resources, once they were released. [Please note: the facility in question is a level 2 medium-security facility that operates as a "release center," housing persons convicted of drug crimes and non-violent offenders and prisoners set to be released shortly. This facility offers more incredible support for prisoners than was noted in other interviews, such as educational programs, technical training, and apprenticeship programs.]

It seemed to the former chaplain that inmates demonstrated genuine decisions to follow Christ while in prison. However, there was a falling out or failure to follow through once they left. According to the former chaplain, the ones with the most success after prison were those with a support system on the outside. Not many churches would follow up with prisoners or a place where the chaplain could pair up an inmate with a church willing to help, primarily because of the safety and liability requirements.

So, when asked about redemption in terms of restoration for those exiting a regional or county jail, the former chaplain suggested that this may consist of some confession of faith by the prisoner, with perhaps a connection to some groups that might come in and adopt a prisoner and help him or her in some way—whether through correspondence or to offer them help once they got out. However, in most cases, there was a breakdown in this relationship once the inmate left prison. This breakdown was also evident when the chaplain recommended that the former inmate contact a particular church that would provide the needed support. In many cases, a residence where the inmate could find housing has been located a great distance from where the church was located. So there was again a disconnect, and the needed support was not always available. As has been the case for many years, these types of ministries are inconvenient to those who want to pursue them, limiting the number of volunteers and the ability of churches to participate.

The former chaplain said that at one time, there were only five (5) nationally known jail and prison ministries in the United States: Prison Fellowship, Good News Jail & Prison Ministry, Chaplain Ray Ministries—now known as International Prison Ministry, Bill Glass "Behind the Walls" ministry, and M-2 Ministries.

M-2 Ministries, or "Match Two" ministries, was once headed by a former inmate named Sam Huddleston (Huddleston, 2013). Huddleston was given a five-years-to-life sentence at 17 years old and assigned to Deuel Vocational Institution in California. He served four years, nine months, and one day, and during this time, he surrendered his life to Christ and dramatically altered his life path. In his biography, it states, "Before entering the pastorate, Samuel was appointed as the Executive Director of a statewide nonprofit organization...which matched adult inmates and wards (youth) with outside volunteer visitors...(He) remains the only former prisoner to ever lead a California Department of Corrections program" (Huddleston, 2013).

The goal of the "Match Two" ministry was to match inmates coming out of prison with people or churches on the outside. This former prisoner saw the need and thought that this type of program would be an effective way to provide support for prisoners once they came out. This type of support for former inmates was essential in the restoration process. The International Network of Prison Ministries (INPM, n.d.) advertises hosting 4,864 prison ministries, chaplains, ministry volunteers, and helpful ministry resources in 111 countries on their website (INPM, n.d.).

Preparation for Launch

What types of resources or support are available to inmates to reduce or prevent recidivism? Based on the limited resources available to the former chaplain, the absence of current literature or support for those coming out of prison on the local level was somewhat surprising. One resource on the topic of successful transitioning provided by the chaplain was a booklet written 35 years earlier entitled, *Making It: A Handbook for Parolees* (Testerman, 1985). This author viewed a copy of the booklet copyrighted in 1985. However, Google Books indicates a copyright date of 1990. You can view it with the following link: (https://books.google.com/books/about/Making_it.html?id=mf4XHQAACAAJ).

It seemed ironic that two organizations would make books available, published in 1985, to modern readers in this new century. One of these books would describe getting out of prison but from a perspective of 35 years in the past, describing the task of looking for a job using classified ads and the Yellow Pages. These items hardly exist in our social media-driven world today. However, the other booklet would describe making this prison experience, your monastery, which would change the life of a rebellious young man who found himself in prison while seeking to establish his independence—but through which prison would give him everything he needed to find peace.

According to the former chaplain, another program offered for a time through the local prison was a "Life Empowerment" program, which included a Christ-centered substance abuse class. This program sounded similar to the "BRAVE" program mentioned earlier, which significantly affected Tim while he was in prison (BOP, 2016). The chaplain was allowed to screen individuals before they entered the program because he did not want inmates in that program who were not going to take it seriously. The determination of who would be picked and how this was determined was not available. After the class, the inmates could meet with mentors already in the program to explain rules, regulations, and expectations to the prospective inmate(s). This procedure was stopped primarily because of jail security concerns. The program selection process sounded discriminatory, but only if opening the program to everyone would weaken the expected impact. It could be suggested that only a few Tims and Jeffs are seriously focused on getting out of prison and staying out and doing something meaningful with their lives. Nevertheless, how will they know they can change if not given the opportunity?

Programs That Are Working: Commonwealth of VA

There was great news regarding the recidivism rate in the Commonwealth of Virginia. In a press release from February 2020 (Virginia Department of Corrections, 2020), Virginia reported the lowest recidivism rate in the country at 23.1% (tied this year with South Carolina). With the way the process works on a local level, as described by the prison chaplain in Virginia Beach, successful recidivism seems more accidental than intentional. The Virginia Beach Sheriff's Office does promote on its website that they provide a wide variety of programs to aid in the rehabilitation of offenders (Virginia Beach Sheriff's Office, 2020). However, the effectiveness of such programs is not yet known.

The former chaplain mentioned a new re-entry program he was unfamiliar with, not knowing the source or whether it was faith-based. The contacts are not through his office, but his office becomes the point of communicating such programs. The chaplain is there to minister to prisoners and is the receiver of many hopeful and helpful efforts with Bibles and faith-based magazines. Other programs are promoted through the prison, whether federal, state, or local initiatives. As previously mentioned, the success of recidivism programs is not documented at local levels.

However, on the state level, there is a successful process that has been in development since the hiring of DOC Director Harold Clarke in 2010. A press release cited the V.A. Secretary of Public Safety, who stated, "Today, offenders are re-entering society more prepared than ever to lead productive lives" (Virginia Department of Corrections, 2020).

The press release described the successful recidivism process as including "effective re-entry services, educational programming, and treatment offered in VADOC facilities and effective supervision by VADOC probation and parole officers in the community post-release" (Virginia Department of Corrections, 2020). In a subsequent report (Celi, Miller, and Cazares, 2020), the process for successful cultural transformation was described in greater detail.

Virginia Department of Corrections Director Harold Clarke began in 2012 by implementing a three-fold approach:

An analytics-based analysis of the causes of high recidivism with the various risk factors (Celi, Miller, and Cazares, 2020) noted why some former prisoners would recidivate while others did not.

Next, there was an integrated feedback approach drawing insights to program improvement from several stakeholders;

Moreover, the implementation of a program called the "Healing Environment and Dialogues initiative" was founded by Peter Garrett and Jane Ball (prisondialogue.org).

Their efforts seem to be working, with the data recognizing this lowest-in-the-nation recidivism rate. Ironically, on the Virginia Department of Correction's main website https://vadoc.virginia.gov/, two jobs posted on July 23, 2020, proposed that a Building and Grounds Supervisor role would start at a higher salary ($39,600) than the top starting salary for a Corrections Officer ($36,394).

Faith-Based Programs That Are Working: Prison Fellowship

Outsiders may never forget Chuck Colson as the Watergate felon, a political saboteur linked to the obstruction of justice that surrounded the disgraced President Richard Nixon. The New York Times described the former inmate turned evangelical leader upon his death in 2012 (Weiner, 2012). Colson will never forget himself as the liberated man whose heart was radically changed through his internment, trial, and prison time (Colson, 1976).

In Colson's autobiography, called *Born Again*, Colson tells the story of his conversion to Christ (Colson, 1976). He was a hardened ex-marine Captain, a tough guy in the White House, protecting his president; who, upon hearing about the message of salvation, wept bitterly in his car and could not even find the keyhole to drive away (Colson, 1976). Pre–conversion, Colson relished his role as Nixon's hatchet man (Aitken, 2012). However, as the Watergate scandal caught up with, and surrounded Colson, so did the Holy Spirit. Colson would later say that the greatest joy he had found in life was seeing how God had used him to touch the lives of others (PrisonFellowship.

org). His surprise was not in the awards he received or in the great people who showered praise on him: Colson was most amazed that God would use this broken man and convicted felon to transform the lives of others (Colson, 1976).

Colson's prison experience led him to create Prison Fellowship International in 1976. In his memoir, Colson wrote that he found himself increasingly drawn to the idea that God had put him in prison for a purpose and that he should do something for those left behind (Colson, 1976). Prison Fellowship is now the nation's most prominent Christian nonprofit serving prisoners, former prisoners, and families (PrisonFellowship.org).

According to their website, Prison Fellowship works to restore America's criminal justice system and those it affects (PrisonFellowship.org). They provide a ministry outreach to prisoners within the prison and after they are released. Much of their ministry focuses on connecting prisoners with Christ and conversion. However, besides their efforts to encourage and promote transformation through salvation and a connection with Jesus Christ, in selected prisons, Prison Fellowship offers training for incarcerated men and women to pursue what they call a 'holistic life transformation process.' Their efforts encourage those inmates to lead lives of purpose and productivity, both in and outside of prison.

Prison Fellowship has evidence of success with recidivism noted on their website (PrisonFellowship.org). In data on their web page, they cite some statistics—with data 17 years old and older—that state where prisoners participate in the in-person Bible studies they offer, they reduced recidivism by 66% (PrisonFellowship.org). In another study, prisoners who participated in a particular program sponsored by Prison Fellowship were noted to have a re-arrest rate, which was half of a matched comparison group (PrisonFellowship.org). The author here could not identify more recent data.

Having a national scope and a recognized leader in Charles Colson with his high-profile transformation brought tremendous regard to the Prison Fellowship program early on. In our interviews together, ex-convict Tim suggested that Prison Fellowship offered very little support to him while in prison. Again, as has been noted here, whether programs are being actively offered locally or nationally, it appears that the individuals who are motivated to turn their lives around are the ones who have managed to overcome the odds of getting out and finding success—while wearing the

"Scarlet Letter" label of ex-convict on their record.

In the case of Prison Fellowship, someone who saw the need was in a position to do something about it and forged an effort to try to help others because he saw that the path out of prison to success was broken, and bridges needed to be built. With inmates named Jeff Henderson and Charles Colson and an insignificant young man named Tim, sheer determination and force of will seemed to make this transition work. Without effective programs like Prison Fellowship and their training for reconciliation and re-adjustment—for prisoners and members of their families—we might say that the key to successful reintegration has been thrown away. However, the bridge to the island has been torn down, creating a cycle that's hard to break.

Faith-Based Programs That Are Working: Hope for Prisoners

The president stood at a podium in the Rose Garden and told the man that he did not look like a bank robber. Of course, it is difficult to imagine that a man in a double-breasted suit, standing next to the head of the Free World, would look the part of a prisoner (Saunders, 2018). Don't prisoners wear orange jumpsuits? Nevertheless, the person he spoke to had been in and out of prison, but today would mark one of the most remarkable transformations in prison reform history—and now he was paying it forward (Ponder, 2020).

Jon Ponder was a three-time loser—having been to prison three times before the final release, which changed his life forever (Ponder, 2020). Ponder had been doing drugs, running from the law, and getting arrested since he was 12 years old (Saunders, 2018). Ponder started drinking, doing drugs, and stealing to support his habit when he was 12 years old (Ponder, n.d.). Police came to his high school and arrested him for armed robbery. He was an addict and on his way to becoming a career criminal.

At 38 years old, he was hunted down, surrounded, and arrested for a string of bank robberies (Ponder, n.d.). He was facing extended jail time. While waiting in solitary confinement prior to his sentencing, Jon had a miraculous transformation after reading through the Bible and other Christian materials. Random individuals pushed these materials through the slot in his prison door. Only God can explain how these materials made it into the hands of a man isolated in solitary confinement, and only God can genuinely redeem a person. However, just because a person's heart is changed in prison—as noted by the former chaplain's story above—does not mean that the person always walks a straight path after redemption.

At sentencing, when asked if he had anything to say, Ponder told the judge that he would "spend every waking moment improving the caliber of who I am" (Ponder, n.d.). Even the judge was surprised by his response, and instead of sentencing him to 23 years in prison, the judge sentenced Ponder to only six years in prison.

When Ponder got out of prison and entered a halfway house, the FBI agent who arrested him came to visit and told Ponder that he had been praying for him. Special Agent Richard Beasley told Ponder that "God had called him to the FBI, in part for you" (Ponder, n.d.). Once at opposite ends of the legal spectrum, these men, now brothers in Christ, eventually became the best of friends (Saunders, 2018).

Ponder felt that his redeemed life was not meant to be lived only for himself, and God had given him a burden for those remaining in prison. Like Chef Jeff and his "Felon University," Ponder created a program with volunteer help from those who helped put him away and other law enforcement professionals (Ponder, 2020). After three stints in prison, Ponder saw what prison could do to a man and was determined to do something to help those who made it out of prison—to find success again when returning to the "free" world.

Saunders (2018) noted that research on the program Ponder founded—Hope for Prisoners—found that 64 percent of the program's participants found stable employment (Saunders, 2018). The study also found that 25% of those going through Ponder's program found employment within just a few weeks of leaving prison and graduating from the program (Saunders, 2018). The difference here is a prisoner who understands that bad choices lead to restrictive circumstances. Ponder knew the difficulties facing those former inmates re-entering society, and he committed himself to help others overcome those barriers.

His nonprofit, Hope for Prisoners, provides wide-ranging re-entry services, including mental, physical, and spiritual coaching and training for those who enter the program. What is different about Ponder's program is how active local law enforcement is: Members of the Las Vegas Police Department volunteer their time to support and educate those returning to society. One-third of the volunteer mentors are police officers (Levin, 2020). Here is a picture of redemption—that those who have arrested these prisoners and put them away in prison now are part of the process to help them be productive in society once again.

Stories of people like Jon Ponder, Chef Jeff, and Charles Colson show that the road to success after prison is complex, and it requires the former inmate to work hard to prove the doubters wrong. Nevertheless, these "success stories" also show that success after incarceration means that the ex-convict must find an advocate. Tim discussed two programs designed to help former inmates to get jobs after prison. The programs "Second Chance" and the well-known Prison Fellowship programs were ineffective in helping him achieve success once he got out of prison. It was the grace of God, his determination, and similar to Chef Jeff, the support of an advocate that helped Tim find success after his incarceration.

When I Got Out of Prison, I Visited You

In one compelling longitudinal study of former prisoners conducted in three states (Visher, Debus, and Yahner, 2008), the most successful strategy for long-term employment for the former prisoners studied was returning to a previous employer. The former inmates sought employment through various means, leveraging connections with family and friends. However, these contacts went only so far (Visher, Debus, and Yahner, 2008). The data suggested that restoration to former employment was the most successful for these failed former employees. As noted here, the data suggests that 60% of people who come out of prison return to their former employer. They do that because no one else knows them or trusts them, and they are looking for someone who knows them, and they hope their former employer will trust them and offer them an opportunity to get back on track.

Tim's story is different for two reasons: first, he is unique because he successfully overcame the obstacles. Nevertheless, after finding success in returning to work, he decided to leave all of that and take up the monastic life for real.

Once he left prison, there was a sense of a call to ministry. However, even his efforts to become a priest or pursue Catholic orders were rebuffed, and he could not even get a job in a Catholic Church. He has since become a monk and declared vows of asceticism. Now called Brother Tim, he uses his superior administrative skills to serve others, but he does not receive a paycheck. He depends on God and does receive some support from other churches. He administers a community food pantry ministry that serves the needs of people in a desperately poor area of Hampton Roads, Virginia.

Jesus, Himself mentioned His concern for those isolated in prisons, declaring that the faithful servants of the Kingdom of God would visit those in prison as if they were visiting Him (Matthew 25:34-40 English Standard Version). This certainly raises the value of each individual, whether in prison or not: it was and is our role to look after them and not to forget them—not to 'throw away the key' as it were. We act as if we have lost the key not only when we do not visit them; but also when we do not offer support for those former inmates looking for work in an attempt to return to everyday life. We know that we all have an Advocate with the father (1 John 2:1), but perhaps we might also consider becoming an advocate for a former prisoner when society has lost its key.

In searching for a Biblical model to guide the faith-oriented manager, there is an excellent example in the story of the enslaved person, Onesimus, and Paul's efforts to restore him to his master Philemon.

Philemon was a wealthy and righteous man who participated in and supported the work of the gospel and became a friend of the Apostle Paul. Onesimus had been Philemon's servant. From the letter, Onesimus had stolen from Philemon (v 18) and then ran away. Paul and Onesimus connected while Paul was in prison in Rome. Onesimus converted to Christianity and stayed to support Paul while in prison (Philemon 1:10 GNV). Paul knew it was essential to restore the relationship between Philemon and Onesimus. He acknowledges the harm caused by Onesimus's theft and running away in the letter. An enslaved person under these circumstances faced dire consequences, and Philemon could have had Onesimus put to death (Giszczak, n.d.). Paul appeals to Philemon's faith, offers to pay restitution for Onesimus, and invites Philemon to receive Onesimus back as he would Paul (Giszczak, n.d.). Paul is not asking that Onesimus now be released from his employment as an enslaved person. However, he asks that the runaway thief be reconciled to his master Philemon and restored in the relationship (Philemon 1:15-16 GNV). Although there are no specific steps or "how-tos" here on this approach, the evidence of Paul seeking to encourage restoration and reconciliation should be a model to those who believe in what Jesus Christ has done for us by reconciling us to our Father in Heaven.

Students of the New Testament like to say that church tradition has it that Onesimus eventually became the bishop of Ephesus (Giszczak, n.d.). So Paul's efforts at restoration were not just for the runaway thief at that moment, although there is nothing to suggest the Apostle could have imagined what sparing the life of this enslaved person would mean. Similarly, Chef Robert Gadsby could not have known what it would mean to offer a dishwashing job to a former prisoner named Jeff Henderson.

Chef Jeff himself has come full circle. He has launched a program called Felon University (Felon University, 2018). Felon University is an ex-offender educational platform offering training, consulting, and support for businesses considering hiring former inmates and helping with the process of restoration (Felon University, 2018). Chef Jeff is paying it forward to help others overcome poor decision-making and the stigma of incarceration. Where are the current day Apostle Pauls, and other people of faith, stepping in alongside Chef Jeff and supporting his redemptive efforts?

Brother Tim's story has become well-known, not for what he did in his past but for who he is today. Now, agencies and judges will refer young, incarcerated men and women to him for community service instead of jail time. Tim offers the opportunity for them to turn their history around into a positive future, but there is one catch: When he asks them what they have done, they have to be honest about it. Similar to findings in other research, one thing that comes up in the research about turning one's life around and breaking the chains of the past is acknowledging that you have fallen short and made a mistake—and the ownership of that mistake. This concept is evident in Alcoholics Anonymous, in the drug rehabilitation program Teen Challenge, and was also one of the key findings in research on employees terminated for cause and then rehired (Bucci, 2016). If we cannot recognize our part in poor choices, we cannot find a starting place to learn how to change. If our problems are always someone else's fault, this will not help us turn our own lives around. When Brother Tim asks, "So how did this happen (winding up in jail or being arrested)?" the younger version of himself had better be honest about their poor choices. This is the opportunity to follow a mentor and possibly change their future trajectory. If they lie and deny it, he will not work with them. Tim is offering them a way forward out of trouble. All they have to do is turn the key.

CHAPTER 6

Transformed from the Inside Out

Redeeming Those with Life-Controlling Problems

Abstract: According to Kersten (2011), Adult and Teen Challenge has helped about 50,000 people struggling with these life-controlling problems (Teen Challenge Programs, 2017). It is the world's most extensive drug and alcohol treatment program, with more than 200 locations in the U.S. and 1000 facilities worldwide (Kersten, 2011). In this chapter there are lessons from this life-changing program.

> "No test or temptation that comes your way is beyond the course of what others have had to face. All you need to remember is that God will never let you down; he'll never let you be pushed past your limit; he'll always be there to help you come through it."
>
> —***1 Corinthians 10:13 MSG***

Introduction

As long as men have sought healing properties in plants and flowers, there have also been discoveries of side effects of such efforts in the distilling of plants for drinks and medicine. These discoveries of nature and now chemical treatments for illness have led to the development of drugs for both good and harm.

One of the early leaders in the American colonies, Dr. Benjamin Rush, was noted to have believed that alcoholism was not a matter of personal willpower but was affected by the alcohol itself (Patterson, 2016). Dr. Rush, known as the father of American Psychiatry and a representative at the Continental Congress, grew up in a very pious Presbyterian family

(Butterfield, 2017). However, he was still unique in his view at the time that the concept of addiction was not simply a moral failing.

Throughout early American history, society viewed substance addictions as a moral flaw or a sign of weakness (Genetic Science Learning Center, 2013). Therefore attempts at reversing the addictive behavior ranged from intensive intercessory prayer meetings to sentencing the addict to an asylum, a sober house, or even prison (Patterson, 2016; Genetic Science Learning Center, 2013). According to one academic article (Genetic Science Learning Center, 2013), Doctors used a shotgun approach to treat the addiction, being willing to try just about any combination of drugs and therapy.

It would not be until 1935 that a significant successful program to address the rehabilitation of addicts was started. It became more of a movement than simply the recovery from addiction. That year Dr. Bob Smith and Mr. Bill Wilson, known in the program as Dr. Bob and Bill W, founded Alcoholics Anonymous. Using a spiritually focused approach, this program sought to encourage alcoholics to recover from the addiction and be personally transformed and find the support needed to maintain freedom from repeated addictive behavior.

According to their website (http://www.aa.org/pages/en_US), Alcoholics Anonymous is an international fellowship of men and women who have had a drinking problem. Alcoholics Anonymous's 12-step program is famous all over the world. Since the program's founding, some efforts have ameliorated the "God concept" from the original program. Some programs built on this model have recommended this adjustment. In contrast, other attendees have rationalized their way through the "God-focused" steps (Castleman, 2011). The A.A. organization itself has sought to remain faithful to the principles of the program, affirming this in a book on the 12 Steps written by one of the co-founders of the program (see the Introduction, Twelve Steps, and Twelve Traditions, Wilson, 1953) which has recently gone through its seventy-fifth printing. These principles have worked in the lives of hundreds of people since the first meetings were held in 1935. The founding of A.A. and its successful approach eventually led to similar programs, such as Narcotics Anonymous, Marijuana Anonymous, et al. (Patterson, 2016).

A Modern Understanding?

In more recent history, modern science has weighed in on addiction and its effect on the brain, where the addiction makes fundamental and long-lasting changes. While many modern treatments include approaches and techniques based on scientific research, the effectiveness of such treatments is mixed (Genetic Science Learning Center, 2013).

In an approach that is fundamentally similar to that of Alcoholics Anonymous in terms of a spiritually-centered foundation for overcoming drug dependencies, Adult and Teen Challenge programs use a Christian faith-based recovery model to aid the restoration of and recovery of persons struggling with life-controlling problems (Teen Challenge Programs, 2017). [Please note: the program's name was changed in 2019 to Adult and Teen Challenge. Some of the references will reflect the previous name.]

This program began as an outgrowth of the call on the heart of Pastor David Wilkerson, which was dramatized in the classic film "The Cross and the Switchblade" and has grown dramatically due to its effectiveness. In contrast to A.A., where volunteers host weekly support meetings walking attendees through their 12-step recovery model, Adult and Teen Challenge (ATC) would more accurately be associated with a residential therapeutic community model (ATC, 2022).

The program openly declares on its website that its approach to dealing with "life-controlling problems" relies on the teachings of Jesus Christ, the work of the Holy Spirit, and the study and practical application of Biblical principles. These topics are not ancillary but the central transformative components of their recovery program (Teen Challenge Programs, 2017). The program does not dismiss psychological and medical expertise, but this expertise and associated concepts are viewed from a spiritual perspective.

The Success of Adult and Teen Challenge

According to Kersten (2011), writing for a public policy website, Adult and Teen Challenge has helped about 50,000 people struggling with these life-controlling problems (Teen Challenge Programs, 2017). It is the world's most extensive drug and alcohol treatment program, with 225 locations in the U.S. and over 1400 facilities in 129 countries worldwide (https://www.

globaltc.org/global-locations/). According to the Kersten article, some research cited in Time magazine noted that Adult and Teen Challenge has a 70 percent success rate for those who finish the program (Kersten, 2011). On the official website (https://teenchallengeusa.org/studies/), several studies on the program's effectiveness are highlighted. In a more recent study conducted by Evangel University in 2019, 78% of the sample respondents (N=340) were sober and free from substance abuse after participating in the ATC program (https://teenchallengeusa.org/studies/).

In order to learn more about the redemptive approach to assisting teens in overcoming these challenges, an interview was conducted with the Executive Director of the Mid Atlantic Adult and Teen Challenge program Rocky Russell (R. Russell, personal communication, July 11, 2017). The Mid-Atlantic Adult and Teen Challenge program offices are based in Virginia Beach, VA, and serve the residents of Hampton Roads. Russell may have the perfect skill for operating an Adult and Teen Challenge program. Russell's dad was a corrections officer, and his grandfather was also in corrections. His dad was a big supporter of Florida Sheriff's Youth Ranches, whose mission is to "prevent delinquency and develop lawful, resilient, and productive citizens" (FSYR, 2017). Russell was previously a morning radio show host and manager of several small radio stations and was involved in full-time professional ministry as a church planter before being appointed Executive Director (Mid-Atlantic Adult and Teen Challenge, 2017).

Of the 225 Adult and Teen Challenge facilities in the United States, only 12 of them serve boys ages 12 to 17. So the facility managed by Russell is particularly unique. The boys are brought by family members, with most of them facing drug addiction. About one-third of the boys come to the center from guidance or direction from a court, and the rest come from family members contacting the center. Of the means of contact, about 50% of the contacts are made through phone calls, while the rest of the contacts are made through emails or family members completing referral forms online. About 70% of contacts are made by the mothers of the teens, while Dads make the rest. The teen program has some significant costs associated with it, and also a long-term commitment is required. The program was meant to create space, time, and opportunity for a significant reset.

Different Strokes

Adolescent programs are very different from Adult programs. The younger teen students need to get out of their environment, so a local facility is not utilized for them. For the adults, they might be able to stay at one of the intake centers closer to their home location. Most adult programs conduct the initial phase of the program in the local facility; but then will graduate members to other centers. The teens will remain in the same location for the entire program for 12 to 18 months.

Teen "students" at MATC progress through five phases as they move through the redemptive process. The actual progress for advancing in the program is different in each center. Adolescent centers do not all utilize a phase system within their programs, but many do. The time frame for the program is still 12-18 months. The Student Handbook describes the phases (Adult and Teen Challenge, 2017). The first phase has to do with students understanding the rigorous processes the center operates. The handbook describes how to behave at the center and on church visits, standards for living, dorm life, personal hygiene, school rules (students do also take classes here), how the program will work, and other vital details of how to get along with others while at the facility (Adult and Teen Challenge, 2017). [Please note: the Mid-Atlantic Teen Challenge Student Handbook and phases are unique; not all ATC locations have a phase system or similar handbooks.]

How It Works

According to Russell, the first phase is completed when a student has reviewed the handbook and takes a test, identifying and recalling essential details from the handbook. Being able and willing to follow processes is vital at the center. Students have to understand the policies and know how to conform. Life in recovery is about learning self-control and proper behavior. If students do not behave here, there are few other options for them—they will learn to behave somewhere else, generally in more confining or restrictive environments. Adult and Teen Challenge put tools in the students' toolboxes. They learn how to deal with the events that trigger aberrant and addictive behaviors.

In Phase 1, students are issued a contract when they come to the center for the first time. They read through and agree to the contract and the program's requirements, which moves them on to the next phase of the program. The last four phases of the program are not identified by any specific time frame or spiritual capability. Students begin basic discipleship training in subsequent phases and start to work on school materials.

Students begin going through the personal discipleship program ("PSNL" Personal Studies for New Life in Christ). They demonstrate a good attitude and honor commitments and contracts they have made. The next phase is more discipleship training and then designing and achieving attainable goals for educational achievement. The student is demonstrating some motivation and positively taking the initiative. The student begins to take leadership roles at the center. Next, there are additional discipleship training materials to be completed and more leadership roles to be taken in the center and complete school work. Now an effort is made to restore relationships frayed by the addictive behavior, and the student begins to plan for the transition back to the home environment. As more maturity and self-discipline are demonstrated, students are given more freedom and additional privileges.

There is a staff phase evaluation every month by the treatment team, where they review students' progress and then decide to move students between the phases. It is not a calendar year approach, nor is it based on some spiritual standard or capability. Some of the literature for other Adult and Teen Challenge centers reviewed for this article appear to follow a calendar timeline approach (North Dakota Adult and Teen Challenge, 2009) or a spiritual capabilities type of evaluation (Adult and Teen Challenge of the Firelands, 2017). Although the material in the early phases is prescribed, the students can create a more self-directed approach after a specific timeframe.

There are individual study programs, and then there are group studies. There is an individual program through which students advance, and then group interactions. The process for advancing a student is different in each center, but the phases are the same. Personal Studies for New Life in Christ (PSNL) is the individual program re-branded in 2019. The PSNL program is more of an individualized education and discipleship model. There was some similarity to a 12-step approach, but the materials have been revised more recently. While students work individually through the PSNL, small group studies are also available, called Group Studies for New Life in Christ GSNL. These groups are a subset of the whole facility.

Should any of the other centers offer other programs—some centers were noted as offering other 12-step programs such as *Stepping Into Freedom* and additional training—this is up to each center. There are about 85 standards to which each center has to adhere, but PSNL is the one unifying thread. Adult and Teen Challenge USA have certified teachers for PSNL and GSNL. The rest of the accreditation is focused on OSHA and food safety. It is like a franchise model—same core but fiercely independent.

Redeemed Yes, But Not Necessarily Free

Mr. Russell talked about the difference between redemption and disqualification. People can be redeemed in the spiritual realm, but because they are redeemed, they are not necessarily qualified to step back into the role where they were found lacking. There are not always opportunities for moments of grace, but the program is grace, and having this opportunity is grace.

Offering students an environment free from consequences is not helping them; it enables them. Not only do the students need the process structure, but even some of the staff need structure to be able to do their jobs. Even when staff come in and are not as successful in their role, the goal at this Mid-Atlantic Teen Challenge center is to take everyone to the next level. Many of the staff have been through some treatment program level, so they can relate but still must operate according to the structure. No matter how challenging it is to work with the staff, as they are working through the redemptive process themselves, and whether the staff or the students remain at the center or not, the goal is to offer them growth opportunities and some truth on which they can build and move to a higher level than when they started.

Conflicts Ahead

There is a potential battle within the Adult and Teen Challenge community as more and more Federal dollars are allocated for community treatment programs. At a regional meeting of the Adult and Teen Challenge Eastern Regional centers referenced during our interviews, Mr. Russell recalled one person saying, "Remember—we are not a drug and alcohol program. We are an evangelistic organization." Nevertheless, there is a flow of income coming from state governments for drug and alcohol treatment programs, and Adult and Teen Challenge is a very effective program. So Adult and Teen Challenge are facing a bit of a crisis. They have a successful program that is strongly evangelistic. Moreover, the program is highly effective in terms of recovery.

A secular program might offer to help people overcome bad habits, but there is really no change of attitude in their hearts. There may be repentance from things they have done, but there is not necessarily a spiritual transformation. The goal of Adult and Teen Challenge is a spiritual transformation and a path to complete healing from life-controlling behaviors. While the organized church seeks to lead people to the Eternal God, Adult and Teen Challenge seek to lead them to wholeness. According to Mr. Russell, some students experience spiritual salvation, but that is not the program's primary goal. According to a regional representative of ATC, most ATC centers might disagree with this statement. Can we have changed behavior patterns without truly changing hearts?

CHAPTER 7
Work as Redemptive Intervention

Abstract: A story about one woman's selfless efforts working with at-risk youth, striving to put them on a positive path after they have found trouble (or after trouble found them) early in life. There is also a description of an effective public-private partnership where work provides at-risk youth so much more than simply walking-around money.

Introduction

Most of our focus in these stories has been on programs that support a redemptive fresh start among adults. The data suggest that children's activities can lead to aberrant behavior before they become adults. What kinds of support are being offered to at-risk youth, which puts them on a positive path after finding trouble early in life?

Believe it or not, the effort to define "youth at risk" was itself more difficult than anticipated. In writing in the Journal of Counseling and Development (1994), counselors Tidwell and Garrett argue for consistency with the definition (Tidwell and Garrett, 1994). In their field, a solid definition allows for treatment methodologies that support a young person's presenting problem (Tidwell and Garrett, 1994). According to these authors, the term 'at risk' has been applied to young people as juvenile offenders, School dropouts, drug abusers, and adolescents with personality disorders, among other things (Tidwell and Garrett, 1994).

Standing in the Gap

I became familiar with Kerri through our church. She had read my book on Redemptive Leadership and followed me on social media. She is a program coordinator for an independent nonprofit that serves as a bridge for what the agency classifies as "at-risk youth," ages 18–24 coming out of the juvenile justice system and those about to move out of foster care: "aging-out" they call it. Kerri is a young woman, deeply passionate and concerned with these young people. Passionate young caseworkers like Kerri may be the only kind of people who can make it in this business of heartache and high turnover. She was part of the system for a brief time, so she understood the inherent difficulties (K. Henderson, personal communication, October 15, 2019).

Kerri's agency deals with youth who are aging out of foster care. [Her agency requested anonymity in exchange for sharing information on the current state of this work]. The target age as mentioned is 18–24. In that age group, these youth are free to leave the foster care situation but are not necessarily settled into what may be their next step. Kerri works hard to help them find jobs and build competencies to maintain self-control and stay out of trouble.

If all foster care situations were ideal, children coming out of challenging parental crises would be placed into an environment of nurturing and love, which would give them the ability to know how to proceed once they reach the age where they begin making their own decisions (Annie E. Casey Foundation, 2019). They might even stay with their temporary family for the stability it brings. However, the reality is that many people take on children for foster care because it brings them an additional paycheck.

Children in foster care report that the ambiguity of living away from home in the unfamiliar surrounding is the most challenging aspect of this transition (Annie E. Casey Foundation, 2019). The foster children are not always cherished, and sometimes they do not even feel valued in the homes of these foster parents. Often children are moved among several homes or residential treatment centers, making concentrating on school and building friendships complicated (Annie E. Casey Foundation, 2019). So Kerri's agency, and people like Kerri, struggle to get into the minds and hearts of youth on the precipice, encouraging them to find stability through a good job or by furthering their education in order to learn life skills and build new relationships that will help them to have meaningful lives that contribute to society.

Inconsistent Rules in Care for At-Risk Youth

In the wisdom of care and concern, each state has put together alternative care systems, or foster care, when children are abandoned or when parents are unable to care for them because of their dependencies and difficulties. As of 2017, there were about 442,000 children in foster care, with nearly half of these children in non-relative foster family homes (Child Welfare Information Gateway, 2017). Some people do this out of love, and others do it for a paycheck. Once the child turns 18, and the paycheck stops, sometimes their care stops, and the children are now on their own.

Kids walk in, saying they heard about Kerri and the agency. Their parents kicked them out, and they had no place to go. The state's Child Protective Services refer some because their parents are on drugs or in prison. Some come from other social service agencies because the state or county agencies are overwhelmed by the need. Some young adults find themselves victims of the foster care system—the very system set up to provide a covering and transitional bridge for them. Where else can they turn when the folks they were assigned to are hostile and unsupportive after coming out of a horrible family situation? Once these young adults age out of foster care, one in ten find themselves "couch-surfing with friends" or sleeping in unsafe situations (K. Henderson, personal communication, October 15, 2019).

That is where Kerri and her agency come in. The agency conducts an assessment to know what resources they need to collect to aid these at-risk youth. She beams as she talks about a young man who was taught to fill out an application, whom she taught to complete a resume so he could find a good-paying job (K. Henderson, personal communication, October 15, 2019). Often she will go with her clients when they apply for jobs. Kerri will go into the business first on her own and speak to the manager. She will tell that manager that there are people who want to change their lives and turn them around, but first, they need a job. And then, she will tell the client to go in and apply for the job. Said Kerri: "I feel like every person should know that they are valued and are loved, you know, and that ultimately, regardless of what their past life was like, they can make a brighter future for themselves with hard work, determination, and help" (K. Henderson, personal communication, October 15, 2019). The agency has many other in-house resources, like GED classes and access to temporary housing. There are requirements for the youth to qualify for and maintain their standing to access the resources. However, the entire approach is comprehensive, whether the youth take advantage of one resource or integrate many resources to get on their feet.

Their Guardian Angel

Sometimes, when Kerri is successful, her clients secure a job and completely change their lives. Nevertheless, sometimes, they cannot get the job or keep it. Kerri keeps plugging away with whatever support she can supply despite the setbacks. Her organization is a nonprofit, an independent nonprofit, among many larger agencies. They are trying to stand out, fighting to find funding. They have retained the services of a grant writer, whose full-time job is to find the dedicated funding that will help their agency keep its doors open. Kerri is a hero, but she would say her clients are the heroes. They are the ones who have escaped the system and made it through to get a job and find greater satisfaction than just living from day to day, not knowing what is around the next corner.

Furthermore, that is the reason for this book. This book is written for Kerri and for all of those counselors and prison chaplains, and leaders of agencies who work so hard every day to see lives transformed through redemption. Their organizations often struggle to make ends meet and wonder how they will be able to pay their associates and provide for their clients with their limited resources. We could provide better facilities, more contemporary living conditions, reliable mentors, and better resources. However, they want more than that. They would gladly settle for the limited situation where they find themselves if they could see their graduates succeed after completing their Redemptive Intervention Program.

Sometimes we see it in the university, where parents who had a limited education hope for a better life for their children and make a tremendous sacrifice to help their kids get the education they never had. It is that idea of paying it forward in one sense. In another sense, this is a vicarious act by those working in these agencies since many of the folks who serve in these roles have been through these difficulties. They are passionate, like

Kerri, about the process because they have worked through it and survived it. Although the agency or the program is not perfect, it is a hand-up, a support-based redemption plan, and if their clients stick with them, they know there is a better life on the other side.

An Example of Work as Redemption

One example of a broad public-private partnership to help at-risk youth find success through employment is a Georgia company that hired troubled teens and proved that hard work could overcome hard knocks. There is a structured program in the state of Georgia under the direction of Southwire Industries, and Southwire is one of the world's biggest wire manufacturers. The company has invested $4 million to get the program going, including purchasing a building and outfitting the classrooms. The school district contributes teachers and transportation.

Students can earn money for their expenses, but they must attend class and are carefully monitored. They work part-time in the factory, and the rest of the time, they are in class working on getting their high school diplomas. The district's dropout rate has plunged from 35% to 22%.

It was the company that approached the Georgia School District. The company wanted to be more focused on its philanthropic efforts and do something that would actively improve the lives of those needing the most help and encouragement. Drugs and violence have destroyed the social fabric in these rural areas, and many students fall through the cracks. This is a win for the school district and the students, motivated to earn money, finish their degrees, and pursue higher education or technical work. It is also a win for the business because the students perform much better than the average workers they hire.

The company website contains research that states high school dropouts face significantly limited employment options. The website also touts the program's success, that 40% of the students went on to post-secondary education, 30% pursued military careers, and a significant number of students pursued work with Southwire or other local employers. Like Kerri's work, these initiatives seek to create a future and hope for these students and, ultimately, a better life.

Nevertheless, that better life is not complete unless we can help these youth find work, finish their education, integrate into healthy relationships, and find stability after growing up in chaos. Employers cannot support each of Maslow's famous hierarchical needs for every individual in their employ. However, they can help provide meaning and purpose for individuals who are still trying to figure out why they are here and what they are supposed to do.

Businesses with a social conscience need to allow their employees to volunteer in their communities. However, they can also speak into people's lives and tell them that their lives matter, their contributions to our organizations matter, and they have a greater purpose. That is something that people want to hear; that is something that people need to hear, not only from their caseworkers and program coordinators but also from all of us.

CHAPTER 8
Redemption in Other Cultures

Despising the Shame

Abstract: Much of what has been written here has been viewed in the eyes of an America-centric culture. What about redemption in other cultures? Is that a byproduct of a religious belief and its impact on the culture? Does the culture even consider redemption a viable option if there is no religion in the culture or no spiritual opportunity for redemption? This chapter contains research and an interview on this topic.

"For the joy set before Him, (Jesus) endured the cross, despising the shame."

—***Hebrews 12:2***

> "Shame is a terrible thing to endure, and many of the proudest natures have been subdued when once they have been subjected to it. In the Saviour's case, shame would be peculiarly shameful; the nobler a man's nature, the more readily does he perceive the slightest contempt, and the more acutely does he feel it."
>
> —***C. H. Spurgeon***

Introduction

Throughout this book, the author has considered the concept of redemption and the dramatic effects of redemption on persons through whom this process has worked. Redemption is a religious term used in the Bible to describe the process of spiritual restoration and how it transforms people who allow the process to work in them (Rightmire 1996). Perhaps due to the early prevalent view of America as a nation built on Judeo-Christian values, this concept has also permeated the culture, with author Wilfred McClay describing redemption as a solid fundamental foundation of American culture within our deepest moral convictions (McClay, 2013).

Several things are assumed in writing here; first, although redemption is a spiritual experience, there can be evidence of life transformation in restoring individuals who have turned from aberrant behavior to a productive society. Our culture is equipped for and built with this concept of redemption; we are comfortable with these radical transformations (McClay, 2013). Some of this may occur by one's self-awareness of their desperate condition (Romans 3:23-24). However, this author has documented many occasions where the failed individual needs support and encouragement to be restored to a position of contributing to society (Bucci, 2016).

What if a culture is not experienced or comfortable with redemption? What if a culture rejects the guilt of failure as a motivation to seek transformation and instead bridles failed individuals with shame? Most people who fail but earnestly seek restoration are subject to social shaming resulting in deception, denial, and sometimes even death.

At a networking meeting, I was asked: What about redemption in other cultures? What does that look like? I took the question to investigate the concept and practice of redemption as translated into other cultures. The following are the results.

Living in an "Honor-Shame" Culture

Tyler Klausmeier is a US citizen who lived and worked in Japan for four years. He worked for four different agencies or organizations teaching English to Japanese children in his four years. He taught English to children from babies up to high school age and became acquainted with his students, their parents, other teachers, and many different managers.

Tyler had access to several different managers and the parents' lives of the children he taught. He became familiar with many aspects of this Asian culture. He watched as managers were replaced for mistakes made but never given a second chance. Tyler observed that employees are not ever rehired in Japan for legal or professional reasons. The reason that this does not happen in Japan is that Japan is an "Honor-Shame" culture. If someone quits or gets fired, they will not be rehired—they will not return.

According to Tyler, it is not hard to get fired from his few years working in Japan. In Japan, it is hard to find a job. However, where companies are looking for talent, someone fired from one job might lie or not put the former job on a resume. If a person is fired from their job, their sense of shame will be so great, and the implication that they brought this on themselves in the company is so prevalent that they will not ask to be redeemed. In this same culture, not only could you lose your job for any number of reasons, but if your boss finds out about poor behavior outside of work, you could also be terminated for this behavior unrelated to work.

This breadth of managerial control over behaviors, even outside the workplace, is very common in Japan. For example, in Japan, the penalty for DUI is severe. Again according to Tyler, not many people in Japan drive, but if you do and get a DUI, you could get a hefty fine and have your license taken away. If your boss finds out about it, he will fire you even if this is apart from your work responsibilities. This is certainly unique to their culture, this integration of work behaviors and personal practices.

According to Demetriou (2020), there is a collectivist and hierarchical approach to work in Japan. Employees even refrain from taking earned vacations if their supervisors do not take vacations (Demetriou, 2020). The reasons for all of this boil down to one concept: Shame. In this collectivist culture, one mistake or demonstrated weakness in one area impacts all of your activities and potentially disrupts the collective group harmony.

Disrupting group harmony is shameful, and fear of a manager's scorn causes stoic compliance. Moreover, shame in this culture is so uncomfortable that people may even take their own lives to remove the shame (Louie, 2020). The cultural influence of shame is so strong that even among Asian Americans, suicide is the leading cause of death among Asian Americans aged 20-24 years (Louie, 2020). Suicide in this age bracket is responsible for about 33% of deaths, which is far greater than comparable ethnic groups in that age bracket (Louie, 2020).

Honor-Shame Framed as a Cultural Concept

The Anthropologist Ruth Benedict was thought to be the first to define the Japanese culture as a culture of honor and shame in her classic work, *The Chrysanthemum and the Sword: Patterns of Japanese Culture* (Benedict, 1947), based on her research after the Second World War (Creighton, 1990). As much as the Japanese decried the characterization (Creighton, 1990), after Benedict's work, contemporary studies of this Asian culture have used this terminology and sought to better understand its impact on the Gospel message. The Gospel message is guilt and shame to many, but it needs cultural adaptation (Naylor, 2010).

Simon Cozens is an expert on Intercultural Studies and Missiology (Cozens, 2018). Cozens wrote two related articles on the Shame culture and its origins (Cozens, 2018). Cozens cites the Ruth Benedict book and research from Eugene Nida's anthropological textbook Customs and Cultures (Nida, 2000), suggesting three different types of culture when it comes to their reaction to transgressions religiosity. Cozens cites Nida (2000) as the source of qualifying the different cultures: Fear, Shame, and Guilt. Cozens believes that Nida's Shame cultural response is more emotionally based as if we would feel terrible.

Meanwhile, another Missiologist, Roland Muller (2000), expands on Nida's definition of shame beyond simply an emotional response and links it with a social value. Mueller does this with Guilt and Fear (Muller, 2000). So, in propagating the Gospel, professional Missiologists have qualified three cultural contexts in which the Gospel of Jesus Christ must be navigated: the "Honor-Shame" culture of the East and the "Guilt-Innocence" culture of the West. There is also now a "Fear-Power" cultural identifier in other parts of the world. Professional Missiologists recommend that the Gospel communicator discover metaphors and the correct terminology to adequately present the message of the Cross cross-culturally (Naylor, 2010).

Below is an example of how the traditional Gospel message would need to navigate these cultural dimensions—here, we return to the "Honor-Shame" Japanese culture.

In his blog on missionary contextualization of the Gospel, Mark Naylor (2010) related a story about a missionary to Japan, Norman Kraus (Kraus, 1990). Missionary Kraus realized that the presentation of the Gospel as redemption—the atonement made by Jesus, giving his life to pay the penalty for our sins—did not connect with the culture of the Japanese. Kraus discovered that the Japanese understanding of justice differed from our Western culture. A Western understanding of justice uses the idea of an impartial decision based on legal statutes or precedent. The accountability comes in an obligation that must be met or a debt that must be paid. The Japanese do not perceive something similar to this. As Tyler mentioned, guilt is not banished through punishment for the Japanese, and shame must be overcome by establishing the right relationships and restoring honor (Naylor, 2010).

According to Creighton (1990), Ruth Benedict wrote that the Japanese sometimes react as strongly as any Puritan to a private accumulation of guilt (Creighton, 1990). However, while it might be guilt-reducing, the seeming avoidance of confession would be too publicly traumatic given this extreme sensitivity to social shame (Creighton, 1990). As we see in Japan, and as is becoming a reality in our culture, shame sanctions play a more significant role in regulating behavior in Japan than guilt sanctions. According to Creighton (1990), shame involves an awareness of one's inadequacy or failure to achieve a wished-for self-image. Fear of separation and abandonment accompanies this. In a collectivist culture, the degree of shame would be much stronger than one's feelings of guilt. Guilt is linked to punishment and fear of such. Nevertheless, if one is afraid of losing their status, this will supersede guilt nearly every time (Creighton, 1990). Because the fear of punishment is not as intense as being ostracized or isolated in one's culture, guilt is borne in silence. But if left unresolved, this may lead to self-destruction (Ausubel, 1955; Louie, 2020).

Again according to Naylor (2010), many Asian or Eastern cultures use the Honor-Shame paradigm as the lens through which they view themselves. In these cultures, people assess their value through the way others perceive them. They are not driven by guilt but by shame, which is how any action is perceived by themselves and others within their community (Naylor, 2010). Another missionary cited by Naylor (2010) spoke of his experience in an Honor-Shame culture (Naylor, 2010), describing his efforts to witness the Gospel by working on acting correctly. According to Naylor, this is more of a Western "Guilt-Innocence" context. Meanwhile, those in the Honor-Shame culture sought to act honorably and frame their actions accordingly (Naylor, 2010).

A Triple Play of Culture—with the Same Solution

In the third cultural context—that of "Fear and Power"—acting incorrectly or offensively in this culture is defined as offending existing powers, whether political or social powers or some deity (Muller, 2000).

This could result in personal setbacks or tremendous stress and pressure to conform. This also leads to acts of self-deprivation in order to justify oneself before the offended deity. How does one appease an offended deity? The culture's writings define what offends them, and then individual acts in excessive ritualistic ways to try again to appease their disgruntled idol (Muller, 2000).

Naylor (2010) also references Muller (2000), who describes the story of the Fall of man in Genesis chapter 3 with a view of these separate cultural contexts (Muller, 2000). Muller says that this sin of rebellion in the Garden led to the foundations of cultural condemnation: There was shame in their nakedness (Gen 3:7); there was fear as Adam and Eve hid from God (Gen 3:8); and finally, when their disobedience was exposed—there was guilt (Gen 3:17) (Naylor, 2010). This rebellion is universal, as is our estrangement from God and each other due to it (Muller, 2000). Since all three cultural contexts were present in this Garden rebellion story, the opportunity for redemption and restored relations with God exists here. Moreover, why does shame get all of the attention?

Is Shame Normal for Everyone?

Cozens (2018), previously cited, references a book by Psychologist Michael Lewis (1992), who sees shame as a typical but normal human emotion (Lewis, 1992). Lewis asserts that we are negotiating shame for much of our lives, and cultures are shaped by how children learn to deal with shame (Lewis, 1992). As our modern-day culture drifts further away from a Christian worldview, our youth seem to operate more from the "Honor-Shame" perspective, viewing tolerance as the greatest virtue and not seeking to offend anyone but to get along at all costs (Francis and Hoefel, 2018). In the Shame culture, as noted by Tyler's interview and also in the writings of Rabbi Sacks (2014), if you have done something wrong, do not admit it and do not be found out (Sacks, 2014). There is a great reluctance when there is a trial by public exposure. This has an interesting responsive effect: we become less trusting of people and more suspicious (Sacks, 2014).

Shaming is also prevalent in response to perceived aberrant behavior and is meted out through certain social media platforms. In a highly controversial article reported by the Wall Street Journal (Wells, Horwitz, and Seetharaman, 2021), internal research done by the social media giant Facebook recognized the impact of Instagram on users' body image, particularly teenage girls (Wells, Horwitz, and Seetharaman, 2021). Part of the research noted that almost one-third of teen girls who had body image issues felt worse due to the Instagram social media tool (Wells, Horwitz, and Seetharaman, 2021). WSJ reporters observed data in FB's internal documents, which noted that among teens who reported having suicidal thoughts, a significant percentage of these users traced the issue to Instagram. Teenagers also blamed Instagram for increases in the rate of anxiety and depression (Wells, Horwitz, and Seetharaman, 2021). The reporters suggested that this accusation was an unprompted response but consistent across all the groups surveyed. While other social media apps utilize performance or antics to share with friends, Instagram focuses mainly on the body and a person's lifestyle. Facebook research found that this was detrimental to many young users, particularly young girls (Wells, Horwitz, and Seetharaman, 2021). Here again, self-image is a critically manipulated part of the shaming, as referenced by both Benedict and Creighton in their research (Creighton, 1990).

Where Has Redemption Gone?

As mentioned here in the introduction, while it is true that redemption is a spiritual transformation, in our culture, the term is often also used when people are given second chances or an opportunity to make things right. The author has written on episodes which we call "restoration," including the stories of people who have been fired or terminated for cause and who are then given another opportunity to make things right in a working relationship, to possibly find healing and eventually social restoration and career success (Bucci, 2016).

Much of this has been viewed in the eyes of an Americentric culture. As noted, this view of "redemption" and offering "second chances" within the context of a "Guilt-Innocence" culture looks more like the repayment of the debt owed without the need for some self-abasement. We might speculate that a person's view of restoration or being made whole or right in a cultural content can often be a byproduct of a religious belief system and its impact on the culture. If there is no spiritual opportunity for redemption in the context of cultural religion, then the culture would not even consider redemption as a viable option. In mission work, Naylor suggests that missionaries would either have to teach other cultures a Western view of justice (besides learning their language and subtleties) or interpret the redemption of Christ using some cultural metaphor that would resonate in their cultural context (Naylor, 2010).

In his research, albeit dated, Ausubel (1955) analyzed the basis of guilt and shame and their relationships. His conclusions indicated that guilt should develop in all cultures, given the minimally favorable social conditions (Ausubel, 1955). This would seem to conflict with the professional Missiologist's view. Professional Missiologists believe it is arrogant and wrong to work at convincing people in an Honor-Shame culture to recognize guilt since the Bible addresses all forms of separation from God. However, according to Ausubel (not a Christian author), the reason confession and atonement are seemingly not easily observed within the Asian culture is not that genuine guilt is lacking, since otherwise, it would be relieved by confession (Ausubel, 1955). The Japanese individual does not, according to Ausubel, avoid confession because his guilt is an only shame. He surmises that it is more reasonable to posit that while confession of errors and wrong-doing would be guilt-reducing to the Asians, it would also be highly traumatic given the tremendous Japanese sensitivity to shame (Ausubel, 1955). He suggests that overwhelming feelings of guilt can be relieved less painfully by suicide (Ausubel, 1955). As noted earlier, this trend among young Asians continues to rise. Could we need to release not from shame but the guilt causing it?

Impact of Shaming Within Contemporary Culture

Within our Americentric culture, the specter of shame's imputation by social culture warriors is a powerful tool in controlling behavior and inhibiting creativity. In today's virtual culture, shame has been applied to anyone who seems to violate a predetermined set of postmodern cultural norms (Mueller, 2021). In modern culture, the concept of redemption has been adapted to become face-saving, which represents the actions of an individual to remove shame and be restored to an acceptable role in society

(Mueller, 2021)—if anyone can attain this narrowly defined position. Many individuals who rightly or wrongly act in ways that are deemed socially inappropriate suffer greatly in cultural detachment and, more remarkable still, in seeking social restoration (Mueller, 2021).

According to Yoder (2021), 70% of youth stop attending church after graduating from High School; then nearly a decade later, about half return. While there are many reasons for the loss of young people in the church today (Yoder, 2021), one reason not observed in the research, but which could be possible, as noted here, is this transition from a Guilt-Innocence culture to an Honor-Shame culture. Pastor and author John MacArthur suggest that guilt-engendering subjects like hell and judgment have left the church. The focus has changed to promoting positive psychology, with an adaptation of the outer society stressing individualism over God's authority and moral absolutes (MacArthur, 2014). Even if this style of preaching was still prevalent, Hellfire preaching is ineffective because, as mentioned by Creighton describing Japanese culture, it appears that the strength of guilt sanctions has eroded in our modern culture. In contrast, shaming sanctions have increased influence (Creighton, 1990). According to MacArthur, there is no longer any sense of guilt (MacArthur, 2014).

Quoting a seminary professor, MacArthur writes that hell preaching "is just too negative. Churches are under enormous pressure to be consumer-oriented, appealing rather than demanding" (MacArthur, 2014). Our youth see the church as consumed with image, and there is no room for depression, struggle or doubt (Yoder, 2021). When we fail to live up to an image, the result is the envelopment of shame through the perception that we could not be as perfect as everyone else. Remember the earlier Instagram research (Wells, Horwitz, and Seetharaman, 2021)?

This is also pointed out in research on Bullying (Martocci, 2015). Author Martocci (2015) suggests an increase in narcissistic personality among adolescents because of a cultural shift to focus on the construction of the self (Martocci, 2015). Here is the building of an "Honor-Shame" orientation: author Martocci suggests that people saw *more importance* in building an appearance of worth to others rather than an adherence to a moral code (Martocci, 2015). When a religious perspective was more critical, there was a possibility for acceptance, forgiveness, and redemption. However, Martocci writes that people are responsible for redeeming themselves (Martocci, 2015). Social forces influenced by media encourage the withdrawal of support for individuals who have demonstrated aberrant behavior and are deemed unacceptable or problematic by the social collective, managed in the virtual space by large social media entities (Mueller, 2021).

Redemption vs. Reputation Management

Reversing the social stigma perpetuated in social media outlets in the "Honor-Shame" culture sounds much like our contemporary version of "reputation management" and is not like redemption. Reputation management focuses on trying to distance oneself from the past, particularly in a societal context. With reputation management, the individual asks questions about how they can restore themselves and regain what they believed was taken away. In contrast, redemption says, "The old things have gone; everything is made new!" (2 Corinthians 5:17 NCV).

Christianity does not require restoration tours and public interviews of shame-ownership. Jesus, our substitute, died a shameful death on a cross, with the scripture declaring that "cursed is anyone hung on a tree" (Galatians 3:13, quoting the Old Testament). Peter the fallen and forgiven apostle wrote that God the Father called down from Heaven on the Mount of Transfiguration to honor Christ for His sacrifice (Matthew 17:5; 2 Peter 1:17). If anyone could understand the eradication of the specter, it would be Simon Peter (see Gospel of John chapter 21 for Peter's reinstatement). 1st Peter chapter 2 declares that as Christ was rejected but became the Chief Cornerstone, we who may also be rejected are being built up into a spiritual house—and this is a great honor, for our God will dwell among us! As we seek to humble ourselves before God and accept this merciful freedom, the scripture declares that His Father will honor us (John 12:20-26).

Can the Concept of Redemption Be Appealing in the Asian Culture?

One author on ancient Japanese culture suggested that the forceful intervention of Western technology into 19th century Japanese life shocked their culture out of its hierarchical "Honor-Shame" centered approach to consider more opportunities for restoration within their culture (Ikegami, 2003). Nevertheless, another equally exciting article suggested that this global metamorphosis from the shame culture to the guilt culture was influenced by the onset of Christianity (West, 2015). In truth, Christianity does not ameliorate the cultural shame or fear of a guilt culture. Christianity introduces redemption to a culture (West, 2015). The act of Christ dying on the cross released individuals from the fear of animist or legalistic requirements and converted fear of loss to an earnestness to be made whole and in the right relationship with a benevolent Father (1 John 4:18). Redemption also transformed the desire to pursue cultural honor over shame by recognizing that failure and mistakes fill our lives. However, Jesus took upon Himself our shame (Hebrews 12:2) so that we could enjoy the peace provided by forgiveness.

The verse quoted in the introduction to this chapter is significant in regards to how we understand shame from a spiritual perspective (Hebrews 12:2). Jesus despising the shame means that He disrespected it—He literally "saw the shame as detestable" (Helps Ministries, 2011). That is the key to our liberation from a culture of shame and self-loathing. Since three the experts on Asian culture suggest that it is genuinely guilt that is at the core of this conflict, but public atonement would be detestable to an Asian person, given the significant sensitivity to shame (Benedict, 1947; Ausubel, 1955; Creighton,1990) eradication of the trauma of shame is the only solution. Jesus knew that He had to endure that painful death as the substitutionary atonement for my sins. The only action is recognizing not the shame but being satisfied with His ability to remove the guilt of my sin. Therefore, we can completely reject the shame as well.

Jesus Christ died to set all people free from shame and guilt and the fear of oppression from powerful spiritual forces. Christ has redeemed us from the condemnation that comes when our self-interest berates us for not living up to others' standards; and the fear that, due to our failures, we will never amount to anything. Fear and pride are cited in the "Lead like Jesus" series (Blanchard and Hodges, 1999) as two obstacles to being in a right relationship with God. The self-perceived failures in either pride or fear lead to guilt and shame, while Christianity offers redemption of sins leading to freedom from guilt and shame in the glow of God's unconditional love.

Example of Restoration in an Honor-Shame Culture

Do we have an example of restoration in an "Honor-Shame" culture where the overwhelming restraints of shame once kept people in bondage, but who can now be set free? There is an example of a "culture within a culture" with Native Americans.

Paul Spicer has written extensively on Native American culture based on his proximity to Indian tribes in Minnesota, where he does his research. In an article Spicer wrote on alcoholism among Native Americans (Spicer, 2001), the title describes the restoration of self as an essential aspect of Native Americans who find the opportunity to overcome the draw of alcoholism. In studies conducted over 20 years before Spicer's paper and his research, formal recovery programs were not always as effective in helping Native Americans overcome alcohol problems. However, Spicer has documented some significant transformations (Spicer, 2001).

Among Native Americans, there is a sense that drinking alcohol negatively influences people's lives. However, it is also a strong draw in socialization since many Native Americans are involved in alcohol abuse. Spicer suggests that drinking was a shameful indication of cultural degradation and loss of their testimony (Spicer, 2001). Spicer noted that individuals who found the treatment helpful for their sobriety pointed to an educational experience that brought self-awareness and changed how they view themselves (Spicer, 2001).

There is, throughout the research, evidence of the significance of self-awareness and how awareness of the problems related to alcohol caused these individuals to look at their decision-making on whether they would continue with this addictive behavior. There is evidence that when people made a spiritual connection, either through the church or through an Alcoholics Anonymous group which allows for self-awareness and moral consideration of the effects of alcoholism, it impacted the secession of drinking. Awareness of culture and identity as potential solutions seems to be a theme in much of the literature that Spicer identifies. Nevertheless, a few of the reports of the effectiveness of such cultural identities are supported with evidence through specific studies or control groups to reduce alcohol use (Spicer, 2001).

It seemed that self-awareness caused individuals to surrender to their inability to overcome their problems (Spicer, 2001). Similar to the approach with AA, this may have led to a spiritual experience in the re-connection with their own culture and spiritual knowledge. This aligns with the Alcoholics Anonymous Step 3 of surrender and acknowledging their need for a higher power's help.

How interesting that these findings related to some of the early research on Redemptive Leadership (Bucci, 2016): Spicer's findings suggested that in this process of redemption and restoration, leaders carefully highlighted to those seeking recovery that continued movement back to the aberrant behavior was going to cause them to lose their jobs again; while changing their behavior would not only lead to career stability but also restoration of societal acceptance and a restored family (Spicer, 2001). In Spicer's research, some individuals develop a general self-awareness either through a spiritual experience or through educational experience about the impact of this continued degrading behavior. Failure in restoration would cause the candidates to lose their jobs, face, and possibly lose their families. So as evidenced in the original research on Redemptive Leadership (Bucci, 2016), as with Native Americans, self-awareness led to a recognition of fault and frequently repentance of previous aberrant behavior; and throughout this process, a recognition of a need for a Higher Power or re-connection with spiritual roots (Spicer, 2001).

For these Native Americans, there was a sense of a greater morality of having fallen short or missing the mark, which had its roots in the Christian faith (Spicer, 2001). Several Native Americans interviewed had powerful spiritual experiences, more aligned with turning from alcohol to serve and help their fellow Native Americans. So then, the application of what it meant to be sober was related more to the cultural context of Native Americans and being able to serve others in the community and help them find success and overcome these obstacles (Spicer, 2001). Here pride in culture and shame for the degradation of once-proud heritage is superseded by recognizing how far they had fallen and an earnest desire for restoration, to help others not continue in the same failed habit pattern—sounds familiar (Psalm 51:13).

Conclusion—The End of Shame

Tyler Klausmeier suggested that the extreme efforts to restore honor and negate shame in the Asian culture of Japan are a strange contrast to redemptive leadership. He says that we as Americans would think that getting your license taken away and a huge fine is bad enough. However, in our Western culture, your boss would probably not seek to terminate you—unless the DUI was in a company-owned vehicle. Nevertheless, in that "Honor-Shame" Asian culture, there is a sense that if you do anything to dishonor an organization, you must be held accountable, even if it is something in your personal life. So Tyler did not experience a time in his four years in Japan when he was aware that someone messed up and kept in their job. In 4 years, there was never an excuse where someone had screwed up, whether on the job or off the job and was terminated but then given another opportunity. Tyler had never heard of a restoration case. There was no evidence of any redemption in Japanese culture. The bondage of the shame culture is intense and lethal, as was mentioned earlier (Louie, 2020).

In his book Encounters with Jesus (Keller, 2013), Tim Keller sets up this discussion with a perfect ending. Keller relates the story of Jesus attending the Marriage Feast from the Gospel of John. This is Jesus' first public display of His majesty and miracle-working power. Why did Jesus choose to launch His miraculous ministry at a simple village wedding, Keller asks rhetorically (Keller, 2013)? In that Honor-Shame culture, as the community came together for this wedding celebration, running out of wine would have been shameful; and this would have embarrassed the family while starting this young couple on the wrong foot in that culture. Jesus vanquishes the shame and provides the wine so that the party can continue—but is this all that He did? Keller opines that Jesus did something else in that context—and He does the same for us: He released the couple from the social shaming, and He provided Joy! The wine Jesus provided was better than anything they had previously had. However, Jesus also provides the perfect antidote to shame, not only for that moment in that young couple's life but also for us. As Keller suggests, Jesus blessed this wedding feast with an eye toward the Marriage Supper of the Lamb (Revelation 19). At this wedding feast, Jesus represents our bridegroom, and we are His bride. Throughout the scripture, God describes wanting to be intimate with His people. At the feast, there will be no shame that will separate us from the love of God, only "perfect redemption, the purchase of blood," as the songwriter once said (Crosby, 1875).

CHAPTER 9
After the Thrill is Gone

Abstract: What happens to combat veterans, wounded warriors who can no longer function in a role for which they have trained and singularly focus their attention for some 15 or more years? Furthermore, how can they adapt to this new life of "family man" and average citizen with many limitations—some of which others cannot see or appreciate? A story of a Green Beret who gave his all for his country, and when he reluctantly stopped fighting for us, we also stopped fighting for him. He had to fight the greatest battle of his life alone.

Introduction

It is a holiday classic for millions of families. Hardly a Christmas goes by when the members of our family and perhaps hundreds of families across the country celebrate Christmas by watching the film "White Christmas." If you are familiar with the film, several plot lines blend to bring the cast together to help a retired general (Fogle, 2019).

One of the notable characters in the story is the retired General who has sunk all his retirement savings into a former Vermont gristmill which is turned into a ski lodge. People come to Vermont for snow, and when there is no snow, no one comes. His former soldiers, now successful entertainers, find out that he is losing his shirt in this entrepreneurial venture, and they want to help.

One of the ironies portrayed in the film is how this Major General has gone from being high up in his organization's pecking order to be at the lowest end of the spectrum. One of the main characters meets the retired General carrying wood and mistakes him for the janitor. When introducing the challenge of rallying his former command troops to come to Vermont and support the General's venture, Bing Crosby's character in the film sings an introduction to his pitch, in which he refers to a retired general as "General Who?" The lyrics continue: "We are delighted that he came, but we cannot recall his name."

It is difficult to go from being at the apex of your organizational structure to being considered "General Who?" Whatever may have led to this change of status, whether voluntary or involuntary, that sudden change of managerial position often means a loss of prestige in merit-based organizations. Some people take the change of status in stride. Former football players or Olympic athletes are well known in their communities and continue to earn respect after playing at the highest level in their particular sport. Some suffer from the loss of status, with their sense of self-tied in their former roles, such as Olympic swimmer and gold medalist Michael Phelps (Crouse, 2019).

So then, consider the General, who goes from being one of the top dogs in the Army to being "General Who," as is portrayed in the movie. Some retired military leaders with exceptional skills might score a leadership role with a defense contract. Most military retirees, whether serving a minimum or extended time in the service, become ordinary citizens, which is an adjustment for them. Consider the protagonist in the following interview. He was formerly at the highest level in his group; he was among the cream of the crop, earning the Purple Heart, the oldest and most revered of all military recognition (Borch, 2016). However, when he was seriously injured and acknowledged it, he was suddenly seen as a malingerer. After this, within his organization, he became, in his words, an "F---ing nobody!"

Green Beret Who?

He valiantly served his country, longer than the average tenure for most people in his group. He was a member of the United States Army Special Forces and served 15 years in the military; he was deployed to war zones in Iraq and Afghanistan for three years. He saw plenty of combat activity. He was a Green Beret and would still consider himself in that class of men if not for the repercussions of an IED explosion.

At first, he and his comrades were grateful they survived the explosion.

They thought that, like many other times when they had found themselves in tight spots, they had gotten out alive and could still function normally. Earlier versions of the same "Mine Resistant Ambush Vehicle" (MRAP) would have blown up and sent body parts flying everywhere. In his case, the vehicle he and several others were riding did not fall apart after the explosion.

Nevertheless, the strange thing about explosion trauma is that the effects may not be felt for quite some time. There was a rush of adrenaline and the realization that they had survived another fatal attack on them. There was laughter and joking about how the enemy had missed them again. They had always been in firefights and active combat situations. This is the calling for this class of elite soldiers (Brown and Szoldra, 2018). Their training and actions live up to their motto: "De Oppresso Liber"—To Liberate the Oppressed (Brown and Szoldra, 2018). Our Green Berets call it "to free the oppressed," which is why our nation, "the land of the free," sends these brave soldiers out into harm's way.

They carefully plan when treading into a hornet's nest of 'less than scrupulous individuals,' as he put it. As the advanced team came into hostile territory, it was their job to stir things up, which always led to many bad guys fighting the good guys. The goal was to defeat the bad guys and stabilize a tenuous situation. When they returned to their base of operations after the explosion, their partner force was called out for not following up on them. "Why did you leave us," he asked? "Because we thought you were dead." They had not died that day, but their lives had been altered. It would take some time before realizing the full impact of what had happened.

Initially, he saw things were not quite right, but he did not accept them as problems. Their training is exhaustive, and at each level, only the best move on (Brown and Szoldra, 2018). They are trained to continue to take the fight to the enemy, to be able to shoot a weapon with their right or left hand. This is not just about being ambidextrous—this means that there is no excuse, just because your hand is blown off, for you not to be able to shoot your way out of a situation. They hide pain and weakness because they are committed to protecting each team member as they complete their mission.

Some of the other effects of the blast were starting to become manifest. On a routine helicopter flight around the base, he almost threw up. He had flown in planes, jumped from incredible heights, and never been sick. Suddenly, he got cold, sweaty, and nauseous in that swaying helicopter. He thought back to the incident in the RG-33 MRAP and how, after this, he wondered if he might have been hurt a little bit. Moreover, the realization came that his condition might be worse than he thought.

The soldiers were well aware of the Traumatic Brain Injury (TBI) threat. What is called TBI or PTSD today was previously called "Nostalgia" in the eighteenth century; later called "Soldier's Heart" or "Railway Spine" during the Civil War (Robichaux and Stalnecker, 2017). In later combat situations such as WW1, men with this condition were called "shell shocked" (Robichaux and Stalnecker, 2017). These soldiers had consistently recognized this as a possibility in their line of work. However, after their brush with death, there was no blood, and none of his team members demonstrated any overt effects from the blast as minor as a nose bleed. So what was happening to him?

He later realized that many more symptoms had presented themselves, but he had learned to brush minor aches and pains aside because of his training. One moment, in particular, sticks out: they were conducting close-quarters battle training at night, under night vision, using live explosives. In this type of training, precision, speed, and overwhelming force are keys to subdue the enemy, devastating the hostile force (Brown and Szoldra, 2018). He came into the room and immediately lost his balance amid small arms fire. He made excuses about what happened, and his friends laughed it off. Nevertheless, he knew that something had changed. He knew, at that point, that it was more dangerous for the team if he were to continue with them (Green Beret, personal communication, October 14, 2019).

Pulling the Trigger: Admitting a Need

As he reflected on the time when he came to this realization, he told me that there is a quote about Special Forces being a mistress. At some point, she will leave you for a younger man (GB personal communications, October 14, 2019). This quote has been attributed to James R. Ward, a Lieutenant in the OSS (Office of Strategic Services), a precursor to today's Special Forces, who was quoted as saying this:

> "Men, Special Forces is a mistress. Your wives will envy her because she will have your hearts—She will love you, but only a little, seducing you to want more, give more, die for her. She will take you away from the ones you love, and you will hate her for it, but leave her you never will, but if you must, you will miss her, for she has a part of you that will never be returned intact. And in the end, she will leave you for a younger man" (USASOC, 2019).

Our former soldier lamented that the worst day in Special Operations is better than the best day in any other unit, and the reason is because of this identification: it becomes part of who you are. Leaving such a role and the prestige associated with it made it difficult to admit that you might not be able to operate at this superior level any longer. Nevertheless, as the quote mentioned above states, a younger man will take your place (USASOC, 2019). Maybe not only a younger man but a less-broken one.

When it became too difficult to hide it any longer, he sat with his commanding officer and told him that he would have to step down from his role after a 15-year career at the highest level of service in the military. He had the fiercest desire to continue serving because of his commitment to his fellow soldiers and his team members. There is a deep sense of commitment to the other members of your squad—the way you enter a firefight, the way you move—everything is choreographed. These soldiers are trained for more than self-preservation but extreme loyalty to their small units. You are trained not only to protect yourself, but you are also protecting the right flank of someone else. Your front armor plate is your team member's side plate. So when s/he turns right, you turn left and take a step. It is a constant and careful sequence of steps, and you never stop moving. Deep within himself, our Green Beret knew that if he could not protect his fellow soldiers, he would be letting them down. It was more of the loyalty to others in his squad that led to his dramatic decision.

There is no easy way out of this sophisticated level of commitment. Trying to get a transfer means taking an opportunity away from other soldiers who have had many more exposures to combat than you. Nevertheless, he found himself in his commanding officer's office, head in his hands, tears streaming down his face, admitting that he could not continue in this role. Thus, he stepped away from something he had focused on most of his adult life.

What is the Problem?

Part of his realization of the severity of his injury was the struggles with his personal behaviors: with surprising anger, intolerance, and alcohol and substance abuse. He recognized that something in his behavior had changed dramatically, and he committed himself to working through this to find out exactly what happened and how he could overcome it.

The doctors here are not helping the military. According to our former soldier, they sent you back if the doctor determined that you were good to go. No doctor would ever give you an excuse for getting out of being a Green Beret. You were the toughest of the tough, the best of the best. If you did not have six bullet holes, you were going back. That is just the way it was.

So, diagnosing a traumatic brain injury and then admitting you needed help recovering from that traumatic brain injury was difficult with this group, perhaps more difficult than others. These guys did not admit weakness; they ate weakness for breakfast and lunch. Furthermore, that became difficult to diagnose the problem. According to our Green Beret, the resources available to soldiers coming through this type of injury are limited "if not non-existent." His words were, "I didn't just not get better; I got worse through four years of treatment."

They saw doctors, got checked out, but soldiered on, literally. This situation could be compared to the current debate in professional sports, specifically professional football (Martins, 2018). It was long before they realized that severe brain damage had been done in professional football and the military (McKee, Alosco, and Huber, 2016). Does this suggest that the doctors are part of the problem? Maybe, but a big part of the problem is the men themselves and the invincibility that comes with incredible talent and athleticism (Martins, 2018).

The soldiers in this Green Beret's squad had received purple hearts. They were told, "we are glad you guys are okay but do not screw up again." They were all under-performing, but they had become adept at manipulating people's perceptions that they were okay. He admitted that he was hanging on by his fingernails, and no one wanted to acknowledge what had happened and the damage that had been done. However, it is the only thing he has known for 15 years. He was at the highest level of the most sophisticated fighting force globally. There are only a small number of teams in the world called upon to be ready at a moment's notice to go anywhere in the world where they are needed. He does not have a little time to get better, and it is time to admit what is going on.

How many men would not admit this? How many football players with concussions have gone back in and risked further damage to themselves and their team (Martins, 2018)? How many soldiers have continued on and not acknowledged the damage that has been done? Is it only because of pride or a lack of sensitivity to those around them? Alternatively, does it also have to do with a culture where even the doctors would not acknowledge that a serious problem had occurred? They send you back in if you are not bleeding profusely from every orifice.

When you are a Green Beret, as it is, you mostly miss the birth of children, and you miss personal tragedies at home. It is all about the mission. Furthermore, this is important for the country and these men. There is a pride in these units that they can clean up these messes worldwide. These teams are adept at isolating problem situations and coming out victorious. They are masters at manipulating circumstances to work in their favor to accomplish their mission. However, like the NFL, and its concussion issues, there is a question of whether there should be more oversight to assess the condition of these folks. Could we expect an independent medical advisory unit to operate in such an environment? Could we justify telling our soldiers and their commanders not just to put a Band-Aid on the situation and send that warrior back in for more (Martins, 2018)?

Next Move?

He is now at home for an extended time, not just a couple of weeks, but now on an extended furlough. He notices anger and tension with his wife, that has not been there in the past. The anger and fighting continue, and he is ready to toss the whole marriage aside. They find themselves arguing over stupid things. He realizes that something is wrong with him. He has a headache that will not go away. He has never had a headache, and it is getting worse. The more his head hurts, the more he tries to find out the cause, the more the doctors poke at him, and the worst it gets.

He is trying to be patient, but there is no protocol for TBI treatment. According to one source, no one treatment works for everyone (Robichaux and Stalnecker, 2017). While what causes the trauma is more clearly understood, due to the uniqueness of each individual, each victim is a blank slate, to which various treatments and therapies are applied to see if something will work (Robichaux and Stalnecker, 2017). It is not only veterans or professional athletes who suffer TBI trauma—the data suggests that up to eight percent of the population will deal with a traumatic event each year, and up to 70% of adults in their lifetime (Robichaux and Stalnecker, 2017).

While all kinds of doctors seek to check him out but guess what the problem may be, our soldier is driven to figure this out himself. That is a part of his training, just part of who he is. He is researching brain damage and its effects, and he realizes that emotional regulation is the first symptom that accompanies brain trauma. Furthermore, this is what he has been experiencing. Now, finally, the doctors are saying PTSD. Here is the label, so let us get on with some treatments and see what works. Nevertheless, it was frustrating to label him and then dismiss him—not providing the help and support needed to overcome these changes.

There is a danger, in the process, of trying to get help for this condition. If you hold what is called in the service "the profile," and if you are physically unable to do a portion of your job, then a doctor gives you a sick note for your commander which tells him that the soldier cannot do this part of the job. The note does not give the commander any more information because the laws say they have no right to know any of this. However, this leads to a medical board proceeding, where a board of doctors evaluates all of the data and the tests given, and they determine whether the soldier can perform the required tasks. If s/he can, they "throw" them back in there. However, if he cannot, you need to get rid of them; the commander then starts the "Medical Retirement" process. It feels more like a disciplinary process. Imagine that—our Purple Heart recipient gets hurt, so now it is time to "retire" him/her out of the service. However, this is not the "gold watch" type of retirement process: it feels more like punishment to our faithful Green Beret. Is that the only approach that can be taken? Ultimately, if by no fault of your own you cannot perform the required tasks, you are forcibly retired out of the service, even though you were a hero for surviving the blast. Does this make any sense?

Road to Redemption—Recovery

As this author sought to identify the sources of successful treatment and what strategies helped this soldier transition from a fastidious, mission-focused warrior to a broken vessel and then back to a competent contributor, he pleaded that to list all the agencies that helped or did not help would be pointless. Some of the organizations no longer can provide the same services. Doctors' offices change leadership, and charities lose funding. Some veterans' organizations proclaim they raise funds to help the wounded, but this money does not always reach its target. Furthermore, this is being kind!

There is no one answer for those seeking recovery from this mysterious condition; there is only the encouragement to pursue solutions that do exist but are difficult to navigate. Our soldier did what he was trained to do: explore every option and capitalize on every opportunity. It might mean swallowing pride and saying "I do not know" or "I need help," which are things formerly independent competent people hate to say. Those trained to be self-sufficient survivors in this environment know that they can and will survive no matter the outcome, but they cannot and will not readily admit that they cannot still do something or must depend on others for help.

According to the Brain Injury Association of America (BIAUSA, 2020), no two brain injuries are alike. These are complex injuries, requiring some guesswork from the medical team to try and ascertain an outcome while noting that the determination of a long-term prognosis could take months or years (BIAUSA, 2020).

According to the National Institutes of Health Information on Traumatic Brain Injury (NIH, 2020), people with moderate to severe brain injury will need rehabilitation therapy to recover from the injury's effects. One of the rehabilitation therapies utilized is retraining in a way that models similar activity to what is now past damaged capability in order to reconstruct acuity and neural pathways. Our former Green Beret learned to do several things to support his rehabilitation program.

He makes it sound easy, but he has been through this struggle and has sorted through the details. When we are children, he says, we learned to play and act out things in our play. We learn how our body works and how, if something breaks, we learn to make adjustments. As we grow older, we forget what play has taught us—that to continue to grow, we have to make adjustments.

The brain has a tremendous capacity for rewiring. We become comfortable with the brain as it currently functions, and rarely do we seek to expand its capacity. It takes some extra effort to compensate when things are not working correctly. However, adding extra challenges like learning a sport or adapting to a new habit helps to expand brain capacity. These activities can help rewire some previous habits that may have been lost due to TBI.

Our former Green Beret took up archery to help with his recovery, and he now coaches this sport for DOD Warrior Games athletes. Our former soldier tells me that archery is 90% mental—"and the other 10% is in your head." Anybody can pull a bow and launch a pointy stick towards a target with relative confidence that it will head in that direction. Nevertheless, staying focused and disciplining the mind to achieve an objective and then rigorously training to accomplish that objective is part of the rehabilitation process that helps with the recovery from a traumatic injury of any type.

Not What They Appear

The author is older but not severely injured. From personal experience, we use less of our potential capabilities every day if not fully invigorated or challenged. Compare the average healthy adult to a previously well-trained and now disabled veteran seeking to recover some sense of their former capabilities. Many of these soldiers may be grappling with combat trauma, having narrowly survived an exploding IED meant to kill them. Their bodies may appear normal, or they may carry themselves as if nothing unusual has occurred. However, the struggle to recover and not quit is a daily challenge deep within.

The Mighty Oaks Foundation (www.mightyoaksprograms.org) has former military officers—devastated by the effects of war—who now band together to create positive changes in the lives of service personnel with peer-based discipleship and other types of interactions (www.mightyoaksprograms.org). The founder of Mighty Oaks, Chad Robichaux, has also suffered from traumatic brain injury effects (www.mightlyoaksprograms.org/speaker/chad-m-robichaux).

He has dedicated his life to working on behalf of combat and trauma victims and encouraging service members who have been affected by battle-related injuries. In order to personally demonstrate the body's ability to recover from such traumatic injuries, Chad has become a professional MMA Champion and founded this organization to reach out to those who have been affected by war injuries (www.mightlyoaksprograms.org/speaker/chad-m-robichaux). You see his passion and the efforts of many former soldiers who have survived military casualties, know the systemic breakdowns in treatments, and now labor extensively on behalf of their brothers in arms.

In a book written to document their stories and encourage service members on the road to recovery (Robichaux and Stalnecker, 2017), the authors identify some essential facts that address specific actions which are helpful following TBI injuries. The first step in recovery, according to these authors, is for the victim of this TBI to acknowledge that they are different and that things are different after suffering a traumatic brain injury—and some things may never return to "normal" once they have suffered through this injury (Robichaux and Stalnecker, 2017). This point should be obvious, perhaps. However, each of us may believe that there is some sense of routine to which we can return, which will justify the effort to get some care to resolve the issue. People are different once a hamstring is pulled, a knee is repaired, and once they have experienced trauma. They may not be the same and may feel that bone ache when the weather changes. Medicine can work wonders to provide some restorative sense of normalcy and give a person back much of their mobility. However, medicine is still a practice and an effort to re-establish or simulate what has been broken or taken away.

Another fact to acknowledge, according to these authors (Robichaux and Stalnecker, 2017), is that an injury like a traumatic brain injury is not something that can be dismissed. A severe injury such as TBI affects us, like a death in the family affects us. Those affected cannot just pretend it did not happen. It is essential to acknowledge that it did happen, as hard as it may be to admit it and be vulnerable. In the case of overcoming drug addiction or alcoholism, many programs begin with the admission that we are human, that we are broken, and that we need help to start on a path of recovery (Wilson, 1953). This is where we are with TBI. This is what our Green Beret needed to do. The hardest thing for him to do was to acknowledge weakness and vulnerability.

Another fact, as identified by the founders of Mighty Oaks Ministry to wounded soldiers, is hardship in life is a common experience for all human beings (Robichaux and Stalnecker, 2017). Adopting a victim mentality is not a healthy approach to recovery (Robichaux and Stalnecker, 2017). Although some may have suffered a significant trauma or severe injury, we are all human beings created in the image of God, a Faithful Guide who knows the steps of the righteous ones and orders them—and God delights in the way of the righteous (Psalm 37:23 ESV). From a spiritual perspective, all human beings are on a path of recovery or restoration. God's guidance is to lead us to repentance (Romans 2:4). God guides us to recover from hurt and sin and the traumas inherent in human life. There are trauma, trials, and sorrow on earth (John 16:33 NLT), but God plans for us to fully recover from a life of sin and separation into a relationship with the one who created us.

Finally, the author's position is that research on traumatic brain injuries indicates that people who suffer trauma remember the events related to their trauma and program them into their brains (Robichaux and Stalnecker, 2017). Why is this important to know? There are times past the traumatic event when something triggers the repetition or remembrance of this event (Robichaux and Stalnecker, 2017). Retraining to overcome injury and understanding the triggers is critical so that we as humans can operate as we were naturally made to do. Moreover, it is also necessary to recognize that brain triggers could cause lapses or even the fear and loathing associated with the damage that had occurred in the past.

Nevertheless, this fascinating brain given to us by God allows us to retrain and drill something into our thinking until it becomes automatic. This can help persons with TBI retrain and overcome their fears to live a complete life. This same training is how emergency responders can continue to run toward danger while everything within them loathes danger, and maybe they even fear it. This retraining allows those affected by traumatic brain injury to reprogram their minds and move toward more positive and productive activities (Robichaux and Stalnecker, 2017).

It is vital to continually grow through the injury and the trauma and apply what was learned to more fully express one's unique and vulnerable human nature and to apply remaining capabilities positively. Turning back inside and relating to victimization is not a way toward positive contributions. It is impossible to relate the suffering of a captured soldier or one who has survived a bomb blast and to relate it to someone who suffers because of parental abuse or other emotional stress. There are some similarities in how the brain responds, but they certainly are of differing degrees. And yet, each individual has an opportunity to find help and support, move forward positively, learn and grow, and utilize their skills and abilities to help others, particularly those who have gone through such trauma and may not see a way forward.

Conclusion

The glory of fame and recognition, personal achievement, and great success have worn thin. Most of us may not ever achieve the type of acclaim to which we would want it to end. Nevertheless, it can and does happen to some famous individuals. Consider the lament in the song penned by the Eagles rock group, *After the Thrill is Gone* (Henley and Frey, 1975). Henley would later write that as much as their fame skyrocketed, some of the luster had worn off after a while. More than 40 years after this song was recorded, the Eagles are still famous. None of them would claim to be as unknown or forgotten as our "General Who" mentioned earlier. What is shared here is the loss of importance of things once held onto so dearly. There are now new things to learn, the past to be cherished but not held onto so fiercely. And as mentioned, that past victory or cherished event "... will leave you for a younger man" (USASOC, 2019).

According to this former Green Beret, the real question is, "what are you or I willing to do to get better moving forward?" He tells me that "how you do anything is how you do everything. Anything less than [giving] everything is nothing." Let us be encouraged by this example of a true and noble warrior, now fighting a different battle; as well as the example of another former Green Beret, who turned the energy from his injury into becoming a professional MMA fighter, martial arts instructor, and motivational speaker and author, who now seeks to educate soldiers and their families on the paths to recover from PTSD (Robichaux and Stalnecker, 2017).

CHAPTER 10

No Such Thing as an Overnight Success—Nor Failure, Nor Restoration

Abstract: In this chapter, the story of a famous second overall pick in the first round of the 1998 NFL Draft with a failed career and a ruined life represents that restoration is possible, but nothing happens overnight. Neither success, failure, nor restoration is simply a matter of flipping a switch. It takes the dedication of therapists or coaches and the affected individuals to rigorously work to identify those hidden demons and learn new behavior patterns to not respond to negativity or failure the same way as in the past.

Introduction

According to Chris Myers (2017), everyone loves an overnight success story! Myers writes about entrepreneurs and what may seem like instant wealth, fame, and success from the outside. However, as he continues, Myers notes a long road of failure and persistence, which leads to some minor recognition, which may lead to a break (hard-earned) that opens up to greater recognition, and then—voila! It appears to some like an overnight success (Myers, 2017). Myers cites Reid Hoffman, co-founder of LinkedIn, who describes the entrepreneurial journey as walking through the "Valley of Death" (Myers, 2017). Fellow entrepreneur and now a venture capitalist and investor Ben Horowitz (2014) called this entrepreneurial journey from start-up to potential success "the struggle" in very graphic terms (Horowitz 2014).

It is very tough to move from starting and building a business and gaining customers to ultimately turning that business into a success. This is why so many small businesses fail. The statistic on first-time start-up business failure that 90% of first-time businesses fail is disputed but is often cited as an actual statistic. The researcher found several authors that quote this 90% statistic (Griffith, 2014; Patel, 2015; Hartley, 2016). Nevertheless, some will dispute this figure as well. Author Ryan Jorden (2014), a managing partner in a Venture Capital firm, cites SBA statistics in a LinkedIn blog post (Jorden, 2014), stating that about half of all new businesses survive five years or more, and about one-third survive ten years or more. Another author, Meszaros (2016), cited the U.S. Bureau of Labor Statistics, saying that about 50% of all new businesses survive five years, and about one-third survive 10-years or more (Meszaros, 2016). Wherever the actual data falls, the fact is that small business failure is genuine, the struggle to overcome obstacles and achieve success in any field is real, and there is nothing overnight about it. Luis Romero says that overnight success, particularly in entrepreneurship, is a myth, believing this myth is one of the most significant obstacles to business start-up success (Romero, 2016).

The same can be said about overnight success in nearly any field. What seems to the public as an overnight success story is years of practice and training. Most often, endless hours were spent working to improve their craft before some opportunity might come along and greater awareness is made. According to Malcolm Gladwell in his book *Outliers* (2008), the Beatles had performed over twelve hundred times before their first burst of success in 1964 (Gladwell, 2008). Musician and entrepreneur Derek Sivers practiced singing and playing lead guitar for 15 years, going through voice coaches and mentors, taking weekly lessons, and practicing tones and scales - until someone who heard him for the first time noted that "some people are born with the gift of singing, or they are not. You are lucky to be born with it" (Sivers, 2020). Sivers, a musician, guitar player, producer, and entrepreneur, left this encounter, realizing that many had told him to give up on his dream along the way. Suddenly he was an overnight success: Where did those 15 years go (Sivers, 2020)?

Destined for Notoriety

Meanwhile, some people burst onto the scene, apparently destined for great success. Such a person was Ryan Leaf (Ritchie, 2018). Leaf is well-known to those who prognosticate about football and draft picks. Leaf was a star quarterback at his university, leading his team to a fantastic season in 1997, culminating in his team appearing in the highly esteemed Rose

Bowl (Raley, 2020. Although the team lost this game, his stature as the Pac-12 Offensive Player of the Year and as a Heisman Trophy finalist made Leaf a highly sought-after player selected second in the 1998 NFL Draft, right after Peyton Manning (Ferry, 2019). Leaf and Manning were neck-and-neck as to who would be chosen first in the National Football League Draft. The worst team, the Indianapolis Colts, chose Peyton Manning after Leaf refused to call them back for an interview. This might have been a sign of Leaf's immaturity, which would become more evident as he began his professional football career. Leaf suggested that if the team had probed a little more deeply, they might have found out more about his refusal to accept responsibility for losses and other tell-tale signs of a potential problem (Peter, 2017).

The San Diego Chargers took Leaf with the second pick that year, and he imploded (Dalton, 2020). The story has been well-documented. Leaf's pride and inability to handle adversity left him in a situation where he tried to escape from the failure that everyone assumed would never happen (Raley, 2020). There was poor on-field performance, yelling at reporters, embarrassing off-field incidents, and suicide attempts (Ferry, 2019). His high-profile expectations and exuberant self-confidence were met with embarrassing publicity and no way to escape—until he met pain medication.

Leaf took Vicodin for painful football injuries and then became addicted to it. His low point was when his addiction to pain medication led to a felony burglary conviction (Ferry, 2019). Leaf was indicted on burglary and controlled substance charges in Texas in 2009 (City News Service, 2020). Later he would find more trouble, being arrested twice in 2012 on burglary, theft, and other drug charges (Dalton, 2020). As a result of his poor life choices, he found himself on a cold concrete prison floor, where he would spend the next 32 months.

Finding a Path Forward to Recovery

Leaf will say that what turned his life around was his encounter with his cellmate, a former Iraqi War veteran serving a sentence for a fatal drunken-driving conviction. This man encouraged him to come to the prison library to help other prisoners learn to read (Ferry, 2019). However, perhaps the most remarkable success is that after being written off as a complete bust and failure, Ryan Leaf emerged as a man working on using his life on purpose to help others (Peter, 2017). He was willing to associate his name and sorted reputation with drug rehabilitation programs and to lend a hand to others who needed it (Peter, 2017; Ferry, 2019). What was more remarkable was not that Leaf recognized his low point in prison but the many hours of therapy and support that he received in order for him to reconstruct his life and redeem the time that was remaining for him (SOC Telemed, 2018). After his release from prison, Leaf sought treatment for his addiction with a grant from the NFL (SOC Telemed, 2018). Leaf was hired to represent the NFL Legends group to promote these available resources like money for treatment programs—which one of his interviewers acknowledged that he had utilized as well (NFL, 2019).

Leaf not only pursued treatment for his addiction problem but pursued employment with Transcend Recovery Community, which labels itself as the best sober living in Los Angeles, Santa Monica, Beverly Hills, New York, and Houston (Transcend Recovery Community, 2015). Leaf contacted Transcend when he heard they were willing to hire addicts in early recovery (Peter, 2017). This is not simply about Ryan Leaf's discovery in prison that his life was more than his self-focus and pride and the agony of failing to live up to others' expectations. This story is about organizations on the front lines like Transcend Recovery Community that take those failed individuals like a former 1998 first-round NFL draft pick who was addicted to painkillers and work with them to help them restore their lives so they can contribute to society.

Where would our society be if not for the therapist that worked with Ryan Leaf and those less famous and others of us who struggle with emotional character flaws that need to be addressed in order to overcome these life-controlling habits?

No Such Thing as Overnight Success

Just as there is the fallacy of overnight success: that people can suddenly hit it rich or become optimized in their particular field, there should be a similar fallacy when it comes to the overnight restoration. Just like success takes years to build towards, restoration through therapy and interventions sometimes takes repeated tries and is not automatic. However, we should not write off individuals who failed spectacularly nor dismiss any effort they make to seek restoration. They may need ongoing support and help to optimize their potential.

Entrepreneur of the Year and successful businessman Gerald W. Chamales is Chairman and Founder of Rhinotek Computer Products. In this $45 Million business, roughly one-third of the workforce comes from halfway houses, work-furlough centers, and recovery programs. This author wrote about Mr. Chamales in his first book (Bucci, 2016). These employees are assigned a mentor and enrolled in a training program. There is a rigorous follow-up but lots of determination due to the opportunity given when others would not take the chance. "This is not philanthropy. This is a sound business principle that started because it was the right thing to do, and now we realize it is the smart thing to do" (Marchetti, 2005). Chamales knows the value of a second chance and the challenging work involved in the redemptive process. Chamales is a recovering alcoholic who worked his way into the executive suite from a life of poverty, welfare, and food stamps. Chamales knows what it is like to be at the absolute bottom; through his business pursuits, Chamales reformed his own life, but now he also has the opportunity to help restore the lives of many of his workers. Says Chamales: "You could say we recycle human beings. Instead of giving them a handout, I am giving them a hand up" (Pennington, 2002).

After he found himself on that cold prison cell floor (Ferry, 2019, Leaf needed an opportunity to address his life-controlling problem. He needed someone to take the work done by the therapist in reconstructing his purpose and actualize it by offering him job opportunities and a voice. Ryan Leaf has used his voice to represent drug recovery programs (Ferry, 2019). He has flourished within the opportunities given to him as a TV analyst and commentator on college sports (City News Service, 2020). Does that mean that Leaf's life is without problems? Leaf found himself in more trouble with a recent domestic dispute, pleading guilty to a misdemeanor (City News Service, 2020). Since we are not perfect, we must recognize that each person has failed several times (Romans 3:23 New International version). Continued support and forgiveness are critical whether a person is new and has a meltdown or seems to fall into silly mistakes continually.

Dr. Fredric Neuman, a psychiatrist who directs the Anxiety and Phobia Treatment Center at White Plains Hospital (Neuman, 2017a), writes about self-destructive behavior in his blog for *Psychology Today* (Neuman, 2017b). Some men and women do self-destructive things, and our culture blames Ryan Leaf for his braggadocious attitude and subsequent failure

(Rexrode, 2019). Even inexperienced therapists, according to Neuman, believe that these people repeat these mistakes out of a desire to fail or a wish to suffer (Neuman, 2017b). Therefore, the inexperienced therapist blames the patient, and so do we (Neuman, 2017b).

Ryan Leaf suffered from mental health issues and pride that was never put in check because of his athletic success. After failing his own and other people's high expectations, bouncing around the NFL, and finally losing this once-promising career (Ferry, 2019), he was surrounded by criticism and multiple journalists denouncing him as a failure and a colossal disappointment (Willis, 2019). Leaf sought to hide his shame behind his addiction, which led to more failure and prison (Ferry, 2019). It took health professionals to see the patient behind the disease and help support Leaf in his efforts at recovery (SOC Telemed, 2018). Leaf took hard-earned self-awareness and humility to recognize his need and seek treatment. He continues to acknowledge that he needs help and is still an addict (SOC Telemed, 2018).

Neuman (2017b) wrote that while inexperienced therapists continue to seemingly blame the patient for their continued excess through self-destructive behaviors, the truth is that these are not pleasurable recurrences (Neuman, 2017b). People demonstrating aberrant behavior are not seeking to suffer, nor do they have a desire to fail. A good therapist will help clients understand that self-destructive behavior is not necessary to maintain or rebuild their self-respect. Change is possible, and support is available (SOC Telemed, 2018). With the assistance to facilitate a change of habits and faulty thinking, there also needs to be an understanding employer and a strong community of support available, especially for those who find themselves continuing with minor occurrences of the same destructive behavior (Neuman, 2017b).

Who Sees Their Potential?

Without some wise and kind broadcasters recognizing Ryan Leaf for the value he could contribute (Peter, 2017), or without the NFL hiring Leaf as an NFL Legends advocate (NFL, 2019), where would Ryan Leaf's battle to turn his life around leave him? With the support of organizations such as Transcend Recovery Community, many people like Ryan Leaf now have a second chance to contribute value to themselves, their families, and others

(Peter, 2017). With his new platform with NFL Legends, Leaf has a new purpose: helping others avoid the pitfalls in which younger football players may find themselves and directing them to resources and the support they may need (NFL, 2019). That is what these organizations help individuals to do. Nevertheless, recovering draft busts like Ryan Leaf need help to recover, and they need to be hired to share this new purpose with their world.

CHAPTER 11
It is God Who Makes Things Grow

Abstract: The following chapter describes the origins of a unique entrepreneurship model, reflecting how the power of business can release people into flourishing careers and provide for them second chances and what a business influenced by the Kingdom of God might look like. It is the story of two men who grew up together, followed different paths, met again through God's power, and became business partners. There was a failure, drug abuse, and notable miracles that could only come from God.

> "For the vision is yet for the appointed time, and it hurries toward the end, and won't prove false.
>
> Though it takes time, wait for it; because it will surely come, and it won't delay."
>
> —***Habakkuk 2:3 New Heart English Bible***

Introduction

This is the story of two men named Chris. They grew up right near each other, living in the same neighborhood. They rode bikes together and did kid things together. They hung out together while they were in middle school. One Chris went to a private Christian school, while the other went to public school. In this sense, they were different. Even as kids, there was some rivalry between them but no real hostility.

Both grew into a specialist with the talents God gave to them. One was frustrated because racial attitudes and nepotism limited him, and one was frustrated because he was limited due to addiction. It took a tragedy to bring them back together. However, they shared a lot in common: not just growing up in the same neighborhood, but their interest in the Kingdom of God and in operating a business according to its kingdom principles.

Chris T is a pastor, but not in the traditional sense of the word. Chris and his wife pastor a small group of dedicated disciples. Chris uses principles of the word of God and things that he has learned from his successful business practices to take a group of people through a series of stages and then release them to start kingdom businesses. Once they have completed the discipleship course, Chris T launches them into their own business. Chris T also provides lots of mentoring and continual support. In two cases, Chris has given these disciples their own business for them to operate. This includes many individuals with little or no business background, including former heroin addicts. The businesses have also consulted and employed ex-convicts who struggled to find work elsewhere.

Before you think that Chris T is entirely crazy, the network of businesses that Chris and his partners have launched returns profits from which Chris can continue to launch new ventures. Moreover, the results are phenomenal: Each business is earning a profit, and each of the business owners has been restored to a point where they are fulfilling their purpose and using their talents to bless their families, their customers, and others. This entrepreneurial model was recognized under the 2018 CBFA Conference theme of "Making All Things New Through Business." Chris T and his partners in Kingdom Horizon are launching new businesses in complete obedience to God, operating each based on their view of the word of God, with a radical belief in kingdom generosity and a great appreciation for the power of business to set people free.

The Birth of the Vision

Chris T's life would turn out so differently than he thought. He had big dreams for himself. Chris attended college to play basketball and dreamt of helping his team win a championship. His team did win a championship—but Chris was not there to enjoy it. Chris's mom passed away while he was in school, and his dad had some run-ins with the law. Chris needed to get to work to take care of his dad, who could not secure a job after being arrested. While working in property management, Chris started his first business—a cleaning business for which his dad could work. Finding employment for his dad was impossible since he now had a record. Chris felt led to start this business for his father. He hoped it would allow his father to feel like a real man again, free from his past mistakes and redeemed by being gainfully employed without being dependent on others.

Chris T then saw the dream of athletic success change into the dream of corporate business success. He became a sales executive for a Fortune 100 business. As a young man, he climbed the ladder quickly and was very driven to achieve success and recognition in this corporate environment. Chris attained everything that seemed to mirror success in business: a six-figure salary, the American Express travel card, and more.

Chris T recalls his Fortune 100 company job, "I got the position and failed miserably in the first year. I grew the business. However, it does not matter; you are unsuccessful if you do not hit that mark. Thus, after seven months, [they] moved me to the corporate department, so I can now call on corporate clients versus government clients. So, I prayed [that] God would lead me. So, by the end of 18 months, I had sold a product that had never been sold before in the United States, and I had closed over a million dollars of business. They [recognized me] with the 'Achieving Customer Excellence' award—given to the top 10% of salespeople in the North American region."

"Nevertheless, they initially refused to put me on a leadership fast track. They said I was not qualified and did not go to the right school, and I did not have what it took. They did not recognize how many of us knew what we were saying. [The scripture says] humble yourself, and He will exalt you in due time (1 Peter 5:6). So you humble yourself, and you study up, and you do everything [that] you are being asked" (Pastor Chris Taylor, personal communication, May 16, 2018).

Chris T hit the wall in corporate life and sensed discrimination based on his background and the school he attended. He struggled with rejection and his bitter feelings. However, God was doing a work in his life that had little to do with Chris's frustrations due to his lack of corporate growth.

His mind and heart searched for the reason for this discomfort to no avail. So Chris T went back to his spiritual heritage and conceived the idea of operating a business according to the principles that he saw in the Bible. As Chris expressed during our time together, his past understanding of traditional business was that it took from people rather than giving to them in a generic sense. Now, what Chris envisioned was a business that could thrive by applying the principles in God's word. That is why his operation is so unique. He is constantly looking to give things away and bless people.

Chris T is obedient to the word of God and seeks to act according to the law of reciprocity. The Bible quotes Jesus as saying. "Give, and you will receive. Your gift will return to you in full—pressed down, shaken together to make room for more, running over, and poured into your lap. The amount you give will determine the amount you get back" (BibleGateway–Luke 6:38 NLT). This kingdom principle is at the core of how Chris and his partners operate their businesses.

Several business books and websites advocate for following this "law of reciprocity" as the only way to do business—and these are secular sources (Korisko, 2013; Spears, 2013; also Cialdini, 2006).

While Chris T was struggling to reconcile his faith and corporate endeavors, suddenly, his great grandmother needed care and a place to live. Climbing the corporate ladder became secondary. First things first—Great Grandma needs a place to call home!

Chris T recounted the day he heard what to do next, "Literally, as I was driving down the street, I heard a voice say to me "call that sign" (a real estate sign out in front of a home that was for sale). I had just purchased my family's home. This is about 2011, and I did not have any more money. It was a very nice neighborhood, a 3000 square-foot home, and I am driving down the road, and Lord says to me, 'call the sign.' I told Him no. The second day He said, 'call the sign.' I told Him no again. Furthermore, on the third day, I sensed God saying, 'I am not going to ask you again.' Thus, I obeyed this time. It was delayed obedience, but I did obey. That home ended up housing my great grandmother for the last four years of her life" (Pastor Chris Taylor, personal communication, May 16, 2018).

Chris learned from the owner that by the time the house was sold, after paying a realtor, closing costs, and including the money still owed on the house, she would only walk away with about $8,000. Chris T told her that he would give her $15,000 and use the house to care for his great grandmother, honor the Lord, and make it available to others, as God directed. So Chris bought a house worth $240,000 for only $15,000. You may be saying that he is not operating according to kingdom principles as I know them. Nevertheless, it was purely by faith that Chris T contacted the seller when her house would not sell. While he owned it, the home housed four families and was later sold. Three widows and an ex-convict, who gave his heart to the Lord in the living room, lived in that house. The home was also used to minister to a young Muslim man from Egypt. More significantly, while caring for his great grandmother, God began to speak more clearly to Chris about the pursuit of ministry. The message was: stop running.

Not only was he able to use the house to bless other people, but after the house was renovated and sold at a profit, Chris T went back and blessed the original owner with an additional $25,000. So when she was only going to net perhaps $8,000 from the sale of her house, she made $40,000. Chris was able to use some of the money from the sale of the house as seed money for another business for which he and his partners serve as mentors and overseers.

Chris T explains the significance of having a firm foundation: "Part of what we are doing is making disciples of servants and believers. It is not easy to lead people in the truth of the Gospel without having a foundation, and the Scriptures are our foundation. It is very challenging to have people with the discipline required. Thus, as members and individuals join our ministry and show themselves to be faithful with little, we have been led to give them more responsibility, which comes in leading a business" (Pastor Chris Taylor, personal communication, May 16, 2018).

Chris T is not just teaching people about kingdom principles and business. It is one thing to teach people about business, but it is another thing actually to give someone their own business. For Chris now, he gave two of his mentees their own business in two cases. In two other cases, the disciples took the lead in the business while Chris T and his organization kept an equity share of the business. Chris T puts his teaching and money where his mouth is in each situation. He is showing the utmost confidence in these disciples and is equipping them to be able to run a business.

Chris explains, "We believe that one of the key components to freedom in the Gospel is to work for yourself. As individuals who are faithful to the Scriptures, we believe that just as Solomon asked for wisdom instead of money, so it is my duty and responsibility to share that wisdom with the flock of God that God sent me. Thus, our job is to help these individuals do exactly what God has done for us: to free us from Mammon's spirit, a drive for money, and a drive for success. We encourage them to seek what God has given to us, a spirit of power and love and a sound mind (2 Timothy 1:7 NKJV). We encourage them to seek first the kingdom of God and His righteousness, and all these things will be added to them as the scripture says (Matthew 6:33). As God has added them to me, it is my responsibility and a duty to ensure that those [who] are following me are going to be added to from the father. It is just remarkable [when] you know the Lord has blessed you, [so you can] give away what you started with" (Pastor Chris Taylor, personal communication, May 16, 2018).

Benefactor of the Vision

Chris D is the owner of Kingdom Time, the second of the businesses launched by this entrepreneurial ministry called Kingdom Horizon. Chris T connected with Chris D right after his younger brother died. After Chris D experienced a long struggle with opiates and heroin, several efforts to get clean, and the loss of every successful job or opportunity he had, he was at rock bottom; and now he had lost his brother.

Chris D details his life right before he knew he needed to make a change, "So this is several months after I got out of rehab, then my brother died, and I mean I was a mess. So then the woman that I was in love with and talking to about getting married left me. She had stayed with me through the many efforts to get clean, and now she was gone. So at this point, I was like, life is not worth it. Yeah, I will try something new" (Chris Dilkes, personal communication, May 18, 2018).

Chris D asked God for a mentor or somebody to help him as he tried to stay off the drugs and get his life and career back on track. The two men had known each other as kids. Now fast forward 15 years: they were not close in any way. Nevertheless, here was Chris T at Chris D's brother's funeral. Chris D was hungry for change. He had lost everything dear to him. The only job opportunity available for this innovative and talented man was grilling hot dogs at a country club.

Although this mentoring was not precisely what Chris D expected, the two men began to reacquaint. There were initial issues of trust to overcome.

Moreover, Chris D, out of rehab and trying to stay drug-free, was still struggling with lapses back to heroin and spaced out trying to suppress drug cravings by taking Methadone and Suboxone, drugs prescribed to decrease the severity of Opioid withdrawal symptoms. However, a unique bond was built over the discussion of God's Kingdom and business practices. Chris D shares that Chris T "had come out of the business world, and he had worked for an IT company as a government subcontractor in sales and stuff like that. I ended up losing my job because of my addiction. So initially, the focus was ministry, but we are constantly talking about business. It was ministry, but it was also mentorship. We ate lunch several times a week at a pizza place right near his house. It was pretty selfless for both of us. It was selfless for Chris T to come and have lunch and talk to me about the struggles going on in my life" (Chris Dilkes, personal communication, May 18, 2018).

Chris T told Chris D, "I think God is calling me into the ministry, and here is what I am doing." Chris D was also being drawn closer to Chris T. and felt like he could support his old friend as he pursued this call.

Chris T moved ahead with his ministry plans and started a Bible Study in his house. At one point, Chris T has three disciples, Chris D, and two others. Chris T shared a message about money and giving, some of the principles he was working through as he began to define further the vision God had given to him. The message was so unorthodox that two Bible study attendees quit coming. One of the people was so upset that they demanded that Chris T give his offering back. The two Chrises were acquainted with these principles and had been praying about how to live these out in their business practices. They were talking about life and faith and business and giving. The two guests did not want to hear this, and one went from giving to taking back.

Chris T left his Fortune 100 company and its management development track to work locally and care for his great grandmother in the home he had purchased. Chris T became licensed and then ordained into the ministry. He and Chris D began working together more, and together they developed a master plan for Chris T's home church. Chris T developed the Master Plan, while Chris D provided graphics and charts and helped Chris T put the plan together administratively.

Some of the concepts were drawn from the men's weekly meetings, ideas found in the scriptures, and principles taken from Chris T's corporate management program. There was also much time invested in prayer. The approach again was so radical that the leaders in the church rejected it out of hand. When this plan was presented, one of the people in the meeting was the Senior Pastor's granddaughter. She would later become Chris T's wife, and he would help her launch her own business—Kingdom Fitness and Wellness.

Out of this experience, the trio now would venture out and start holding their services in Chris T's home. They would also set up a consulting business called Kingdom Horizon. In the same way that Chris T had provided consulting, and an assessment for his home church, the first projects for Kingdom Horizon were along the same lines. The two Chrises would compliment each other: Chris T provided consulting and developed plans, while Chris D provided graphic and web design skills to support the plan presentation and implementation. This business would become an entrepreneurial consulting company, a place where new business opportunities were discovered, researched, and developed.

Chris T describes the blessings of being obedient, "God told me to start [Kingdom Horizon], and God started sending clients. God sent a woman that wanted to start a business offering tutoring and teaching services to help kids get into college. So I helped her start that business. Then a friend from high school who was playing the NFL was trying to start a business, so I helped him" (Pastor Chris Taylor, personal communication, May 16, 2018).

Chris T coaches people on starting businesses, forming LLCs, and conducting marketing. However, he is still giving things away. Chris T believed that God sent these folks to him and helped him put food on his table. Nevertheless, God was also asking Chris to act in obedience. Over the next two years, Chris believes he gave away about $160,000 in time, website development (with Chris D), and actual cash, samples, and promotional materials. Chris negotiated the lease and wrote the check to help start his wife's business—Kingdom Fitness and Wellness. Funding for the initial businesses came from selling the house that Chris T bought by faith with very little money.

However, the most unusual step of faith is yet to come. When previously, exploring these ideas in a Bible Study lesson on giving caused two men to get up and leave immediately. This was only the beginning of God's work on Chris T's heart regarding his trust in God's promises.

The Vision Becomes a Reality

Through the relationships built by Chris T in the property management business, an opportunity became available to buy out a watch business in the Pembroke Mall in the heart of Virginia Beach. Chris T explains the warning he felt he received regarding being a good steward, "In reading the Gospel of Luke, chapter 16, I see that I have had these passions. Many passions, as it relates to business. I love watches. I asked God for a watch business. Furthermore, He said, 'Okay.' But there is this sense from the Lord that if I have not been faithful in handling worldly wealth and managing what belongs to someone else, then I will not receive anything from the Lord."

"And so I was always taught that is better to give as the scripture says, but we do not always follow that it is also better to receive. My great grandmother always told me that if I can always find a way to add value to whatever I have, I will never lose. Thus, I took that scripture to heart, and God spoke to me. When Daddy says everything you want, you have to give it away first. So as these individuals choose to follow me and are obedient, I sensed God say, 'If you want that watch business, I am going to give it to you. However, you need to give it away" (Pastor Chris Taylor, personal communication, May 16, 2018).

Negotiations with the owner of the watch business were complex, and it was uncertain whether Chris T would finally be able to acquire the business. Amid the final negotiations, Chris T senses that God leads him to give Chris D the business he just purchased—free and clear. Remember that lesson on giving that was so tough for several people to hear?

Chris D is not at all surprised: "When God moves on your heart and says [to be obedient], you have to be at a point where you are ready for that. So then it does not surprise you [when someone else responds to God like this]" (Chris Dilkes, personal communication, May 18, 2018).

A former drug addict still working on kicking the habit, a former addict who knew nothing about jewelry: he did not know anything about repairing watches, even what sterling silver was, or the difference between gold and white gold. The negotiations would include training the new owner on how to operate such a business—with the potential to earn six figures. Wow! Was Chris D ready to run his own business, just a few months removed from starting to rebuild his life after losing everything to a life-controlling habit, major disappointments, and a recommitment to Christ?

Chris D questions whether or not he was ready for such a large endeavor, "I mean, there had been years of mentorship. I may not have felt as I should. (Not) I felt equipped, but you know God's at the helm, and you know, he (Chris T) is not going to (just) hand over a business to me because I am still stuck. I am not using street drugs, but I am taking medicine from the doctor (Suboxone) [to control] these things, and I was continuing to take that [right up until the business purchase was final].

Chris D recalls the night he was given a tremendous gift, "I was in contact with him [Chris T] during that [negotiating to buy the business]. One night after Bible study, I was driving home, and he [Chris T] called me, and he said, 'Chris, I am giving you this business.' It was like, 'what?', and he said, 'I am giving you this business.' And I said, 'Okay.' I did not know what that meant. That was in December 2016. In January of 2017, we started; and so I had 20 to 30 days to get prepared."

Chris D remembers still not being completely drug-free, "I was taking Suboxone, and I was not completely drug-free until November 2017. The business was purchased in January of 2017, and Chris T continued to consult and help manage the employees. He also continued to sow financially into inventory for the business throughout the first year. Chris T was aware that I was still struggling with getting completely sober while running the business. It was an act of faith to give a business to me while I was not drug-free" (Chris Dilkes, personal communication, May 18, 2018).

That was the second business started of the ministry of Kingdom Horizon, an extension of the planning and studying of scripture and the mentorship. There are now four businesses, and a new business is coming online very soon. The classic entrepreneurial types are not running these businesses. Several of the business owners have little if any background in business. The few things they have in common are having worked for someone else and having failed—Chris D is a former heroin user, while several other employees and consulting clients are ex-convicts. They not only have frustration and failure in common—but thankfully, they also have Chris T in common as well.

Additionally, they have Chris T's unique views of scripture and kingdom principles and how to live these out in business. Of the four businesses, two were given to the disciples; and in two, the parent company Kingdom Horizon maintains an equity share. Profits from the businesses can then be used to start other businesses as the Lord leads.

Applying This Story

So there seem to be three main storylines in the journey that these two men named Chris have taken. The first story tells how the power of business can release people into flourishing and provide for them second chances (Bucci, 2016). This discipline of business which we teach, encourages entrepreneurs to supply society with necessities; in business, we explain the transformational process of raw materials into valuable products. Through this process, a business can provide people with jobs and livelihoods—the means to prosper and fulfill their calling (Nickels, McHugh & McHugh, 2016). Here, the business enterprise is meant to serve others in this earthly realm; and ultimately carry out the creation mandate (Gen 1:28-30). It is also here that business owners must be generous and fruitful, productive and wise stewards in harnessing the resources given by God (Pearcey, 2004).

The second storyline has to do with the picture of what business influenced by the Kingdom of God looks like and what should it look like? This story describes a unique entrepreneurial model that bears fruit, with a vision for those men and women who commit to the process to gain personal and business success when they whole-heartedly work to integrate Biblical principles into their businesses. Part of this expression requires them to give generously without expecting a return. This message does not resonate with everyone. God blesses their obedience by blessing their businesses from start to finish for those who have embraced Him.

The third story has to do with this principle of reciprocity. Several of the characters in the story grappled with giving: not just putting some change in a cup for a coffee tip, but significant acts of giving. Moreover, those who participated in this large-scale giving received back much more than they gave away. Do we know that the scripture encourages this (Luke 6:38), but are we courageously committed to it? How does the need to achieve profitability juxtapose this principle of giving to the point where it does not make sense? This small band of entrepreneurial disciples, led by their obedient pastor and business mentor, are witnessing the fruit of this unabashed generosity. To them, it is not simply an act of kindness but obedience to a sovereign God, who asks us to obey and expects that we will. Additionally, God alone gives us the opportunity to create wealth (Deuteronomy 8:18), and He alone who makes things grow (1 Corinthians 3:7).

A Follow-up to the Original Story

In a follow-up to my original interviews, I met with Chris T almost four years to the day after our first interview (Pastor Chris Taylor, personal communication, August 10, 2021).

The jewelry watch business ended up going online, partly due to the COVID-19 virus and part of it was just to facilitate sales. In the first series of interviews, we did not look into the prospect of opening a smoothie business. However, this was the latest business that Chris T began to develop to accommodate some of his neophyte business disciples and maximize the skill set of the individuals he was training on business. Our second set of interviews was in the same mall corridor where Chris T opened his first smoothie shop and just a few steps from where the jewelry watch business began. They had a good working relationship with the mall leadership, and as businesses were declining in the mall, the opportunity to set up the smoothie business presented itself. Chris D also took resources from the watch business, and they became partners in investing in these new businesses. It was Chris T, Chris D, and Chris T's wife, Kim. Chris D has become part of their family. He has been grafted in as a member and regularly participates in family activities.

Chris T established the smoothie business and worked there alongside several disciples that he was growing into business leaders. One gentleman had mental health issues and struggled with depression—his wife attended Chris T's Bible study group and came to him one day expressing her need to change positions. She was employed as a simple clerk at a coffee shop but could not support her family and her husband, who was not working due to mental health issues. Chris T offered them both the opportunity to be part of the business. He worked to train both of them in the smoothie business.

God continues to bring people along into Chris T's sphere of influence. A man named Matt had just gotten out of prison and was failing at everything he tried. Matt was falling back into bad habits with alcohol. He was also in an adulterous relationship, but he did not want to make any changes even though his marriage was failing. Simply through a series of unexpected circumstances, he had an opportunity to speak to Chris T. Out of desperation, he asked for work. Chris T. offered him an opportunity but told him that this was no joke and that he must be on time and work at this. While Matt did not stay with Chris, he worked very hard, regained some skills, and now has his own business.

It seems that anyone who comes into Chris T's sphere of influence leaves his presence a better person. He works with broken people who need restoration. Eventually, they are either working with both Chrises to take on a new business venture or branch out into the business world and become successful independently.

Suddenly the smoothie business is taking off. The partners are listening to the voice of God as they understand it, and they are moving contrary to trends in business. First, they took the smoothie business out of the mall and into a stand-alone location. They are doing their due diligence, but they are not doing it because they are crazy. Individuals and now community leaders are coming to them and offering them prime locations and lower rents because they have heard of their successes.

When one well-known national smoothie chain closed in an area, the community contacted Chris T. about coming in and moving his business into that location. They had now set up four locations and were starting a fifth when we last spoke. They were also invited to a national conference of major food chains, even though they are just a few smoothie stores and were just getting started in the food business. Nevertheless, they are learning to ask the right questions, and the Lord is blessing their efforts as they invest in the transformation of people—using business as means of restoration.

CHAPTER 12

The Elephant in the Room

Can We Forgive and Forget in the Internet Age?

Abstract: This chapter has to do with people who want the opportunity to start fresh. The problem is not their lack of desire because they lack nothing but an opportunity. The problem with people judging others for their past failures is using their past as an excuse not to help but to continue on the judgment train. It seems easy to judge another who "should never" have done something. They want to get past their past, and what they need is someone who will help them.

> "Judge not, that you be not judged. For with the judgment, you pronounce you will be judged, and with the measure you use, it will be measured to you. Why do you see the speck that is in your brother's eye, but do not notice the log that is in your own eye?"
>
> —***(Matthew 7:1-3 ESV)***

Introduction

Is it true that an elephant never forgets? How would we know? One website is reportedly known for identifying the origin of such phrases (Know Your Phrase, 2021) and did not have an answer to the origin of this idiom. There was some conjecture that the phrase sounded similar to an actual phrase, "a camel never forgets an injury" (Know Your Phrase, 2021). So much for the internet is the source of all truth! The website continued to identify reports of elephants that displayed remarkable recognition of persons and locations after a decade of separation (Know Your Phrase, 2021), but this again is not documented data. There was documentation of a similar expression as far back as 1883 (know Your Phrase, 2021) and not much else.

Another website—Scientific American, seemingly more authoritative (Ritchie, 2009)—did offer some anecdotal evidence of the excellent recall of these pachyderms, as well as other research, notes, and statements declaring how scientists believe that the recall power of the elephant is a part of how they survive in the wild (Ritchie, 2009).

Some memories live on well past their expiration date. These can be good memories or sad ones. The internet has become a repository for visual images and video recordings of good and bad memories. These recollections can inspire subsequent generations; they often bind people to past mistakes when they hope to move beyond youthful indiscretions.

Is Transparency Good or Bad?

In a futuristic look at the impact of the internet (Anderson and Rainie, 2008), a survey of 578 leading Internet activists and commentators and 618 additional stakeholders (1,196 respondents) were asked to assess a series of proposed scenarios for the year 2020. One of the scenarios projects that not only would there be greater transparency in the future, but being "outed" for some past indiscretions through social media, would no longer do as much damage as it did in the past and would offer more personal integrity and forgiveness (Anderson and Rainie, 2008). Respondents were evenly split on the effects of greater transparency back in 2008. Some experts believed that transparency was a force that was unstoppable and would make everyone more vulnerable. Some believed that this concept of privacy was doomed but would somehow influence people to live lives in which integrity and forgiveness would be more likely (Anderson and Rainie, 2008).

We have seen that privacy was indeed threatened, but so was forgiveness. If the internet could be compared to anything, it is not so much an 800-pound gorilla as it is akin to the elephant that never forgets. One high school teacher in a St. Louis school was found to have a past life issue by one of her students searching her background on the internet. This mistake has already cost her a teaching job in another school district, and now this history has been repeated.

Exposing a Past Life

Tera Myers is not her real name, and she cannot go by her real name because people will find out. People will find out that at a point in time when she felt she needed to do something desperate in order to survive, she participated in pornographic videos (Holland, 2011). Tera says that she has come to know God and has been on the Dr. Phil show speaking about the transformation in her life while asking for help to get past the situation in which she finds herself (Holland, 2011).

She finds herself now trying to get past her mistakes and move on. The problem is that no one will let her get past her past life. They do not offer her an opportunity to start new or fresh; they only throw her old life back in her face and judge her. All she is trying to do is start a new life. Tera is on the run: she runs from place to place, starting again until she is found out.

The writer cites a St. Louis paper quoting Mrs. Myers, who says she has tried to turn her life around and found God (Holland, 2011). The unfortunate thing is that others cannot forget, and they speak of understanding her bad decisions and her trying to change. However, then St. Louis school district representative Paul Tandy made a statement like this: [School district representative Tandy] said the district hopes to use the incident as a teaching lesson. "We are trying to remind them of real-world consequences, that the decisions you make will be around in the electronic world forever," [Tandy] said (Sheehy, 2011).

One author referenced an online comment attached to their story. The post went like this: "I think she should have her second chance. She has proven you can screw up royally early in life and turn it around into a positive. I am wondering what some of the other teachers may have been involved with at college or before their teaching careers that, if known, might 'distract' students they teach! We have all done stuff we regret, and how to overcome it counts" (Giegerich, 2011).

Is it true that our mistakes and questionable decisions, when posted on the internet, leave us vulnerable for the rest of our lives? This penalty seems more severe than a convict spending several years in prison. At least the convict gets to go free, although others often cannot forget what they have done, and they must report it on every application which asks, "Have you ever been convicted of a crime?"

While doing further research for this book, the author retrieved the information in this part of the chapter from a blog post written ten years earlier. We sought to update the links to verify information; there were still many websites with information about this incident, some ten years after it occurred. There is even a Wikipedia page describing this particular incident with the history of Ms. Myers as far back as her sordid past would allow (see here–https://en.wikipedia.org/wiki/Tericka_Dye). Indeed the "internet elephant" never forgets. Are we okay with this? So, what are we going to tell people to do in order to move them forward and escape their past?

In our next story, a person revealed a previously hidden bias on a live television broadcast. This is not a good thing. Nevertheless, in their effort to get past their own mistake, address their personal biases, and move forward, the internet has decided that this is impossible.

Exposing a Hidden Bias

Thom Brennaman thought the mic was off. The broadcast team was coming out of a commercial break as he began his duties to broadcast play by play for the Cincinnati Reds baseball team whom he represented (Martin, 2020). We always think the mic is off when we want to say something silly or stupid or sometimes something hurtful to a close friend, or when we make snide comments to someone we believe thinks like us. It is a way we lift ourselves at the expense of another.

According to Paul Daugherty, a baseball radio booth can be like any male sports locker room, filled with raging testosterone and arrogant puffery (Daugherty, 2020). However, this kind of talk is always a heart issue when we want people to think that we are on their side as we denigrate someone else and put them down to lift ourselves. This kind of speech is never right, whether we are secretly mocking others or stereotyping an entire group of people.

According to author and pastor Tim Keller, this does occur in the New Testament (Keller, 2013). When Nathanael, the skeptic, was approached by Philip in the Gospel of John (1:46) about the coming of Jesus as a fulfillment of prophecy, his disdain for the hometown of Jesus was apparent: "Can anything good come? Out of Nazareth?" (John 1:46).

Nathanael sought to lift his opinion of himself by putting down anyone who comes from Nazareth.

Thomas Brennaman made the same mistake, but he was heard by a live regional audience in Brennaman's case. He seemed to know this was career suicide moments afterward (Daugherty, 2020). What he said was inappropriate, he would later acknowledge. He would try several times to apologize. As he grappled with what had happened and stumbled to recover, Brennaman had to call a home run ball hit right in the middle of his apology effort (Kalaf, 2020). He would the next day apologize again, this time writing his apology in a Cincinnati Enquirer opinion column (Kalaf, 2020). Here Brennaman would follow a well-worn path trod by many who have made cataclysmic public mistakes.

In an article in USA Today, author Kelly Whiteside (2012), an expert in reputation management, discusses the parameters for a comeback. Whiteside quotes Karen Kessler, who has experience helping individuals restore their reputations. "The strategy is different for every case, but there are certain kinds of principles that transcend whatever field of work," Kessler tells Whiteside. "The overview is confess, contrite and compassion" (Whiteside 2012).

Transgression, then disgrace, then repentance, exploration of the issue to gain further insights, and finally hoped-for social redemption— the whole self-destructive cycle, in order to be mainstreamed back into the public eye—is a recognized part of the 21st Century drive for public acceptance by many notable personalities. Whether people in drunken hubris, careless abandon, or planned deception speak folly and then find themselves in the public doghouse, repairing reputations after scandal is as much a part of our daily news as is the congressional fights over raising the debt ceiling. There seems to be an agreed-upon process used by the accused offender and their public relations firm for extricating the offending party from the lead story on the News Channel's web blog (Borrelli 2010). More reputation management than actual recovery and transformation (Whiteside 2012).

Whether Brennaman should be fired for his actions is really between him and his bosses. Contract clauses indicate compliance with certain norms and professional behavior (Daugherty, 2020). Brennaman was immediately fired, and perhaps there could have been less of the nuclear option with the provision of a work furlough or suspension for some time. The Cincinnati

Enquirer Editorial Board called for his termination—calling him "damaged goods"—but suggested that we should forgive him (Cincinnati Enquirer Editorial Board, 2020). How understanding?

What is sinister about the whole incident is this advancing social media idea that Brennaman should never be restored. This puts Brennaman right alongside Tera Myers. The author of the Slate article questioned Brennaman's sincerity in his multiple apologies, with no opportunity for restoration insight (Kalaf, 2020). That seems to be where we are as a culture (ProCon.org, 2020).

People make mistakes; all of us do. Our failings as individuals and as a nation make us human and, as Trennert says, forever a work in progress (Trennert, 2020). We would rather others not know about our mistakes, particularly public mistakes. In Tera Myer's case, her past life was exposed. Desperate for money or not, some folks cannot get past their previous line of work. As was written earlier, the measure they use to judge Mrs. Myers will come back and be used on them at some point (Matthew 7:2). In Thom Brennaman's case, his heart was exposed. What he thought in his heart was exposed for all to hear, for the Bible says clearly that "out of the abundance of the heart his mouth speaks" Luke 6:45 ESV.

Respect for others' faith backgrounds, lifestyle choices, and a tolerance for a diversity of viewpoints was a hallmark of our free society (Trennert, 2020). This should coincide with a level of tolerance, not necessarily acceptance, of criticisms and teasing. I cannot judge the heart of what was said, whether, as Mushnick suggests, it was spoken as a wise guy or as a hate monger (Mushnick, 2020). Increasingly, public mistakes which involve an actual or implied belittling of another culture or protected class unleash extreme social shaming, "calling out" these offenders as publicly as their inappropriate actions.

ProCon.org (2020) suggests that the "call-out culture," as it is known, gives a voice to those disenfranchised or less powerful people who are seeking to hold others accountable (ProCon.org, 2020). On the other hand, this website quotes former President Barack Obama, saying that these activities are not productive and they are not activism—this is more like casting stones and is not bringing about social change (ProCon.org, 2020).

According to Mushnick (2020), irony is the selective way this social justice is applied (Mushnick, 2020). The rush to social judgment seems swifter if the actions are perceived to be more malicious than circumstantial. While some may classify this social action as a new form of boycott, the "call-out culture" approach to social compliance is a slippery slope that can lead to the same intolerance the persons initiating the call-out claim their victims have demonstrated (ProCon.org, 2020).

Are We Better Than Those We Judge?

The temptation which felled mankind in the Garden of Eden is similar here: by eating the fruit of the social gatekeeper; we put ourselves into the same situation which cost Adam and Eve their freedom—we seek to become like a god knowing good from evil (Genesis 3:4). What we think is good and evil appears to be a moving target in our age. In 2020, according to Daugherty (2020), there are no second chances when it comes to slurs. However, the most dehumanizing part of the entire episode is not offering forgiveness and holding someone to an impossible standard from which there is no opportunity for redemption.

Padecky (2020) writes that the case of specific high-profile individuals' words speaks louder than their actions. They will be socially punished for an extended time for saying the wrong word at the wrong time. Their words or action were perceived as hurtful and inappropriate when said, and this is acknowledged. However, should their punishment be forever? Or is there a redemptive process by which fallible human beings can recover from these mistakes? If not, society has become as intolerant as we claim they are.

Here we remember several biblical figures whose choice of words could have been to their eternal detriment—but instead received redemption, forgiveness, and a new passion for living for Christ: How about the Apostle Peter, denying he even knew the Lord with whom he had walked for three years? (See Luke 22:54-62). Or how about the man who would become the most significant evangelist and teacher in the new movement? Paul, as Saul breathed out threats and murder against the members of the Way (Acts 9:1), yet God would use him to reach gentiles and kings by the hand of the Lord (Acts 9:15). If the hateful speech of the Apostle Paul could be forgiven and his life used for God's glory, we must recognize that with God, all things are possible (Matthew 19:26). We, who were made in God's image (Genesis 1:27), should reflect some of His majesty and mercy and demonstrate forgiveness and redemption among those who have fallen short of our expectations (and God's glory—Romans 3:23).

For some reason, talk of forgiveness and redemption in this world more closely represents overcoming a past night of poor play or returning to victory in the playoffs. Nevertheless, God's mercy is from everlasting to everlasting (Psalm 103:17); and He not only forgives but forgets and eradicates sin! Micah 7:19 says: "He (God) will again have compassion for us and subdue our iniquities. You will cast all our sins into the depths of the sea." Other verses indicate how merciful God is and willing to forgive our sins if we will repent of them, forsake them, and turn to Christ to save us. Other examples include: "Come now, and let us reason together, says the LORD, though your sins are like scarlet, they shall be as white as snow; though they are red like crimson, they shall be as wool" (Isaiah 1:18). Furthermore, this one: "As far as the east is from the west, so far has He removed our transgressions from us" (Psalm 103:12). Please keep our sister in the faith Tera Myers and her children, in your prayers.

Individuals such as Thom Brennaman and Tera Myers have acknowledged that past actions represent a real character weakness. Mistakes were made through desperation or arrogance, but forgiveness is being sought. Both Myers and Brennaman qualified themselves as people changed by God, with Brennaman calling himself a 'man of faith'—a qualification ultimately dismissed by one author as having "no relevance as to whether he would say something so bigotedly homophobic" (Kalaf, 2020). This also disparages the cause of Christ, whom we represent.

Not Just Talk—But An Opportunity

As fallen and error-prone humans, our role is to offer Mr. Brennaman and Mrs. Myers forgiveness—this was even the admonition of the Cincinnati Enquirer Editorial Board in the case of Mr. Brennaman (2020). Moreover, it is also our challenge to hope for restoration and some courageous employers to offer these people and those broken and failed individuals like them employment opportunities.

As we discussed in the previous book (Bucci, 2016), someone had to believe in Robert Downey Jr. after being arrested multiple times for drug offenses and cycled in and out of jail (Odovitch, 2003). Iron Man director Jon Favreau was willing to fight to get Downey the role, which cemented his return from what one reviewer called "the dark side" (Bucci, 2016). It is also well known that no one would touch former football quarterback Michael Vick after his arrest and imprisonment, having served time for crimes related to the funding of a dog-fighting operation on his property in Virginia (Bucci, 2016).

Nevertheless, this "second chance" opportunity was personal to coach Andy Reid, who had himself faced challenges with his own sons' incarceration. That personal life event would eventually prepare Reid to consider taking on Michael Vick as a redemptive project for his team (Bucci, 2016).

The mercurial Steve Jobs spoke at a commencement event for Stanford University about how his termination removed him from the company he founded. He expressed remorse for failing to lead the company (Bucci, 2016) successfully. The circumstances for the termination and the subsequent opportunity to begin again were laid out by the CEO of Apple, Gil Amelio (Lashinsky 2013). Here is a man raised by adoptive parents, with a brilliant mind and excessive paranoia, who overcame the rejection by the company he founded. With his second chance, he chose to invest his life back into his former company and transformed not only his former company but also an entire industry (Bucci, 2016). There needed to be a reckoning in Jobs' later life before his return to Apple could have been such a change agent. But there also needed to be the offer of a second chance—not just nice words or "hope you make it" talk, but an actual job opportunity to start again.

According to the Apostle Paul, the ultimate mission of Christ was to give "His life to free us from every kind of sin, to cleanse us, and to make us his very own people, totally committed to doing good deeds" (Titus 2:14 NLT). Christ's act of redemption was meant to break the chains of sin and selfishness and offer forgiveness and complete removal of the stain of sin. We diminish the eternal impact of Christ's sacrifice when we do not allow others to receive forgiveness and a release from their errors and public transgressions. Moreover, in our culture, we diminish the dignity of these persons created in God's image when we do not forgive past transgressions and then when we fail to help them reintegrate into society by performing the work of their hands.

CHAPTER 13
The Scarlet Thread

Abstract: Sexual offenders—is there any hope for redemption? What does restoration look like for sexual offenders? In prison, they refer to them as offenders instead of inmates—an interview with a prison chaplain who has had to understand redemption in a new context.

Introduction

Unfortunately, not every story ends on a positive note. According to an article on fairy tales (Conrad, Mills and Green, 2007), the fairy tales that we love to read to our children, and enjoy, were surprisingly not written with such family-friendly endings in their original form (Conrad, Mills and Green, 2007). These authors suggest that in the original version, Cinderella killed her first stepmother so that the father would marry someone else who was nicer—the housekeeper (Conrad, Mills, and Green, 2007). That certainly changes the plotline for us. Again, not the warm and fuzzy finale to which we have become accustomed.

Finally, these authors write that Hans Christian Andersen's original version of the Little Mermaid goes entirely differently. The prince marries a different woman, and the Little Mermaid tries so hard to become a human that she suffers significantly in her attempts and throws herself back into the sea, where her body dissolves (Conrad, Mills, and Green, 2007). The revelation of these morbid endings compared to the joyous conclusions we are aware of was surprising to us in our research. However, the details were verified in other similar articles (Devine, 2016; Jones, 2016).

Full Circle

We started this book with the background behind the original "Wizard of Oz" story (Baum, 1900; Zipes, 2007). We used the "Wizard of Oz" story to describe individuals bound by despair and frustrations, some of their makings, who were offered restoration through a redemptive intervention process. The opportunity—to contribute back to society, fulfill their calling, and bear positive fruit in the lives of others—was given to these characters by a "Dorothy." They represented non-profit groups and ministries committed to restoring people like them. Their lives and purpose were not labeled failures and not limited or restricted by the wrong choices or circumstances outside of their control.

It seems appropriate that we finish with more fairy tales and their truths, as we did when we began this journey. However, in this case, the idea here is that not all fairy tales resolved their original storylines with joyful conclusions. In truth, the fairy tales by Grimm and Anderson were not written with actual positive outcomes but had to be rewritten to resolve that way. This is also the case with the last group of people we will discuss: sexual offenders. There are no tangible positive outcomes for individuals accused of sexual crimes, no matter the severity, who, for the rest of their lives, are labeled as sexual predators.

Allow me to add a disclaimer here: we, in no way, seek to diminish the nature of the heinous crime of sexual assault or take the actions of sexual predators lightly. As you will see in this brief chapter, our society and the current legal system use a broad brush when identifying people as sexual offenders. When this term is used, it covers many types of incidents, from stupid actions to violent crimes. Once someone receives this label, it is with them for the rest of their lives. Not every story ends on a positive note for those labeled as such.

Defined

The phrase—sex offender—describes any individual convicted under a statute that requires sex offender registration, which lasts anywhere from ten years to natural life, depending on the state and the offense (Fleming, 2018). According to the National Incarceration Association (Fleming, 2018), this generic label is given to a wide range of offenders, from mentally ill people to flashers, sexually motivated killers, adults having relations with underage teens, and also dangerous child rapists (Fleming, 2018). What might be called the production and distribution of child pornography are, in some cases, attached to a 20-year-old male taking and sharing sexual photos of his 17-year-old girlfriend (Fleming, 2018). Not correct—but also not violent.

Nearly 1 million individuals remain on the sexual offender registry. Even though, according to the NIA and some prison chaplains' research, these offenders are statistically unlikely to re-offend mainly because the offense may have been due to stupidity or of another relatively minor nature.

Interview with a Chaplain

The author spoke with Dr. Kathy Williams, the Head Chaplain at the New Castle Correctional facility, a privatized facility with 3500 men (K. Williams, personal communication, January 30, 2015).

Ninety-six percent of the inmates at this facility are in custody for sexual crimes—felony-level offenses. About 200 men are in a level 1 security building outside the electrified fence. These are low-level felonies. About 500 men are housed in two maximum-security buildings, and these men have no interaction with the general population. Then about 2500 men are housed in 11 buildings with 220 men per bldg.—54 per pod with two tiers of about 25 each. There is also a mental health facility with 128 men.

When this interview was given, three chaplains were assigned to the facility—one assigned for outlying areas: minimum, maximum, mental health area, the infirmary, and an assisted living unit.

The other 2 focused their ministry on the general population of 2500 men. Dr. Williams has been at this facility for over ten years and has 30 years of experience in prison and jail ministry.

What does Redemption Look Like for Sexual offenders?

Dr. Williams said that the chaplains refer to the men as offenders instead of inmates. There is a great diversity of faith backgrounds served by chaplains at the prison: Native Americans, Muslims, Wiccan, and general Christian believers. All total, this represents up to 47 different types of faith backgrounds. With so many diverse groups represented, even the concept of redemption means something different to the individuals here (K. Williams, personal communication, January 30, 2015).

It is essential for her to define the term "redemption" for her population (3 dimensions)—secured by the blood of Christ; also acknowledging this change in verbal terms, and then the actual behavior change. Some of this is the work of sanctification. How does this work of redemption translate to their lifestyle?

Dr. Williams said that now she understands redemption differently than she had. She had to learn new things to understand redemption in the context in which she works (K. Williams, personal communication, January 30, 2015). She learned that the most untapped source of power that a Christian leader has is the love of God. We can only talk to people through the love of God with no agenda. We do not have to prove that we are right. The law has defined right and wrong: the US has more laws on the books than any civilized nation. However, only the spirit of God heals. Until we reach for the spirit of God above the law, we will never achieve redemption (K. Williams, personal communication, January 30, 2015).

The experts believe that a sex offender cannot change, interpreting this through the law. Nevertheless, the angel asked Mary if anything was too hard for God (Luke 1:3-7 English Standard Version)? Could Mary become pregnant as a virgin? Well, she did. Jesus declares the same to His disciples (Mark 10 27).

Behind the Walls

The Chaplain said that some men in the facility are corrupted and then are caught up in the perversions. Their minds are broken, and the safest place for them is where they are. Moreover, some men are here in prison for poor judgment. Substance abuse and pornography are the gateways to sexual crime. They say, "If I were not drunk or high, I would have never done this."

For many men, redemption involves healing. This is a multi-layer process. Deliverance is like being shot out of a cannon. However, once you land on the ground, you have to walk. She tells the men that they cannot just speak a prayer and that things will be all right; discipline is required. The men must make up their minds that they want to change and pursue healing (K.

Williams, personal communication, January 30, 2015).

Deliverance comes through Christ; then comes healing and reconstruction of your life. Then finally finding wholeness. The wholeness stage is when people realize that they have been redeemed. They may not realize that redemption has occurred until the wholeness part, but they have to live through the first three phases by faith. There needs to be the faith to wait through this process and determination to stay in the process (K. Williams, personal communication, January 30, 2015).

Dr. Williams was shocked by the number of people in professional ministry—who are now in prison. The devil does not have a sex life, and he does not care about yours. What he cannot tolerate is men with a destiny. The minute their eyes are on porn, the devil plants shame or guilt. We have no one to tell. So the devil locks down our destiny with shame or guilt. We need to direct people back to redemption.

Dr. Williams did her Master's Thesis on recidivism rates in Indiana through the eyes of the Indiana sexual offender registry and parole violators. Her premise was that recidivism rates are inflated based on how frequently sexual offenders violate their parole. The data says that sexual offenders violate parole at a 70–80% rate. However, only 1% of sexual offenders violate their parole based on a new sexual crime (K. Williams, personal communication, January 30, 2015).

She reviewed a year's worth of parole hearings to assess data. She found some interesting results:

The average person on parole has one page of compliance requirements once released. In comparison, the sex offender would have that 1 page plus seven additional pages—8 pages of compliance requirements once they are released.

Most sexual offender parole violations were based on a number 10 requirement: communications. The sex offenders did not tell their parole officers that they were moving or that they did not pay their fees (etc.). They are ashamed and limited in their communication skills from the beginning.

Only 1% of sexual offenders violate their parole based on a new sexual crime. So her data suggests that there is an inflated rate of recidivism.

The recidivism rate for sexual offenders who commit another crime is around one percent. The public hears the vast numbers. The compliance restrictions almost cause them to violate parole from the moment they walk out the door.

The sexual offender registry restrictions are the same for a man caught with a prostitute as for a man caught for child seduction. Some of the restrictions are based on studies done in the 1980s. So the sexual registry is based on "stranger danger." However, few sexual crimes are committed strangers to strangers. In most sexual crimes, the offender is known by the victim. The registry could be modified to reflect this and stop labeling men, but few politicians are willing to make changes because of public opinion (K. Williams, personal communication, January 30, 2015).

Dr. Williams said that the men struggle with the idea of repentance for sexual offenders. They struggle with not forgiving themselves. The spirit heals, but the law blocks healing. How long does someone have to write divorce on an application? It seems that the situation is similar with sexual offenders.

Fleming (2018) wrote on the NIA site that there were some signs of positive change in the life sentences of the sexual offenders. In Los Angeles, there was support for a bill passed to modify California's lifetime-for-all sexual offender registry (Fleming, 2018). This law would permit most offenders to be removed sometime within their natural lives. Nevertheless, it is still challenging for sexual offenders to find employment once released from prison (Fleming, 2018). Someone takes a risk hiring a sex offender—they have to be straight with them.

The Scarlet Thread

In the heavenly realms, we are transformed when we repent, but it sometimes does not show itself so convincingly in our actions. We expect people to change after leaving the altar in the church; in truth, it may require counseling and work to change habit patterns. In some cases, change is much more difficult.

As Dr. Williams has said, many of these men are unable or unwilling to change. This is reinforced in one article by Dr. Ludwig Lowenstein, a psychologist, author, and expert in this field (Lowenstein, 2010). As Dr.

Williams said, in prison, the men struggle with repentance. Some of that is because of their temptations or internal conflicts, and some may be because the law indicates they will never change.

So we have this juxtaposition. Change is available, but it is more than simply saying a prayer. There is more work that needs to be done. Those more willing to change, and who want a better life, should be given the opportunity if their crime was simply an act of immaturity or stupidity. We do not know how to measure that, but we hope that it will be through the actions of wise hearts and heads to determine these things and remove some of the obstacles. It is unfortunate for all to carry the label of a sexual offender for the rest of their lives.

The Bible mentions scarlet thread as part of the curtains in the Tabernacle (Exodus 26) and part of the high priests' ephod for his worship and the offering of sacrifices (Exodus 28). While the Bible does not explicitly explain the use of these various chords, some commentators believe that the scarlet color represents Christ's atoning work on the cross through the shedding of His blood (GotQuestions Ministries, 2022).

We know that the biblical figure Rahab was a prostitute (Joshua Chapter 2), and we know of her heroic actions in protecting the spies and saving her family (Meyers, 2021). Here is another mention of the scarlet thread. We do not know her as a sexual offender but as a sex worker. Nevertheless, the connection of the scarlet thread is still a powerful one.

According to the law office of George Gedulin (2017), Nevada is the only state in the US where prostitution is legal. However, while many states still list soliciting or providing prostitution as a crime, it does not constitute a sexual offense in most states unless the act involves a minor. Six states consider soliciting prostitution a sexual offense.

Rahab was the head of her household. She was concerned about her household and their future, knowing that the God of Israel would capture Jericho and destroy it. Here Rahab the Harlot, a self-employed sex worker, protected the spies, searching the city of Jericho, and identified her trust with the Israelites' protection by lowering the spies out of her window using a scarlet chord. The spies promised protection for this woman and her family by suggesting that this same thread should hang in the window of her home; and that her household would be kept safe in the coming invasion (Joshua 2). She obeyed and hung the chord in her window. When the Israelites captured the city, Joshua commanded his men to search for the house with the scarlet chord in the window (Joshua 6).

Is it just a coincidence that this scarlet thread seems to be apparent throughout the Bible, representing Jesus Christ and his Redemptive sacrifice for all of mankind (GotQuestions Ministries, 2022)? Rahab would become one of five women mentioned in the genealogy of Jesus (Matthew Chapter 1). In James's letter to the dispersed church, she is also mentioned as someone justified by God and made righteous (James 2:24-25). We trust that the scarlet thread will also be something to be clung to by those finding themselves in the despair of the label of sexual offender. Whether or not the opportunities for restoration occur on earth, in the heavenly realms, the work has already been completed.

CHAPTER 14

A Second Chance is the Best Choice

Abstract: This chapter highlights a mix of successful organizations which have chosen to build their success on failed but now redeemed workers.

> "Make it your goal to live a quiet life, minding your own business and working with your hands, just as we instructed you before."
>
> ***—1 Thessalonians 4:11 NLT***

> "Make the tree good, and its fruit good; or make the tree bad, and its fruit bad; for by its fruit you will get knowledge of the tree."
>
> ***—Matthew 12:33 BBE***

Organizations Offering Second Chance Hiring

Jim Dahl purchased a small neighborhood bakery in Milwaukie, Oregon, in 1955. The bakery served as a place of employment for Jim's four children. Son Glenn took over the business while son Dave found trouble and served four prison terms. When Dave was released from prison, his brother Glenn welcomed him back into the family business. It was not Dave's first choice, but ex-cons rarely have any opportunities for work outside of prison. This was the genesis of Dave's Killer Bread, as Dave and his brother developed a new product line that eventually became more significant than the small family bakery. The business is now the world's largest organic bread brand. It all happened because Glenn offered Dave an opportunity for redemption (Dave's Killer Bread, 2018).

There seem to be two types of redemption common to us but at opposite poles. There is the redemptive work of Christ on the cross, whose substitutionary atonement met the obligation for my sinful life. This is the message that drives mission activity across the globe. We hear of another redemption, often cited in news articles and popular media, and this redemption is more aligned with earthly vindication. We read about the redemption of a character in a movie or book or a game where a sports player obtains redemption through victory.

So there is this paradox of redemption in our experience: there is the work of Christ to redeem and transform a soul, which takes place instantaneously, while the earthly human results may struggle to match up. However, when we consider redemption in our cultural context, it is often an effort to find redemption in the public square, which is not complete like the redemption provided through the work of Christ.

Wellman (2014) suggested that a random person on the street might qualify redemption as an act of atoning for a fault or mistake. In finance, redemption would represent the repayment of security before its maturity date. Suppose you asked the average person about redemption. In that case, they might suggest that the term contains the idea of repurchasing something or rescuing something or someone, or making something or someone more acceptable. Wellman distinguishes a general understanding of the term with the Christian perspective on redemption being a repurchasing of life by a Savior (Jesus) in exchange for an individual's commitment to Him. He includes the thought of rescue but specifically focuses on a rescue from sin. The redemption that God offered through the death of Christ is something of great value, which is very costly and should not be taken lightly.

In a random review of articles on "redemption" (minus qualifying words like 'coupon,' 'red,' and 'annual report') collected using the RSS news reader Feedly, there were 51 articles discussing the redemption of a character in a movie or book, or a game or sports player's redemption opportunity through victory. There were also 21 articles describing a coupon or product redemption; there were also nine church names or songs about redemption or poems. Only one article described some aspects of what Wellman describes as the Christian definition of redemption (Wellman, 2014).

One thing we have failed to see in these two extreme views of redemption is the broken individuals that God has placed before us who have "missed the mark" and failed to follow societal norms. These people have failed to adhere to customs or existing laws: volatility in the workplace, excessive drunkenness, drug addiction, minor or significant felony convictions, or worse.

All hiring managers must realize that no one is perfect, and all employees need directive manager behaviors early in their tenure and ongoing coaching to be successful. It is an error to think that our recruiting efforts draw from a standard distribution curve (Blanchard et al. 1985) and that finding the best employees is like getting a taller ladder to reach the top of the fruit tree. The data suggest that aberrant, non-compliant behavior, called "deviant" behavior by Aquino, Lewis, and Bradfield (1999), is expected in organizations. In the workplace itself, one study indicated that as many as 75% of employees have engaged in some form of aberrant behavior, this ranging from excessive absenteeism but also theft, fraud, embezzlement, vandalism, sabotage, and other efforts to cause harm to their employer (Harper, 1990; Hayes 2008).

In the workplace, employee discipline programs seek to "redeem" or restore terminal employee behavior towards compliance with corporate culture and organizational norms for success on the job. Conventional approaches for handling terminal employee behavior recommend that managers talk to their subordinates about the problem behavior first (Yukl, 2002). If this approach is not initially practical, the manager generally follows three recommended paths: pursue progressive discipline with the employee up to and including termination should the behavior not be redirected; reassign the employee; or dismiss the employee outright if they are an "at-will" employee (Falcone, 2010).

The Case for Providing Redemptive Opportunities for Former Criminals

According to the National Employment Law Project (Rodriguez & Emsellem, 2011), the authors suggest that providing individuals the opportunity for stable employment has been proven to lower crime recidivism rates according to their research (Rodriguez & Emsellem, 2011). As an example confirming the NELP research, in a study conducted in Illinois, out of some 1,600 individuals released from state prison and monitored for the survey, only 8 percent of those who were employed for at least a year were found to have committed another crime (Rodriguez & Emsellem, 2011). This was compared to Illinois' current recidivism rate of

54 percent (Rodriguez & Emsellem, 2011).

The challenge of finding employment for those with criminal records is staggering. According to a report by the Brookings Institute (Goger, Harding, and Henderson, 2021), more than half of the formerly incarcerated are unable to find stable employment within their first year of return, and three-fourths of them are rearrested within three years of release (Goger, Harding and Henderson, 2021).

Some legislative efforts to assist former inmates in finding stable jobs include the "One Stop Shop Community Reentry Program Act," introduced to the 116th Congress in 2020 and re-introduced in the current legislative session (Grisales, 2021). Another similar initiative has been the "Ban the Box" legislative efforts (Stout, 2015; Rodrigues, 2015). This means eliminating the box on employment applications asking if the applicant had ever been convicted of a crime. This ban the box movement has already affected 17 states and over 100 cities and counties in the US as of the time this article was written (Rodrigues, 2015).

Organizations That Are Active in Providing Redemptive Opportunities

CEO John Shegerian, a former addict, believes that you can recycle everything, including lives. One-third of his full-time and part-time employees at his current company, *Electronic Recyclers International*, is in the company's "second chance" program, which includes former convicts and former drug addicts. These second-chance workers have a 17 percent turnover rate, half that of employees recruited through traditional means (Brown, 2008). In a story about Shegerian's social entrepreneurial work, it was noted that he was also the co-founder of another program supporting former criminals seeking employment—Homeboy Industries (Pierce, n.d., Shegerian, 2021). Shegerian's latest venture is an online aftercare program for addicts providing addiction recovery resources called "addicted.com" (https://addicted.com/about/).

Shegerian challenges business owners to actively consider recruiting and developing persons from this untapped talent group, noting that tax credits and insurance are available for businesses willing to hire former felons. A government-sponsored Federal Bonding Program offers employers who hire "at-risk" employees free insurance against the loss of money or property to help protect the company if an employee commits a crime against the business (Pierce, n.d.). In unrelated research by a firm that studies employee retention, the research found that workers with prior criminal convictions were more productive than workers without a criminal record (Giang, 2012).

The following are descriptions of more organizations aggressively addressing the problem of the employability of former drug addicts and criminals and some of their success stories:

Delancey Street–http://www.delanceystreetfoundation.org/hww.php

The Delancey Street program is open to persons with felony convictions, persons with gang backgrounds, or persons having problems with drugs or alcohol. This re-employment model functions as an extended family (Delancey Street, 2007). The programs are run entirely by its residents. According to program founder and Director Mimi Silbert, "everyone is responsible for teaching everyone else. This is a horrible world, and it needs people who want to pull everyone up" (Fowler, 2011). Silbert requires each person to have responsibility for another person's success; she also demands that each resident confront every other resident about every violation of their behavioral rules (Fowler, 2011). The program works to break the code of the street, which Silbert has boiled down to two principles: care only about yourself, and do not rat on anyone. As the newest residents come in, the newer associates just entering the program teach them different tasks and activities. At Delancey Street, speaking up about rule-breaking and taking responsibility for behaviors is essential. The people who have been helped also have helped numerous people under them (Patterson, Grenny, Maxfield, McMillan, and Switzler, 2007). The program was started in 1971. The recidivism rate in the first thirty years was less than 20 percent. This rate has increased in the last 12 years.

League Collegiate Outfitters–**h**ttp://www.league91.com/

LCO has partnered with Central American University to seek out gang members that no longer want to be a part of that lifestyle, put them through an intensive rehabilitation program, and finally offer them employment in their factory (League Collegiate Outfitters, 2014). The company has recently merged with the Legacy company to form L2 Brands (L2 Brands, 2021).

Exportadora Rio Grande Company–*h*ttp://www.riograndefoods.com/en/

Former gang members at Exportadora Rio Grande company are packaging food for export to the United States and Canada. These former gang members are not afraid to admit that they have made mistakes, and they endure the disbelief of their fellow citizens that they have turned their lives around. In one article, the plant manager said that the workers had become dedicated and efficient employees (Iqbal, 2012).

Central City Concern–http://www.centralcityconcern.org/

CCC is a non-profit agency that provides comprehensive solutions to ending homelessness and achieving self-sufficiency in Portland, Oregon. The program helps participants build strong peer relationships that support the necessary steps to help former addicts and homeless clients and their families transform their lives and become stable employees and self-sufficient community members (Central City Concern, 2021).

Urbean Café–http://www.akronmetro.org/metro-urbean-cafe.aspx

The Urbean Café provides quality foods and beverages to a community of people using public transportation and anyone who stops by for a visit. It is staffed by those learning to become employable. The Urbean Café operates as a job training outlet to enhance the participants' lives and increase their work readiness. They work to further the mission of Broken Chains Ministry, assisting formerly incarcerated individuals by restoring them to the community (https://www.brokenchainsministry.org/). The program operates out of Akron, OH. (Scott, 2012).

Goodwill Industries International–http://www.goodwill.org/

Goodwill works to enhance individuals and families' dignity and quality of life by strengthening communities, eliminating barriers to opportunity, and helping people in need reach their full potential through learning and the power of work. They focus on training and coaching ex-offenders through their Re-Entry program.
(https://www.goodwill.org/blog/news-updates/kingsport-tn-goodwill-helps-participants-succeed-through-re-entry-program/).

Homeboy Industries–http://www.homeboyindustries.org/

Homeboy Industries serves high-risk, formerly gang-involved men and women with a continuum of free services and programs and operates seven social enterprises as job-training sites. Although several additional locations have been set up, their main focus is in the Los Angeles, CA area (McGray, 2012).

Rhinotek Computer Products–http://www.rhinotek.com/

At Rhinotek Computer Products dba IDT Print Solutions, roughly one-third of the workforce comes from halfway houses, work-furlough centers, and recovery programs. The company founder, Gerald W. Chamales (mentioned earlier in the book), is a recovering alcoholic who worked his way into the executive suite from a life of poverty, welfare, and food stamps. This untapped population of workers is assigned a mentor and enrolled in a training program. There is a rigorous follow-up and lots of determination due to the opportunity given to these employees when others would not take the chance (Marchetti, 2005). The business is currently under a new brand name, Equity Value Group (http://www.equityvaluegroup.com/Home_Page.html).

Electronic Recyclers International–http://electronicrecyclers.com/

Through his past addiction, CEO John Shegerian (previously mentioned) lost everything he had gained from several successful business start-ups. He actively recruits those like himself with sordid pasts (Brown, 2008). One-third of full-time and part-time employees at Electronic Recyclers International are in its "second chances" program, including ex-cons and former addicts (Brown, 2008).

Creative Matters Agency–http://creativemattersagency.com/

Creative Matters Agency operates out of Beit T'Shuvah, an addiction treatment center in Los Angeles. CMA is a social entrepreneurial enterprise that helps people in recovery learn advertising-related job skills while learning the basics of employability. They offer twice-weekly "check-ins" discussing the pressures of work and relationships to keep things real for recovering addicts (Zaimont, 2014). Their main webpage declares that they are "a creative agency built for non-profits and staffed by recovering addicts."

Televerde–http://www.televerde.com/

Televerde was highlighted in a Forbes Magazine article (Barret, 2010). The call center was identified as utilizing the skills of women from the Arizona State Prison in Perryville. In a subsequent blog post after the article came out (Kent, 2010), one of the company's senior leaders argued that the business model used by Televerde demonstrated good economic benefits for the state of Arizona. Televerde saved taxpayers over $20 million annually by keeping hundreds of women from returning to prison by providing them marketable business skills and jobs on the outside once they finished serving their prison sentences (Kent, 2010).

The company seemed to face some criticism about providing these jobs to inmates and not allowing people who are not incarcerated. The criticism suggested that the company was keeping its cost structure minimal by utilizing prison inmates. However, the company met the state's minimum wage requirements and saw tremendous social benefit in its business model. Their website states that in 2020 the business "transitioned from a telemarketing-focused provider to a holistic business solutions company." The company website describes partnerships with the UK Ministry of Justice to expand their prison workforce program to sites in the UK. It also describes how they have expanded their prison workforce program (https://televerde.com/insights/in-the-news/could-a-call-center-inside-homestead-prison-help-female-inmates-get-back-on-track/). According to this article, Televerde has eight US call centers staffed by prisoners in Arizona, Indiana and expanding to Florida.

Sweet Beginnings–www.sweetbeginningsllc.com/

This Chicago-based firm, doing business as **beelove** (https://beelovebuzz.com/), produces honey and honey-based skincare products. Potential employees must complete a job-readiness program before being hired and receive job-placement services during their time with the firm.

I Have a Bean Coffee Store–www.ihaveabean.com/

Formerly Second Chance Coffee Company, the Wheaton, IL company roasts, sells and ships its brand of premium coffee. In addition to hiring ex-offenders, the company works with post-prison support organizations to provide additional counseling and other support for their employees.

Felony Franks–www.felonyfranks.com/

This Chicago-based hot dog stands opened in 2009. The company was founded by the owner of a paper company who had a previous positive experience hiring ex-convicts. Unfortunately, the business was closed in 2017 due to the cost of doing business. (https://www.chicagotribune.com/suburbs/oak-park/ct-oak-park-felony-franks-tl-1109-20171106-story.html)

Belay Enterprises–www.belay.org/

A faith-based non-profit located in Denver, CO, has created businesses to employ ex-convicts to provide opportunities for those who are shut out of the job market because of significant barriers to employment, including addiction, homelessness, and prison time.

Weifield Group Contracting–https://www.weifieldcontracting.com/

As seen in the video, "To Whom is Given: Business for the Common Good" (AEI, 2017), Weifield is a national leader in cutting-edge electrical construction working in three western states. The video tells how the company hires individuals with challenging past life circumstances and participants from area therapeutic programs, such as Stout Street Foundation, Peer 1 Residential Program, Goodwill Industries International, Denver Rescue Mission, and a variety of other organizations, into their apprenticeship program—see also the press release noted here (Weifield Group, 2021).

Virgin Group ***(Petroff, 2016; James, 2011)***

Sir Richard Branson has publicly encouraged the managing directors of his Virgin Companies to hire ex-convicts (Petroff, 2016). Branson tells the story of offering a second chance to an employee caught stealing, and the employee became one of the company's best workers.

Other Redemptive Models for Disaffected Workers

Pursuing redemptive strategies to break the chains of past failure has led to creative alternatives in offering second chances. In a program that meets at the Cleveland Correctional Center, current prisoners prepare business plans which they will pitch to local business leaders as a part of a certificate program in entrepreneurship from Baylor University (Nothstine, 2015b). The program is called the Prison Entrepreneurship Program (PEP), and its purpose is to offer the opportunity for these incarcerated men to become business owners themselves.

The biggest challenge for people getting out of prison is that in many states, once these men leave prison, they will need to report when asked if they have ever been convicted of a crime. As previously mentioned (Rodriguez & Emsellem, 2011), in their effort to find a job, a standard background check will expose a prison record, no matter how long it has been since they committed a crime. Because it is difficult for those getting out of prison to get jobs, these former convicts often will go back to a life of crime because they cannot make money in traditional ways. Programs like the Prison Entrepreneurship Program seek to enable prisoners to become independent business owners and positively contribute to a society that had previously incarcerated them.

The success of the PEP program is remarkable: almost 75 percent of the Prison Entrepreneurship Program graduates are employed within 30 days of their release, while 100 percent are employed within 90 days. The three-year success rate of the program is as high as 95 percent. The return on the investment is 340 % for every dollar donated to the program (Nothstine, 2015b).

Like several of the programs mentioned in this book, this is not simply a handout; neither is it a catharsis for faith-oriented business professionals. One of the program's components is a character assessment program called the Leadership Academy. The inmates do assessments and are confronted with weaknesses and faults that need to be changed and for which they need to be accountable. A simple handout or a training program does not offer the necessary redemptive change. There may be weaknesses or blind spots in the individual's life that need to be addressed.

This program has proven that a well-thought-out comprehensive program can successfully redeem those whose lives were previously broken by bad choices and tragic circumstances.

Entrepreneurship as Second Chance

A group called Defy Ventures goes into prisons. It encourages convicts that they can re-invent themselves, turning a former life of self-employment as a drug dealer or street hustler into a positive employment opportunity to become an actual entrepreneur (Hoke, 2017). Their success stories are incredible, and their track record is impressive. Founded by Catherine Hoke in 2010, Defy Ventures operates in seven states (Grow Ensemble, 2021). According to a website that highlights "B" corporations (Grow Ensemble, 2021), they work with what they call "entrepreneurs in training," some of whom are currently in prison and others in post-prison release programs. They have seen a significant reduction in the recidivism rate among their clients compared to the national average and claim the employment rate for their program graduates is 82% (Grow Ensemble, 2021). So while this is not precisely the same situation as the failed entrepreneurs we discovered in the Texas research, these are failed entrepreneurs in their own right, according to Hoke (Hoke, 2017). Defy Ventures works to convince these formerly successful street hustlers—that they have transferable skills from their old ways into this new life of honest employment (Hoke, 2017). Moreover, the data support these claims (Grow Ensemble, 2021).

Conclusion

The hope with the writing of this book is that it will get the attention of employers, both large and small, to consider offering second chances as a part of their hiring approach (JPMorgan Chase, 2021). Recently JPMorgan Chase was in the news as they continue to expand their efforts at offering second chance opportunities to qualified people with criminal backgrounds (JPMorgan Chase, 2021). A press release from the company highlighted data stating that nearly 70 million Americans have criminal records (Friedman, 2015). This author had previously cited the National Employment Law Project (Rodriguez & Emsellem, 2011). Ten years ago, they estimated that 65 million people, 1 in 4 adults in the United States, have a criminal record. So this more recent data can be validated. According to the same study (Rodriguez & Emsellem, 2011), in a Society of Human Resources Management survey, 92 percent of their member companies perform criminal background checks on some or all job candidates (Rodriguez & Emsellem, 2011). The significance of these background checks has a variable influence on their decisions to hire.

According to the SHRM survey, the confirmation of convictions can have a very influential impact on whether to extend a job offer to the candidate or not (SHRM, 2010).

The JPMorgan Chase press release uses data to highlight how offering education skills training and employment opportunities to people with convictions or criminal backgrounds helps reduce recidivism and, therefore, make communities stronger (Davis et al., 2014). As was also mentioned in this book, the opportunity for employment after prison significantly reduces recidivism and a return to crime (Holodny, 2017). After successfully initiating a pilot program in Chicago, Chase has launched its second community-based hiring model in Columbus, Ohio (JPMorgan Chase, 2021). The program has had great success, as the company announced that 10% of the employees hired across the Chase system were second chance hires in 2020 (JPMorgan Chase, 2021). Their commitment to this effort is to be applauded.

How do some people take pride in restoring old cars or homes, yet this work of rebuilding a failed worker becomes an act of separation and not restoration? A leader in the missions organization Operation Mobilization, Jonathan Thiessen, noted that traditional missions are changing, as is the role of the traditional missionary. This suggests that there may be a great opportunity for redemption and restoration within our organizations. This work of rebuilding and restoring broken people may be the most challenging. Consider the work that Jesus did with His disciples for three years, and even He had trouble maintaining their focus. Finally, all of them abandoned Him upon his arrest. Nevertheless, by the sea at the fireside, the one who openly violated His specific warning was restored to excellent service to all of us. Where would we be without the ministry of the Apostle Peter; or the delicious taste of Dave's Killer Bread?

If redemption is an essential value to you, where does it appear in your leadership style? Applying discipline and offering workplace redemption should not increase penalties until behavior change occurs; acknowledging the error offers a path towards restoration.

Want to see a great example of redemptive leadership in Scripture? Take a look at the efforts of Nehemiah. Right from the first chapter (1:10-11), Nehemiah acknowledges God's redemptive work in His people, and here he expresses a desire to be a part of this work. He spent his career in Jerusalem rebuilding and restoring—not only walls and worship but also his people. In Matthew 20:28, the work of redemption cannot be separated from leadership: this was precisely the serving work Jesus came to do. This is exactly the work we have been commissioned to do (Ephesians 4:11-14 ESV).

CONCLUSION

The Beauty of a Restored Life

"He is Useful to Me in My Work"

"Only Luke is with me. Get Mark and bring him with you. He is useful to me in my work."

—2 Timothy 4:11 GWT

Abstract: The failure rates of new businesses and the potential staggering number of those who have started and failed in business, never to try again, are interwoven with the Biblical story of John Mark and his usefulness to the Apostle Paul (2 Timothy 4:11). John Mark lives as a metaphor for all those crying out to find relief not only from abuse, failure, and life-controlling problems—but from the shame and labels of worthlessness they still carry as "formers...."

Introduction–How Many Entrepreneurs Fail?

We teach students about the perils of the entrepreneurial journey, knowing from the data that failure is a significant part of the journey. Data suggest that somewhere between 50 and 90% of entrepreneurial ventures fail the first time around. Can the variance be so significant?

Author Sean Bryant (2020) cited the Small Business Administration (SBA) in his article on the failure rate of business start-ups. According to this data, in 2019, business start-ups' failure rate was around 90% (Bryant, 2020). The SBA defines a small business with 500 employees or less (Bryant, 2020). Bryant drilled down into the data to specify when these new businesses would face failure, and it was not pretty: according to the data, 21.5% of start-ups fail in the first year, 30% in the second year, 50% by the fifth year, and 70% in their 10th year (Bryant, 2020).

Author Ryan Jorden (2014), a managing partner in a venture capital firm, cited earlier SBA statistics in a LinkedIn blog post (Jorden, 2014). Another author, Meszaros (2016), cited the U. S. Bureau of Labor Statistics, saying that about 50% of all new businesses survive five years, and about one-third survive 10-years or more (Meszaros, 2016).

Regarding business failure, even the data cited by the SBA, as revealed by Jorden (2014), is subject to some interpretation. Jorden cites a 2002 study by Small Business Economics which discovered that about one-third of closed businesses were successful when they "failed." One expert said that many businesses reported having closed while successful calls into question the use of 'business closure' as a meaningful measure of business outcome. In deep diving into the data, many owners may have executed a planned exit strategy, closed a business without excess debt, sold a viable business, or retired from the workforce (Jorden, 2014). So from where is that 90% number coming (Bryant, 2020)?

As much as Jorden (2014) and Meszaros (2016) agree on this 50% number, in another article in Fortune Magazine, Griffith (2014) reports that 90% of new businesses fail within the first five years. According to this article, a significant number of start-ups fail, and the main reason for this, according to data in the article, is that the founders created a product for which there is no market (Griffith, 2014). The article describes some other, additionally significant, reasons for failure. Griffith is not alone in her projection on the new business failure rate: the researcher found several authors that quote this 90% statistic (Griffith, 2014; Patel, 2015; Hartley, 2016).

Failed Once—But the Second Try More Successful

Meanwhile, data suggests that those failed entrepreneurs who try again are much more successful on their second try. According to Harvard researchers Gompers, Kovner, Lerner, and Scharfstein (2006), entrepreneurs who succeeded in a previous venture have a 30% chance of succeeding in their next venture. First-time entrepreneurs only have an 18% chance of succeeding, while entrepreneurs who have previously failed and yet try again have a 20% chance of succeeding (Gompers, Kovner, Lerner & Scharfstein, 2006). It is perhaps through the 'school of hard knocks' for first-time entrepreneurs that things learned the hard way through loss or failure on the first business attempt results in tremendous success with subsequent attempts (Gompers, Kovner, Lerner & Scharfstein, 2006).

A longitudinal study with data collected in Texas, (Lafontaine and Shaw, 2014) tracked 2.33 million retail establishments founded in the state by small owners over 21 years. The researchers found that of the almost 2 million business owners that were tracked, about 25 percent start more than one establishment (Lafontaine and Shaw, 2014). The research also found that once someone became an entrepreneur for a second time, they were more likely to become an entrepreneur for a third time, etc. (Shepherd, 2004). Shepard summarizes the context from which entrepreneurship is currently taught when he quotes from entrepreneurship textbooks that failure is the vehicle where entrepreneurs learn and move forward to more significant and more successful ventures (Shepherd, 2004).

A Remarkable Discovery— Entrepreneurs Failing and Not Trying Again

Many true stories and urban legends support rising from failure to ultimate success. Some examples often cited include the following entrepreneurs (Ellis, 2017; and George, n.d.):

Steve Jobs	Benjamin Franklin
Thomas Alva Edison	Bill Gates
Richard Branson	Walt Disney
Oprah Winfrey	Fred Smith

As an inventor, Thomas Edison is well known for his successes, but not so much for his failures (DeGraaf, 2013). When we think about Edison, we do not often realize all of the challenges he had to work on, including hundreds of failed attempts to see his projects through to fruition (DeGraaf, 2013). Edison is famous for responding to a question about his many failures and mistakes in perfecting his inventions by saying, "I have not failed ten thousand times. I have successfully found 10,000 ways that will not work" (DeGraaf, 2013). Henry Ford reported that "Failure is simply the opportunity to begin again more intelligently" (BrainyQuote.com). In these "failure to success" stories, we are reminded that failure is sometimes a stop along the road to success for those who work through it. Nevertheless, trying again is not assured as a part of this narrative.

Back to this longitudinal study by researchers Lafontaine and Shaw (2014): their research found that over the length of the study (about 21 years), specifically in the state of Texas, of the business failures that were studied, 71% of those who founded a business and failed the first time were determined not to try again (Lafontaine and Shaw, 2014; Schrager, 2014).

It would seem that those of us who teach business with a Christian perspective, who have often referred to statistics about learning from failure, would want to know a little bit more about this troubling statistic regarding entrepreneurial failing and then not trying again. We have research results to suggest that business owners who fail in their first start-up attempt have more success the second time because they have learned from their failures (Lafontaine and Shaw, 2014; Schrager, 2014).

Learning from failure to find success the next time out is a popular theme for those of us who teach entrepreneurship. The data above is popular data for us to cite, and indeed, some scriptures refer to how losing something will lead to gaining something better (Matthew 19:21-29; Mark 8:35).

However, there are lingering questions about whether this data points to entrepreneurs trying once and never trying again, which might represent a phenomenon not considered in our entrepreneurial education. New businesses that fail at an alarming rate have always been discussed when we present entrepreneurship statistics in our business classes. This final data point has not been discussed, not yet confirmed as a nationwide source by this author, but valid nonetheless (Lafontaine and Shaw, 2014; Schrager, 2014). While focused on survey work in the state of Texas, the data from LaFontaine and Shaw (2014) is still quite alarming, that 71% of those who failed at starting a business do not pursue an opportunity to "do-over" but will live with this failure for a long time.

Is There Entrepreneurial Redemption?

What type of entrepreneurial redemption is taking place for those who have failed?

In Burchell and Hughes' research (2006), they noted higher levels of entrepreneurial activity in the US than in Europe; US respondents to their research were more tolerant of failure than the European countries surveyed (Burchell and Hughes, 2006). They noted that there were favorable attitudes toward giving a second chance to business failures, but these were linked to the growth of GDP (Burchell and Hughes, 2006). Nevertheless, paradoxically they noted that countries that were more intolerant of giving second chances after business failures were associated with a higher proportion of the population involved in business start-ups. The tolerance of failure was perceived to be unrelated to GDP growth (Burchell and Hughes, 2006).

These researchers noted that the highest correlation in their research between attitudes and entrepreneurial behavior was a negative relationship between offering second chances and the proportion of the population who had started businesses (Burchell and Hughes, 2006). They proposed that this could be due to the severity of economic experiences. They noted that economic psychology has found that economic losses have a longer-lasting and more significant effect on an individual's attitudes than economic gains (Burchell and Hughes, 2006).

Finally, Burchell and Hughes (2006) found that while there were higher levels of entrepreneurial activity in the US than in Europe, more economic activity related to entrepreneurship did not associate with more tolerant attitudes toward failure. The only place where evidence of more positive attitudes toward second chances was synonymous was within countries with higher national GDP growth, leading respondents to express more positive attitudes about those who had failed trying a second time (Burchell and Hughes, 2006). The authors suggested that part of the explanation of this attitude could be that individuals within the economic sphere may have lost investments or paid for goods they did not receive. This might explain why even with higher levels of entrepreneurial activity, individuals who had experienced loss from a business failure became more intolerant of those involved (Burchell and Hughes, 2006). This could be justification for why in the Texas study (Lafontaine and Shaw, 2014), it was noted that 71% of those who started a business and failed the first time did not try again. Perhaps they perceived that they had let others down and lost others' investment funds. It could be the shame and guilt over handling all of those funds and projections of gain from a successful start-up that did not occur.

In the book, *Losing isn't Everything* (2016), Curt Menefee describes sports personalities as better known for the losing end of a sports score than winning. Most people tend to observe the winners and rejoice with them, particularly those of our home teams. Menefee's work is interesting as it considers the event from the viewpoint of the losing team or individual and the impact of failure on these people. Many struggled with the loss and its social and psychological implications. If losing a game has such a tremendous impact, what about losing or failing at business when one has invested one's heart and resources?

A Plan for Second Chances

Considering such a phenomenon and its impact on investors within European Union governmental policies, there is some action. In Europe, laws are being changed to encourage entrepreneurs to avoid bankruptcy and fund depletion to start the second time on a sure footing. A report was commissioned by the European Commission, Enterprise and Industry Directorate-General (Report of the Expert Group, 2011). The report analyzed what could be done to provide second chances for entrepreneurs in their member countries. In this report, a discussion of Eurozone business bankruptcies was commissioned (Report of the Expert Group, 2011).

The report states that even though a tiny percentage of bankruptcies are fraudulent (only 4-6%), solid public opinion links this action of business failure to fraud. Those who have honestly sought to protect their assets and the debts of those who have invested in them are discouraged from restarting a business because of discrimination and this stigma of public opinion. According to the report, there is also an impact on potential new start-ups. So the report recommended policy changes and adjustments to bankruptcy legislation to support entrepreneurial second chances and the return of the honest but failed entrepreneur (Report of the Expert Group, 2011).

The report has four parts: Part-1—recommends putting an "Early Warning System" to escalate a potential bankruptcy before it becomes insolvency. Part-2—recommends an out-of-court settlement process, which would work like arbitration, to allow the entrepreneur to work with creditors and investors to find points of compromise to allow the ability to make decisions to support the growth of the business and avoid this stigma of failure (Report of the Expert Group, 2011).

Part-3—recommends in-court procedures that help reorganize the business to support every effort by the entrepreneur to engage once again in business activity to create cash flow that enables repayment of debts and investors (Report of the Expert Group, 2011). And finally, Part-4—strong recommendations regarding the perception of the post-bankruptcy experience on the entrepreneur. This is undoubtedly less tangible—more of a societal change but something that legislators can influence. So, a more modern system of honoring the "honest" entrepreneur with greater access to financing; while rooting out the more dishonest entrepreneurs. Insolvency "specialists" can determine the true nature of the balance sheet with improvements in laws allowing for liquidation and discharge procedures to give the sincere, earnest entrepreneur a fresh start (Report of the Expert Group, 2010).

Opportunity for the Church—Only If

While not the same type of "second chance" program, which has already been considered here, a group called Defy Ventures goes into prisons and encourages convicts that they can reinvent themselves; turning a former life of self-employment as a drug dealer or street hustler into a positive employment opportunity to become an actual entrepreneur (Hoke, 2017). Their success stories are incredible, and their track record is impressive. Founded by Catherine Hoke in 2010, Defy Ventures operates in seven states (Grow Ensemble, 2021). According to a website that highlights "B" corporations (Grow Ensemble, 2021), they work with what they call "entrepreneurs in training," some of whom are currently in prison and others in post-prison release programs. They have seen a significant reduction in the recidivism rate among their clients compared to the national average and claim the employment rate for their program graduates is 82% (Grow Ensemble, 2021). So while this is not precisely the same situation as the failed entrepreneurs we discovered in the Texas research, here are failed entrepreneurs in their own right, according to Hoke (Hoke, 2017). Defy Ventures works to convince these formerly successful street hustlers that there are transferable skills from their old ways—in a new life of honest employment (Hoke, 2017). Moreover, the data support these claims (Grow Ensemble, 2021).

However, who is working with that 71% of entrepreneurs who fail and never try again? This could be a unique role for the church, but some churches would need to change their view of entrepreneurs (Stolze, 2021). If the church changed its view of business people as simply a means to their end, from being a tool to aid in achieving their own ministry goals, perhaps the church could see these broken people as needing encouragement and perhaps linking them with successful entrepreneurs to mentor and help them find success the second time around. Hannah Stolze says the same in her research, based on her experience (Stolze, 2021). Stolze writes that growing up in church; it was her experience that business was viewed as a means to provide money for their kingdom work, but not a ministry in itself—as a viable kingdom model of work (Stolze, 2021).

How ironic that the formerly mentioned Defy Ventures and missions groups worldwide cultivate entrepreneurship to help people find stable income and rise from poverty. Meanwhile, those who have tried and failed at starting a business do not often receive encouragement, backup, or recognition for the effort. Perhaps this is due to similar perceptions in the US as in Europe: bankruptcy and poor cash management create strong public opinion linking these actions to fraud (Report of the Expert Group, 2010). We already discussed how economic losses have a longer-lasting and more significant effect on individual attitudes. Individuals who had experienced loss from a business failure became more intolerant of those involved in business failures (Burchell and Hughes, 2006).

Data from several studies suggested that second-time entrepreneurs are much more successful. This was evidenced in the Texas small business study (Lafontaine and Shaw, 2014), which correlated with more positive attitudes toward those who had failed trying a second time (Burchell and Hughes, 2006). Even if these failed entrepreneurs do not return to a business venture, the church has the standing and opportunity to coach and counsel people through their failure to a successful career in another field. Business failure should not carry a life-long specter of personal contempt. Wissman (2017), a previously failed but later successful entrepreneur, philanthropist, and concert pianist, wrote that it is challenging for those failing in business to disassociate the situation from themselves as a person. Often entrepreneurs blame company failures on themselves, which is natural. Nevertheless, allowing oneself to become personally attached to the failure will make the processing of this failure much more difficult (Wissman, 2017).

A Failed Trailblazer Seeking Another Opportunity

The classic entrepreneur stereotype will be a person with persistence who has a vision of what opportunities exist in the marketplace. According to the "Entrepreneur Next Door" (see link below) assessment, there are two broad entrepreneurial personality types: the generalist and the specialist. The designer of the assessment, Bill Wagner, breaks that down further with four general types, using descriptors such as "Trailblazer," "Go-getter," "Manager," and "Motivator." Some successful entrepreneurs, such as Debbra Sweet (debbrasweet.com), describe themselves as the trailblazing entrepreneur. (theentrepreneurnextdoor.com/personalitytype1.html)

Author Kelli Richards identified the characteristics of these Trailblazer entrepreneurs as those who create new markets and forge their paths. In order to accomplish this, these trailblazers need to be ingenious and visionary; they also need to be resilient and collaborative (Richards 2015). It is interesting to consider these characteristics of the following story about Trailblazers.

Here we interject the story of a team of trailblazers, a type of entrepreneur who envisions a product or service not currently available as serving the needs of a target market, desperate for change. As Steve Jobs once famously said, "people do not know what they want until you show it to them." In this case, this trailblazing team launched the first Gospel missions' journey with something that their target market needed but had rejected: the long-awaited Savior of the World, Jesus Christ. This target audience was the people of Israel—God's chosen people—but they rejected this trailblazing message (Matthew 15:24). Thus, these trailblazers cultivated a new target market and found great success (John 1:11-12). However, along the way on this first missionary journey, our hero failed miserably, at least according to the COO leading the team—the great Apostle Paul. When the opportunity presented itself to join up on a new venture, the leadership team caustically split over having our associate join them again—leading to a fissure and a spin-off venture. Could our hero find value again for the contribution he could make to this venture? Our hero's name is John, also known as Mark, author of the gospel that bears his name.

A Trailblazers Journey–Catching the Vision; Failure and Restoration

Mark is a gospel writer. We understand that he gained a lot of his insight from Peter since he would not be part of the group (Nelson, 2019). In Acts chapter 12, it tells us that a critical prayer meeting was taking place at his mother's home, to which the imprisoned and then suddenly freed Apostle Peter went after this surprise release (Acts 12:12 English Standard Version). Mark was raised by a godly woman who believed in prayer and made her home available to the church (Macfarlan, 2013). In that same chapter, Mark was invited to travel with Paul and Barnabas (Acts 12:25) and then eventually traveled with them on their first missionary journey. At some point, Acts chapter 13 tells us that Mark determined to leave the journey and head home (Acts 13:13); and no rationale is given. However, hurt feelings lead to an intense conflict about Mark's future usefulness upon their return.

In Acts chapter 15, there is an opportunity for the work of Paul and Barnabas, among the Gentiles, to be reviewed and recognized. After the council in Jerusalem, Paul and Barnabas received the blessing of the Apostles, and the leaders in Jerusalem, to continue the work they were doing. Once they had shared this great news with their church in Antioch, they decided to return and visit the cities where they had previously preached the gospel (Acts 15:36-40).

Commentator Laymon (2021) suggests that the language from Barnabas was persistent. Barnabas very strongly made it known that he wanted to bring Mark along, which led to a sharp disagreement (Acts 15:39). The intensity is surprising, but perhaps we do not understand the two people concerned. Paul appears to be a process-based person, wanting things to be done differently, and Barnabas seems to be more outcomes-based. We also understand that his name means son of encouragement.

The approaches we may ascertain from this limited evidence advocated by Paul and Barnabas are not new or unique to managing people in a business environment. They represent two sides of the performance management debate that continue to ferment tension among managers seeking to improve their approach to managing people.

Some of the most well-known leadership books spelled out these contrasting approaches, providing two separate paths to help entrepreneurs scale their businesses.

For example, in Michael Gerber's book, The E-Myth Revisited, Gerber described the way to small business success as creating a business model and following it precisely. Gerber believed that a business development process would produce quality results every time and transform a small business into an effective organization (Gerber, 2001). Ordinary people, given specific training, and the confidence, to repeat excellent processes, would be able to perform extraordinarily following this model. Conversely, Marcus Buckingham and Curt Coffman, in the book First Break All the Rules, described the best managers as people who focus on outcomes (Buckingham and Coffman, 1999). Managers needed to select the right people for the job, define the outcomes for their employees, and then create a climate in which employees could achieve their objectives. Buckingham and Coffman suggested that management was not about direct control but remote control (Buckingham and Coffman, 1999).

While commentator Laymon (2021) shares research that Mark may have left to warn the home church about the work being done with the Gentiles, we only know what is written for us. Right or wrong, Paul did not trust John Mark to come along on this second journey; and he would not have been effective under Paul's leadership. Barnabas, on the other hand, desires to bring John Mark. There is evidence that Mark and Barnabas were cousins (see Colossians 4:10). Was it a family connection that caused this? It could be that Barnabas saw something in Mark that Paul would not see until later.

We may not read the scripture carefully enough to know how significant this difference between these two leaders was, and the language suggests a heated outburst and significant disagreement (Laymon, 2021). Nevertheless, several positive results came from this work.

The first was two teams of missionaries going out and encouraging new believers and reaching additional people for Christ. The second was through some process of which we are hardly aware; there is evidence that Paul saw value in John Mark's contribution. In Colossians 4:10, Paul encourages the Colossians church to welcome Mark. Later on, in Paul's second letter to Timothy, he asked Mark to be part of his ministry.

We know that John Mark accompanied Peter (1 Peter 5:13), and Nelson quotes early church fathers who wrote that Mark was the interpreter of Peter (Nelson, 2019). Perhaps Mark's gift was the gift of communicating through writing. Paul recommends that Mark come and should bring the parchments (2 Timothy 4:11). So perhaps, as with Peter, Mark was a writer who helped write these Pauline letters or to document the journeys. Whatever his actual contribution was, here we see that Mark was restored and given a second chance, seen in the light of the value of his contribution.

When the Apostle Paul urged his companion Timothy to bring Mark along (2 Timothy 4:11), he told Timothy, "Only Luke is with me. Get Mark and bring him with you. He is useful to me in my work."

(2 Timothy 4:11 God's Word Translation). The word the Apostle used for useful in the Greek, 'euchrestos,' is a compound word built on two different words. The first part, 'eu,' means good or well done. It is used as an exclamation in sentences or phrases. In the second part, the word 'chrestos' means useful, pleasant, or well fitted.

The HELPS Word Study (BibleHub.com) suggested that chrestos describes what God defines as 'kind' from a spiritual perspective and is eternally useful (BibleHub.com). Language expert Vincent writes that we have no adjectives in English that convey this blending of being good and kind simultaneously (BibleHub.com). So to suggest that the Apostle just saw John Mark as serviceable, under the basic definition, would be incorrect. John Mark was very profitable. He was this unique combination of kind and good. We must remember that this is the same John Mark whose usefulness Paul questioned so adamantly that he and Barnabas strongly disagreed and separated over the question of having Mark come on the second missionary journey. We, as observers, are unaware of what occurred to change the mind of the strong-willed Apostle. Perhaps the mentorship and encouragement of cousin Barnabas? Indeed, something was changed in the Apostle's perception, where Paul, now in prison, perceived John Mark as very profitable in his ministry service.

This presents the question: Who is rescuing those failed or failing entrepreneurs from despair and thoughts of failure, particularly those who have tried once but then never tried again?

These valiant servants need a Barnabas to come alongside and encourage them that they may be seen as useful for the service of God, whether working with another start-up, trying themselves again, or even sharing their insights from the work they did.

Conclusion

Eric Ries wrote about his failure in his first business and how it motivated him to look at things differently when he started again (Ries, 2011). Ries was one of the fortunate ones who continued to move forward and try again after devastating failure. He developed a unique approach in his second start-up, which led Ries to reimagine the entire approach to traditional business start-ups. Ries is the author of *The Lean Startup* (Ries, 2011), which recommends a different approach to entrepreneurship and starting a business. This approach to teaching and learning about entrepreneurship is radical and is becoming the focus of many articles and summaries as a novel approach to entrepreneurship.

The interesting point in the current discussion is that Ries acted out of a position of pain and frustration over the failure of his first business (Ries, 2011). He was willing to try again and work through the failure and develop a process by which others might avoid failure should they consider starting a business again. So his model is a viable approach in that he introduces the topic of failure right up front and some of the stereotypes painted about entrepreneurship in the media. In the book's introduction, Ries talks about how entrepreneurship is promoted as a path where talented individuals with great determination, a good product, and hard work can achieve great success. However, he describes from his own experience how this is a myth and how he has seen many entrepreneurs who have struggled and failed miserably (Ries, 2011).

So Ries' work is meant to provide an alternative for those who may have completely failed at starting a business or those who may be inexperienced themselves. However, eager dreamers reconsider the traditional entrepreneurial journey and follow a new methodology—one where "failing fast" is encouraged, but continuous learning leads to ultimate success (Blank, 2013). We must also be cognizant that Ries' mentor was Steve Blank, who has written several books on a non-traditional approach to business start-ups (Blank, 2013; Blank, 2012).

The lessons throughout this research describe how vital support and mentoring are for those "failed" individuals to gain perspective and find in the rubble of their failures the grace and strength to start anew. This is what Steve Blank did for Eric Ries; and what Barnabas did for John Mark. According to Macfarlan (2013), John Mark's failure also lives as a metaphor for all those crying out to find relief—not only from abuse, failure, and life-controlling problems—but from the shame and labels of worthlessness they still carry as "formers…" (Macfarlan, 2013). This would apply to failed business ventures as well.

Eric Ries found a way back from failure through his mentor Steve Blank, who believed in entrepreneurship and believed in him. His recovery from failure has led to a new approach to starting businesses, positively impacting hundreds of businesses. Similarly, the gospel writer Mark found a way back from the shame of abandoning his fellow missionaries through his mentor Barnabas, who believed in redemption and believed in him. John Mark's recovery from this failure has positively impacted countless millions through his writings. There truly is beauty in a restored and reclaimed life.

Epilogue—Redemption Song

The dedication of this book comes from a verse found in the famous hymn by William Cowper, "There is a Fountain Filled with Blood."

> E'er since, by faith, I saw the stream Thy flowing wounds supply,
>
> Redeeming love has been my theme, and shall be till I die.
>
> And shall be till I die, and shall be till I die;
>
> Redeeming love has been my theme, and shall be till I die.
>
> **—(Cowper, 1772).**

The author of this classic hymn, William Cowper, was a recognized poet laureate who struggled with severe bouts of depression. Cowper attempted suicide several times, driving him deeper into despair (Johnson, 2013). Amid this debilitating condition, Cowper befriended the famous slave-trader-turned-pastor, John Newton. Newton, a hymn writer himself (remember Amazing Grace?), perceived that he could help bring his friend out of this darkness by collaborating on hymn-writing (Johnson, 2013). The friendship of Newton with Cowper's articulation of God's great mercy towards him helped move Cowper from despair to mental clarity and a more productive writing career than he could have imagined. Newton was God's redemptive agent in the life of William Cowper, and we have all reaped a great blessing because of this!

The focus of this book was to consider different expressions of redemptive activity with an eye toward the work that is being done to restore broken people to whole and meaningful lives. In some cases, the groups doing such work are faith-based, and for a good reason. Much of the message and the practice of redemption is rooted in the life of Jesus Christ and in His atoning sacrifice for us, Who took our place to bear the brunt of God's wrath deserved for wayward sinners such as we were (Romans 3:24-25). When individuals have experienced the transforming power of God in their lives, most often, they desire to, vicariously, become the hands and feet of Christ to serve those seeking help and hope to change (see Isaiah 52:7 "How beautiful are the feet of them that bring the good news!").

My response to the message of redemption was to write about it. I first began blogging about the subject of redemption after collecting many stories, research articles, and leadership surveys on the topic—this has led to my second book on redemption. Writing these stories was, to me, as it was to William Cowper in 1772—an uplifting and transformative experience.

It is in my heart that this book will become a blessing to those searching for hope and those who offer hope and restoration to others. I know what God has done in rescuing me, and I hope that by writing these stories, I can inspire child-like wonder in each reader for the amazing work of the Holy Spirit, who brings redemption to fruition in our lives. I encourage you to continue sharing these stories with others and your winsome insights learned along this path of redemption.

—Joseph Bucci, March 2022

REFERENCES

Consolidated Chapter Endnotes

Introduction | Things Are Not Always What They Seem

Ackers, D.; & Preston, D. (1997). Born Again? The ethics and efficacy of the conversion experience in contemporary management development. *Journal of Management Studies, 34*(5), pg. 677–701. doi: 10.1111/1467-6486.00068.

Bailey, M. (2017). Actor Tim Allen reveals heartbreaking story that led him to Jesus. BeliefNet [Web Blog]. Retrieved from https://www.beliefnet.com/columnists/idolchatter/2017/04/actor-tim-allen-reveals-heartbreaking-story-led-jesus.html.

Bueno, A. (2020, March 19). Tim Allen shares how he got sober from drugs and alcohol for 22 years. Entertainment Tonight {Web Blog]. Retrieved from https://www.etonline.com/tim-allen-shares-how-he-got-sober-from-drugs-and-alcohol-for-22-years-143371.

FaithIt.com (2016, March 31). Tim Allen shares how cocaine busts, drunk driving & jail time led him to God after decades of doubt. FaithIt.com [Web Blog]. Retrieved from https://faithit.com/tim-allen-reveals-how-cocaine-busts-drunk-driving-jail-time-led-him-to-god-entertainment/.

Giorgio, E. (2008). *The body of Christ unleashed.* Maitland, FL: Xulon Press.

GoodReads (2017, June 17). Phaedrus: GoodRead Quotes. Goodreads. Retrieved from https://www.goodreads.com/author/show/889.Phaedrus.

Hiskey, D. (2010, September 17). Tim Allen was a convicted drug dealer before becoming famous. Today I Found Out [Web Blog]. Retrieved from https://www.todayifoundout.com/index.php/2010/09/tim-allen-was-a-convicted-drug-dealer-before-becoming-famous/.

Lapin, T. (2020, September 3). Larry Kudlow opens up about battle with addiction. NY Post. Retrieved from https://nypost.com/2020/09/03/white-house-adviser-larry-kudlow-talks-battle-with-addiction/.

LifeWay Church Resources. (1984). *Essentials for Excellence: The ABC's of Salvation* **[Brochure]. Retrieved September 3, 2016, from** http://www.lifeway.com/lwc/files/lwcF_crd_ss_EforESpec_ABCs-of-Salvation_pdf.pdf

Lindell, M. (2019). *What Are the Odds? From Crack Addict to CEO.* Lindell Publishing LLC.

Longeretta, E. (2021, March 3). Tim Allen reflects on his 2-year prison stint for drug trafficking, alcohol addiction. US Magazine. Retrieved from https://www.usmagazine.com/celebrity-news/news/tim-allen-reflects-on-2-year-prison-stint-alcohol-addiction/.

Martin, D. (1993). *Tongues of fire: The explosion of Protestantism in Latin America.* Oxford: Blackwell.

NAE (n.d.). What is an Evangelical? *National Association of Evangelicals.* Retrieved May 13, 2016, from http://nae.net/what-is-an-evangelical/.

Chapter 1 | Redemption in the Land of Oz

Baum, L.F. (1900). The Wonderful Wizard of Oz. Chicago: G.M. Hill Co.

Breiding, M. J., Chen, J., & Black, M. C. (2014). Intimate partner violence in the United States--2010. Atlanta GA: National Center for Injury Prevention and Control, Centers for Disease Control and Prevention (CDC).

Briggs, J.R. (2014). *Fail: Finding hope and grace in the midst of ministry failure*. Downers Grove, IL.: InterVarsity Press.

Bucci, J. J. (2011). Evidence of redemptive manager behaviors in successfully reinstating terminated workers (Unpublished doctoral dissertation). Anderson University.

Bucci, J.J. (2016). *Redemptive Leadership: Offering Second Chances as a Value-Added Management Practice*. New York: Palgrave Macmillan.

Campbell, C. (2014, August 12). 'The Wizard of Oz' at 75: Why we can't take the lack-and-white-to-color gimmick for granted. *Film School Rejects*. Retrieved December 22, 2017, from https://filmschoolrejects.com/the-wizard-of-oz-at-75-why-we-can-t-take-the-black-and-white-to-color-gimmick-for-granted-8485ecb537bc/

Cook, D. A., & Sklar, R. (2017, November 10). History of the motion picture. *Encyclopedia Britannica*. Retrieved March 03, 2018, from https://www.britannica.com/art/history-of-the-motion-picture/The-pre-World-War-II-sound-era#ref508104.

DeKerseredy, W.S., & Schwartz, M.D. (2009). Dangerous exits: Escaping abusive relationships in rural America. New Brunswick, NJ: Rutgers University Press.

Lee, W.J.; Phelps, J.R.; and Beto, D.R. (2009). Turnover intention among probation officers and direct care staff: A statewide study. *Federal Probation 73*(3):28-40.

Powers, H. (2019). *Redemptive leadership: Unleashing your greatest influence*. Littleton, CO.: Illumify Media Global.

Powers, R. (2016, October 13). An Overview of What It's Like Inside a Military Prison. *The Balance.com* Financial Empowerment Blog. Retrieved July 08, 2017, from https://www.thebalance.com/inside-a-military-prison-3354204,

Rainer, T. (2014, January 29). *Seven warning signs of affairs for pastors and other church staff.* Retrieved December 22, 2017, from http://thomrainer.com/2014/01/seven-warning-signs-of-affairs-for-pastors-and-other-church-staff/

Reed, E. (2006, Winter). Restoring fallen pastors. *Christianity Today: CT Pastors Blog.* Retrieved December 23, 2017, from http://www.christianitytoday.com/pastors/2006/winter/22.21.html. Originally published in *Leadership Journal*, Winter 2006.

Ritenbaugh, R.T. (1997, August 16). The parables of Matthew 13–Part 1: The mustard seed. Retrieved December 23, 2017 from https://www.bibletools.org/index.cfm/fuseaction/Topical.show/RTD/cgg/ID/3597/Bird-as-Symbol-.htm.

Stockl, H., March, L., Pallitto, C., & Garcia-Moreno, C. (2014). Intimate partner violence among adolescents and young women: prevalence and associated factors in nine countries: a cross-sectional study. BMC public health, 14(1), 751.

The White House, Office of the Press Secretary. (2019, June 13). President Donald J. Trump is helping Americans gain a second chance to build a brighter future. [Press release]. Retrieved from https://www.whitehouse.gov/briefings-statements/president-donald-j-trump-helping-americans-gain-second-chance-build-brighter-future/

What? Color in the movies again? (1934). *Fortune Magazine*, 10(4), 92. Retrieved March 3, 2018 from http://www.astortheater.org/film17.html.

Zipes, J. (2007). *When dreams came true: Classical fairy tales and their tradition.* New York: Routledge - Taylor and Francis Group.

Chapter 2 | The Slough of Despond

Blitz, M. (2014, January 31). Where did the expression "Let the cat out of the bag" come from? Today I Found Out [Web Blog]. Retrieved from http://www.todayifoundout.com/index.php/2014/01/expression-let-cat-bag-come/.

Bunyan, J. and Offor, G. (1853). *The Works of John Bunyan: Allegorical, figurative, and symbolical* (Vol. 3). Blackie and son.

https://books.google.com/books?hl=en&lr=&id=TAY2AQAAMAAJ&oi=fnd&pg=PR20&dq=Slough+of+Despond&ots=J_3J1sJAWD&sig=m243uG0HFlSuqov_6oWIGIsjfsM#v=onepage&q=Slough%20of%20Despond&f=false

Drury, K. (1998). What to do when a leader has an affair. Found in the book, *So, What Do You Think?* Indianapolis, IN: Wesleyan Publishing House. Essay retrieved from http://www.drurywriting.com/keith/affair.htm.

Fisher, M. (1998, September 28). Clinton's Pastor with a Past. *Washington Post.* Retrieved from https://www.washingtonpost.com/wp-srv/style/daily/clinpastor0928.htm.

Gaultiere, B. (2019). Statistics on Pastor's emotional health family and morality. *SoulShepherding: Pastor Stress Statistics* [Web Blog]. Retrieved from https://www.soulshepherding.org/Pastors-under-stress/.

Holwick, D. (1997, September 14). The mightiest can fall, and the most fallen can rise again. The Holy Bible Database Project. Retrieved from http://www.findthepower.net/CP/IL/PostNewABC2_I.php?IL=ON&SeeAlso=GORDON MACDONALD

Houdmann, S. M. (2017, January 04). Can restoration occur after a Pastor has been caught in a scandal? Got Questions Ministries website: gotquestions.org. Retrieved July 28, 2017, from https://www.gotquestions.org/Pastoral-restoration.html.

Hughes, R., & Armstrong, J. (1995, April 3). Why adulterous Pastors should not be restored. *Christianity Today, 39*(4), 33. Retrieved from Academic Search Complete database.

Krejcir R.J. (2007). Statistics on Pastors. *Francis A. Schaeffer Institute of Church Leadership Development.* White Paper retrieved from http://pirministries.org/wp-content/uploads/2016/01/FASICLD-Statistics-on-Pastors.pdf.

LifeWay Research (2019). Pastor's View on Moral Failure: Survey of American Protestant Pastors. LifeWay Research. Retrieved from http://lifewayresearch.com/wp-content/uploads/2020/08/Pastors-Moral-Failure.pdf.

MacArthur, J. (2008). The Master's plan for the church. Chicago,IL: Moody Press. p.288.

MacDonald, G. (1990). *Rebuilding Your Broken World.* Nashville, TN: Thomas Nelson.

Miesel, R. (2005, March). Gordon MacDonald: General Teachings and Activities. Biblical Discernment Ministries. Retrieved from http://www.rapidnet.com/~jbeard/bdm/exposes/macdonald/general.htm

Pastor X (personal communication, September 25, 2020).

Reed, E. (2006). Restoring Fallen Pastors. *Christianity Today*. Retrieved 06-02-2017 from http://www.christianitytoday.com/Pastors/2006/winter/22.21.html

Scared Straight (1978). *Extreme Universal Crisis Intervention.* Retrieved from https://universalcrisisintervention.com/interventions/scared-straight/.

Sheehy, K. (2011, March 9). Hot for Teacher. NY Post. Retrieved from https://nypost.com/2011/03/09/hot-for-teacher/.

Thomas, J.H. (1964). *Pilgrim's Progress in Today's English*, Chicago, IL. Moody Publishing, p.18. http://books.google.com/books?id=tVzTc3WQF4wC

Chapter 3 | Three Strikes You're In

Allen, D. (2003, March 6). Corrections unit aims to put Marines back on course. Stars and Stripes Magazine. Retrieved July 9, 2017 from https://www.stripes.com/news/corrections-unit-aims-top-put-marines-back-on-course-1.2614#.WWKG34TyvIU.

Powers, R. (2016, October 13). An Overview of What It's Like Inside a Military Prison. The Balance.com Financial Empowerment Blog. Retrieved July 08, 2017, from https://www.thebalance.com/inside-a-military-prison-3354204,

Rudolph, A.S.; Glaser, D.N.; and Kerce, E.W. (1994). Navy Correctional Custody Units: Perceptions of Navy Leaders and Analysis of Effectiveness. San Diego: Navy Personnel Research and Development Center. Retrieved July 8, 2017 from www.dtic.mil/get-tr-doc/pdf?AD=ADA278727.

Chapter 4 | God's Magnificent Work Complete

Breiding, M. J., Chen, J., & Black, M. C. (2014). Intimate partner violence in the United States--2010. Atlanta GA: National Center for Injury Prevention and Control, Centers for Disease Control and Prevention (CDC).

Buel, S.M. (2021). 50 Obstacles to Leaving. *National Domestic Violence Hotline.* Retrieved from https://www.thehotline.org/resources/get-help-50-obstacles-to-leaving/.

Cooke, T. (2015). Understanding women's decision making: The intolerable choice of living in a violent house or escaping to the uncertainty of homelessness and poverty. Parity, 28(4), 21.

DeKerseredy, W.S., & Schwartz, M.D. (2009). *Dangerous exits: Escaping abusive relationships in rural America.* New Brunswick, NJ: Rutgers University Press.

LeTrent, S. (2013, January 10). When a friend won't walk away from abuse. *Cable News Network (CNN).* Retrieved from https://www.cnn.com/2013/01/10/living/friend-domestic-abuse.

Murphy, M. (2021). What are the steps to take in escaping an abusive spouse? Mysti Murphy Law Firm. Retrieved from https://www.murphyfamilyattorney.com/articles/what-are-the-steps-to-take-in-escaping-an-abusive-spouse/.

Sanchez, C. (2016, February 3). 8 Steps that Explain "Why She Doesn't Leave." Huffington Post: The Blog. Retrieved July 5, 2017 from http://www.huffingtonpost.com/crystal-sanchez/8-steps-that-explain-why-_b_9143360.html.

Stockl, H., March, L., Pallitto, C., & Garcia-Moreno, C. (2014). Intimate partner violence among adolescents and young women: prevalence and associated factors in nine countries: a cross-sectional study. BMC public health, 14(1), 751.

Chapter 5 | I Was in Prison

10 Famous Ex-Cons Who Turned It Around. (2012, October 12). Retrieved March 24, 2018, from http://www.criminaljusticeusa.com/blog/2011/10-famous-ex-cons-who-turned-it-around/

AALS, (1908). Select Essays in Anglo-American Legal History. Volume 2. Various authors, compiled and edited by a committee of the *Association of American Law Schools*. Boston: Little, Brown, and Company. Retrieved from https://oll.libertyfund.org/titles/schools-select-essays-in-anglo-american-legal-history-vol-2.

Aitken, J. (2012, April 21). Remembering Charles Colson, a man transformed. Christianity Today. Retrieved from https://www.christianitytoday.com/ct/2012/aprilweb-only/charles-colson-aitken.html.

Bilyeu, M. (2014). How celebrity chef Jeff Henderson turned his life around. *Toledo Blade Online*. Retrieved March 24, 2018 from http://www.toledoblade.com/Food/2014/09/30/Flip-it-over-How-Jeff-Henderson-turned-his-life-around.html.

Blumstein, A.; & Nakamura, K. (2009, May). Redemption in the presence of widespread criminal background checks. *Criminology, 47*(2), 327-59.

Burke, M.E. (2005). *2004 Reference and Background Checking Survey Report: A Study by the Society for Human Resource Management*. Alexandria, Va.: Society for Human Resource Management, 2006.

Capretto, L. (2016, October 17). He went from drug-dealing felon to nationally renowned chef. Here's what he's up to today. *Huffington Post*. Retrieved March 24, 2018 from https://www.huffingtonpost.com/entry/ex-convict-successful-chefs_us_58012bc5e4b0e8c198a80664.

Center for Prison Reform (2019). *History*. Retrieved from https://centerforprisonreform.org/history/

Celi, T.S.; Miller, A.P.; & Cazares, R.A. (2020, May). Virginia Department of Corrections Impact of Dialogue Implementation. Virginia Department of Corrections Research–Strategic Planning Unit. Retrieved July 23, 2020 from https://vadoc.virginia.gov/media/1565/vadoc-research-impact-of-dialogue-report-2020.pdf.

Clark, A. (2020, June 25). Justice Reform. How a group of lifers cracked the code of prison reform. Politico magazine. Retrieved from politico.com/news/magazine/2020/06/25/criminal-justice-prison-conditions-national-lifers-association-334021

Colson, C.W. (1976). *Born Again*. Ada, MI.: Chosen Books, an Imprint of Baker Publishing Group.

Couloute, L. (2018, October). Getting back on course: Educational exclusion and attainment among formerly incarcerated people. *Prison Policy Initiative* [Web Blog]. Retrieved from https://www.prisonpolicy.org/reports/education.html

Cove, P.; & Bowes, L. (2015). Immediate Access to Employment Reduces Recidivism. *Real Clear Politics*. Retrieved March 21, 2018 from http://www.realclearpolitics.com/articles/2015/06/11/immediate_access_to_employment_reduces_recidivism_126939.html.

Families Against Mandatory Minimums–FAMM (n.d.). FAMM primer on mandatory sentences. *Prison Policy Initiative* [Web Blog]. Retrieved from https://www.prisonpolicy.org/scans/famm/Primer.pdf.

Federal Bureau of Prisons–BOP (2016). Bureau rehabilitation and values enhancement program. Federal Bureau of Prisons [Web Blog]. Retrieved from https://www.bop.gov/resources/news/20160913_brave.jsp

Felon University (2018). *Felon University: About*. Retrieved March 24, 2018 from https://www.felonuniversity.com/about.

Giszczak, M. (n.d.). Introduction to the New Testament: Philemon. *Catholic News Agency*. Retrieved March 24, 2018 from https://www.catholicnewsagency.com/resources/bible/introduction-to-the-new-testament/philemon

Haney - de-emphasizing the goal of rehabilitation while emphasizing punishment and incapacitation, the availability of quality treatment programs has declined

Haney, C. (2001, December 1). *The Psychological Impact of Incarceration: Implications for Post-Prison Adjustment*. Urban Institute Press. Retrieved from http://webarchive.urban.org/publications/410624.htm

Hawthorne, N. (1850). *The Scarlet Letter*. Boston: Ticknor, Reed & Fields

Holodny, E. (2017, July 30). 'It still haunts me': What it's like to get a job after prison in America. *Business Insider*. Retrieved March 21, 2018 from http://www.businessinsider.com/finding-job-after-prison-2017-7

Huddleston, S. (2013). *Five Years to Life.* Watertown, MA: Perkins Publishing.

Inside Journal: Special Re-Entry Edition. Retrieved from https://www.prisonfellowship.org/resources/support-friends-family-of-prisoners/supporting-successful-prisoner-reentry/get-out-stay-out-reentry-guide/. More from Prison Fellowship.

International Network of Prison Ministries–INPM (n.d.) [Website]. Retrieved from https://prisonministry.net/app/Index/event/showHome.html

Levin, M.A. (2020, September 4). Partnerships between police officers and former prisoners promote safety and hope. The Hill [Web Blog]. Retrieved from https://thehill.com/opinion/criminal-justice/515092-partnerships-between-police-officers-and-former-prisoners-promote.

Lozoff, B. (1985). *We're all doing time: A guide to getting free.* Durham, N.C.: Human Kindness Foundation.

Mattox, J. (1993, August 25). Texas' Death Penalty Dilemma. The Dallas Morning News. Retrieved from https://deathpenaltyinfo.org/the-future-of-the-death-penalty#fn98.

Muhlhausen, D. (2018, June 12). Research on returning offender programs and promising practices. *National Institute of Justice* [Website]. Retrieved from https://nij.ojp.gov/speech/research-returning-offender-programs-and-promising-practices.

Onesimus Ministries (n.d.). History. *Onesimus Ministries* [Website]. Retrieved from http://onesimus-ministries.org/welcome.html.

Ponder, J. (2020, June 15). The police can help rebuild lives. Wall Street Journal. Retrieved from https://hopeforprisoners.org/the-police-can-help-rebuild-lives/.

Ponder, J. (n.d.). *Everything's going to be alright: Jon Ponder's story.* Lavish Three [Web Blog]. Retrieved from https://lavishthree.com/blogs/stories/lavish-your-soul-jon-ponder-story-everythings-going-to-be-alright-part-ii.

Pray, R.T. (1987) How Did Our Prisons Get That Way? *American Heritage Magazine, 38*(5). Retrieved from https://www.americanheritage.com/how-did-our-prisons-get-way.

Prison Fellowship (2019). Seven Ways to Help Your Loved One Adjust to Life After Prison. Retrieved from https://www.prisonfellowship.org/resources/support-friends-family-of-prisoners/supporting-successful-prisoner-reentry/seven-ways-adjust-life-after-prison/

Prison Fellowship (2002). *Steps to Reconciliation: Restorative Justice Bible Study.* Washington, DC. Prison Fellowship International.

Prison Fellowship (n.d.). Phases of [Prisoner] Reentry [Web Page]. Retrieved from https://www.prisonfellowship.org/wp-content/uploads/2017/09/Phases-of-Reentry-2017.pdf.

Prison Fellowship (n.d.). What We Do [Web Page]. Retrieved from https://www.prisonfellowship.org/about/.

Prison Fellowship (n.d.). Statistics: Criminal Justice System [Web Page]. Retrieved from https://www.prisonfellowship.org/resources/newsroom/media-background-information/media-additional/statistics-criminal-justice-system/.

Reagan, R. (1983, June 20). Remarks at a California Republican Party fundraising dinner. Ronald Reagan Presidential Foundation and Institute. Retrieved from https://www.reaganfoundation.org/ronald-reagan/reagan-quotes-speeches/remarks-at-a-california-republican-party-fundraising-dinner-in-long-beach/.

Saldana, M. (2008, August 27). The two faces of Bo Lozoff: Fall from grace. IndyWeek [Web Blog]. Retrieved from https://indyweek.com/news/two-faces-bo-lozoff/

Saunders, D.J. (2018, May 3). Nevada bank robber, FBI agent who arrested him, pray at White House. Las Vegas Review-Journal–reviewjournal.com [Web News]. Retrieved from https://www.reviewjournal.com/life/religion/nevada-bank-robber-fbi-agent-who-arrested-him-pray-at-white-house/.

Testerman, J. (1985). Making it: A handbook for parolees. Good News Mission. Retrieved from https://books.google.com/books/about/Making_it.html?id=mf4XHQAACAAJ.

Virginia Beach Sherriff's Office (2020). Rehabilitation Program: Virginia Beach Sherriff's Office [Web Site]. Retrieved July 23, 2020 from https://www.vbso.net/programs.

Virginia Department of Corrections–DOC (2020, February 3). *Virginia's recidivism rate falls even lower, remains the lowest in the country* [Press Release]. Retrieved July 23, 2020 from https://vadoc.virginia.gov/news-press-releases/2020/virginia-s-recidivism-rate-falls-even-lower-remains-the-lowest-in-the-country/.

Visher, C.; Debus, S.; & Yahner, J. (2008). *Employment after Prison: A Longitudinal Study of Releasees in Three States.* Urban Institute Justice Policy Center. Retrieved March 21, 2018 from https://www.urban.org/sites/default/files/publication/32106/411778-Employment-after-Prison-A-Longitudinal-Study-of-Releasees-in-Three-States.PDF

Weiner, T. (2012, April 21). Charles W. Colson, Watergate felon who became evangelical leader, dies at 80. *The New York Times.* Retrieved from https://www.nytimes.com/2012/04/22/us/politics/charles-w-colson-watergate-felon-who-became-evangelical-leader-dies-at-80.html.

Wideman, J.E. (1995, October). The politics of prisons: Doing time, marking race. *The Nation 261*(14), 503.

Winfrey, O. (2007) Resilient Spirits: An interview with Executive Chef Jeff Henderson. *Oprah.com.* Retrieved March 24, 2018 from http://www.oprah.com/spirit/resilient-spirits/all#ixzz5AgJBln8J

Report on the effectiveness of virginia reentry programs https://rga.lis.virginia.gov/Published/2007/RD210/PDF

For all of their efforts, the 12-month rearrest rates for juvenile probation placements fluctuated between 34.0% and 38.0% since FY 2014. The 12-month rearrest rates for juvenile probation releases fluctuated between 32.0% and 34.5% since FY 2014 (http://www.djj.virginia.gov/pdf/about-djj/DRG/FY19_DRG.pdf).

Chapter 6 | Transformed From the Inside Out

Butterfield, L. H. (2017, April 26). Benjamin Rush. Retrieved July 12, 2017, from https://www.britannica.com/biography/Benjamin-Rush.

Castleman, S. (2011). Contempt Prior to Investigation. AddictScience.com. Retrieved March 09, 2016, from http://www.addictscience.com/contempt-prior-to-investigation/.

Florida Sherriffs Youth Ranches: Home Page. (2017). Retrieved July 17, 2017, from https://www.youthranches.org/.

Genetic Science Learning Center. (2013, August 30) Addiction Treatments Past and Present. University of Utah. Retrieved July 13, 2017, from http://learn.genetics.utah.edu/content/addiction/treatments/

Kersten, K. (2011, April 4). Adult and Teen Challenge Operates on Faith but then Pays for it. Center of the American Experiment. Retrieved July 14, 2017, from https://www.americanexperiment.org/article/teen-challenge-operates-on-faith-but-then-pays-for-it/.

North Dakota Adult and Teen Challenge (2009). Our Program: Life Care. North Dakota Adult and Teen Challenge. Retrieved July 18, 2017, from https://www.tc4hope.org/our_program/.

Patterson, E. (Reviewer) (2016, July 19). History of Drug Abuse. Recoverybrands.com, part of Sober Media Group. Retrieved July 12, 2017, from http://drugabuse.com/library/history-of-drug-abuse/.

Mid-Atlantic Adult and Teen Challenge. (2017). Rocky Russell. Mid-Atlantic Adult and Teen Challenge website. Retrieved July 21, 2017, from https://www.mateenchallenge.com/staff/rocky-russell/.

R. Russell, personal communication, July 11, 2017

Adult and Teen Challenge. (2017). Adult and Teen Challenge Student Handbook. [Pamphlet]. Newport News, VA: Mid-Atlantic Adult and Teen Challenge.

Adult and Teen Challenge of the Firelands (2017, January 28). Program Phases. Adult and Teen Challenge of the Firelands. Retrieved July 18, 2017, from https://tcfirelands.com/program-phases/.

Adult and Teen Challenge Programs: About. (2017). Retrieved July 14, 2017, from https://www.teenchallengeusa.com/about.

Wilson, B. (1953; 2012). Twelve steps and twelve traditions. New York, NY: Alcoholics Anonymous World Services, Inc.

Chapter 7 | Work as Redemptive Intervention

The Annie E. Casey Foundation. (2019, June 6). What is Foster Care? The Annie E. Casey Foundation. [Web Blog online] Retrieved December 15, 2019 from https://www.aecf.org/blog/what-is-foster-care/?gclid=Cj0KCQiArdLvBRCrARIsAGhB_sySxmCsFRWBvoKxlSMRRO3X7roNShqxEisQXzryDd_lGyNmKG_uueUaAqHeEALw_wcB.

Child Welfare Information Gateway (2017). Foster Care Statistics 2017. Washington, D.C. U.S. Department of Health and Human Services Administration for Children and Families. Retrieved from https://www.childwelfare.gov/pubPDFs/foster.pdf#page=1&view=Introduction.

Helman, C. (2014, July 30). The dream factory: How putting kids to work helps them stay in school. Forbes Magazine: Energy Blog. Retrieved November 27, 2015 from http://www.forbes.com/sites/christopherhelman/2014/07/30/the-dream-factory-how-giving-kids-a-job-helps-keep-them-in-school/.

Southwire (2015). Southwire Company: 12 for Life Program. Retrieved November 27, 2015 from http://www.southwire.com/ourcompany/sustainability/12-for-life.htm.

Tidwell, R; & Garrett, S.C. (1994, Mar/April). Youth at risk: In search for a definition. Journal of Counseling & Development 72(4), 444-446. DOI: 10.1002/j.1556-6676.1994.tb00971.x.

Chapter 8 | Redemption in Other Cultures

Ausubel, D.P. (1955, September). The relationship between shame and guilt in the socializing process. Psychological Review, 62(5), 378-390.

Benedict, R. (1947). *The Chrysanthemum and the sword: Patterns of Japanese culture.* London: Secker and Warburg.

Creighton, M.R. (1990, September). *Revisiting Shame and Guilt Cultures: A Forty-Year Pilgrimage.* Ethos 18(3), pp. 279-307

Crosby, F. (1875) To God Be the Glory.

Demetriou, D. (2020, January 17). Employees in the country whose brutal office culture has led to several deaths are beginning to rethink the tradition. BBC Worklife [Web Blog]. Retrieved from https://www.bbc.com/worklife/article/20200114-how-the-japanese-are-putting-an-end-to-death-from-overwork.

Francis, T.; & Hoefel, F. (2018, November 12). 'True Gen': Generation Z and its implication for companies. Retrieved from https://www.mckinsey.com/industries/consumer-packaged-goods/our-insights/true-gen-generation-z-and-its-implications-for-companies

Helps Ministries (2011). Discovery Bible, Hebrews 12:2 Word Study

Ikegami, E. (2003). Shame and the samurai: institutions, trustworthiness, and autonomy in the elite honor culture. *Social Research, 70*(4), 1351-1378. Retrieved from https://muse.jhu.edu/article/558616/pdf?casa_token=GuEP0gfrk0AAAAAA:r-UF3n1AROmDwy5qS1aKQ3ECcA4vSn_83GklPfcqoS6GX1lMONmW1ORJwS0a27GMthjGJWPU77Y.

Keller, T.J. (2013) *Encounters with Jesus: Answers to life's biggest questions.* New York, NY: Viking Books, an Imprint of Penguin Random House.

Kraus, N. (1990). *Jesus Christ our Lord: Christology from a Disciple's perspective* (Scottdale, Penn: Herald).

Lewis, M. (1992). *Shame: The exposed self.* Free Press.

Louie, S.S. (2020, July 13). How Asian shame and stigma contribute to suicide. National Alliance on Mental Illness [Web Blog]. Retrieved from https://www.nami.org/Blogs/NAMI-Blog/July-2020/How-Asian-Shame-and-Stigma-Contribute-to-Suicide

Macarthur, J. F. (2005). Redemption Through His Blood. On *The Believer's Life in Christ* [Cassette]. Panorama City, CA: Grace to You Ministries.

Macarthur, J. (2014, January 25). The disappearance of Hell. Ligonier.org [Web Blog]. Retrieved from https://www.ligonier.org/learn/articles/disappearance-hell

Martocci, L. (2015). Bullying: The social deconstruction of self. Philadelphia, PA: Temple University Press.

McClay, W. M. (2013). Still the redeemer nation. *The Wilson Quarterly, 37*(2), 31–40.

Muller, R. (2000). *Honor-Shame: Unlocking the Door*. Xlibris, 2000

Mueller, T.S. (2021, July 9) Blame, then shame? Psychological predictors in cancel culture behavior. *The Social Science Journal*, DOI: 10.1080/03623319.2021.1949552. Retrieved from https://www.tandfonline.com/doi/abs/10.1080/03623319.2021.1949552

Naylor, M. (2010, August 1). Fear, Shame and Guilt: Cross Cultural Impact for the 21st Century [Web Blog]. Retrieved October 13, 2018 from http://impact.nbseminary.com/89-fear-shame-and-guilt/.

Nida, E.S. (2000). Customs and Cultures: Anthropology for Christian Missions. Pasadena, CA.: William Carey Library

Parker, K.; & Igielnik, R. (2020, May 14). On the cusp of adulthood and facing an uncertain future: What we know about Gen Z so far. *Pew Research Center*. Retrieved from https://www.pewresearch.org/social-trends/2020/05/14/on-the-cusp-of-adulthood-and-facing-an-uncertain-future-what-we-know-about-gen-z-so-far-2/.

Rightmire, R. D. (1996). Redemption. In W. A. Elwell (Ed.), Baker's evangelical dictionary of biblical theology (p. 664). Grand Rapids, MI: Baker Academic.

Sacks, J. (2014, November 4). *The difference between Shame and Guilt cultures.* [Web Blog]. Retrieved September 22, 2018 from http://rabbisacks.org/difference-shame-guilt-cultures-thought-day/.

Smith, C. (2014, July 18). God Can Restore Your Lost Years. [Web Blog] The Gospel Coalition (TGC). Retrieved September 23, 2018, from http://www.thegospelcoalition.org/article/god-can-restor-your-lost-years/.

Spicer, P. (2001, July). Culture and the restoration of self among former American Indian drinkers. *Social Science & Medicine 53*(2); 227-40.

Thomson, L. (2016). One Native American man's journey from shame to healing. International Reporting [Web Blog]. Retrieved from http://intl-clarke.2016.journalism.cuny.edu/2016/10/28/one-native-american-mans-journey-from-shame-to-healing/.

Visher, C.; Debus, S.; & Yahner, J. (2008). Employment after Prison: A Longitudinal Study of Releasees in Three States. Urban Institute Justice Policy Center. Retrieved March 21, 2018 from https://www.urban.org/sites/default/files/publication/32106/411778-Employment-after-Prison-A-Longitudinal-Study-of-Releasees-in-Three-States.PDF

Wells, G.; Horwitz, J.; & Seetharaman, D. (2021, September 14). Facebook knows Instagram is toxic for teen girls, company documents show. *Wall Street Journal.* Retrieved from https://www.wsj.com/articles/facebook-knows-instagram-is-toxic-for-teen-girls-company-documents-show-11631620739?mod=article_inline.

West, E. (2015, September 5). Guilt vs shame cultures: the silent triumph of Christianity. [Web Blog]. Retrieved September 22, 2018 from https://blogs.spectator.co.uk/2015/09/guilt-vs-shame-cultures-the-silent-triumph-of-christianity/

Yoder, M. (2021, May 19). Why youth leave the church: 10 surprising reasons. *ChurchLeaders.com* [Web Blog]. Retrieved from https://churchleaders.com/children/childrens-ministry-articles/166129-marc-solas-10-surprising-reasons-our-kids-leave-church.html.

Chapter 9 | After the Thrill is Gone

BIAUSA (2020). *In the hospital after a brain injury.* [Web page] Vienna, VA.: Brain Injury Association of America. Retrieved January 8, 2020 from https://www.biausa.org/public-affairs/media/in-the-hospital-after-brain-injury?gclid=CjwKCAiAo7HwBRBKEiwAvC_Q8effnZzKP-VnEUpQBfS63p1TKFGdGqupwedvpwVGFpcaL8u_EA9nMxoCTgEQAvD_BwE

Borch, F. (2016, April 30). The Purple Heart: The story of America's oldest military decoration and some soldier recipients. [online] *National Museum US Army*. Retrieved December 26, 2019 from https://armyhistory.org/the-purple-heart-the-story-of-americas-oldest-military-decoration-and-some-soldier-recipients/

Brown, D. & Szoldra, P. (2018 April 25). Why Green Berets are the smartest, most lethal fighters in the world. [online] *Business Insider*. Retrieved December 21, 2019 from https://www.businessinsider.com/green-berets-army-special-forces-intelligent-well-trained-deadly-2013-3.

Crouse, K. (2019, August 19). Michael Phelps is losing World Records, but he's gained other treasures. [online] *NY Times*. Retrieved December 26, 2019 from https://www.nytimes.com/2019/08/19/sports/michael-phelps-records-family.html

Fogle, A. (2019, December 13). 25 Surprising Things About 'White Christmas' That Even Movie Buffs Don't Know. [online] *Good Housekeeping Magazine*. Retrieved December 26, 2019 from https://www.goodhousekeeping.com/holidays/christmas-ideas/g2997/white-christmas-movie-facts/

Henley, D. & Frey, G. (1975). After the thrill is gone [Recorded by the Eagles]. On *One of these nights* [Album]. Hollywood, CA: Electra/Asylum.

Martins, N. (2018, October). Exploring Traumatic Brain Injury in the NFL and military. *HVMN* [Web Blog] San Francisco: Health Via Modern Nutrition. Retrieved January 8, 2020 from https://hvmn.com/blog/research/exploring-traumatic-brain-injury-in-the-nfl-and-military#McKee2016

McKee, A.C.; Alosco, M.L.; & Huber, B.R. (2016, October). Repetitive head impacts and chronic traumatic encephalopathy. *Neurosurg Clin N Am. 27*(4), 529-35.

NIH: US Department of Health and Human Services-National Institutes of Health (2020). *Traumatic Brain Injury (TBI): Condition information.* [Web page] Eunice Kennedy Shriver National Institute of Child Health and Human Development. Retrieved January 8, 2020 from https://www.nichd.nih.gov/health/topics/tbi/conditioninfo/treatment

Robichaux, C.M.; & Stalnecker, J.M. (2017). *The truth about PSTd.* Making Life Better Publications. Retrieved January 8, 2020 from https://www.mightyoaksprograms.org/wp-content/uploads/2019/03/mighty-oaks-foundation-the-truth-about-ptsd.original.pdf

US Army Special Operations Command (USASOC) (2019). *7th SFG (A) History.* [online] Soc.mil. Retrieved December 21, 2019 from https://www.soc.mil/USASFC/Groups/7th/7thSFGHistory.html.

Wilson, B. (1953; 2012). *Twelve steps and twelve traditions.* New York, NY: Alcoholics Anonymous World Services, Inc.

Chapter 10 | No Such Thing as an Overnight Success

City News Service. (2020, October 9). Ex-NFL player Ryan Leaf avoids jail time, gets plea deal after being charged with domestic violence. *The Desert Sun* [Web Blog]. USA Today Network. Retrieved from https://www.desertsun.com/story/news/crime_courts/2020/10/09/former-nfl-player-ryan-leaf-court-domestic-violence-charges/5940433002/

Dalton, K. (2020, June 3). Ryan Leaf's troubled past returns in domestic battery arrest. *Sportscasting: Pure Sports* [Web Blog]. Endgame360 Inc. Retrieved from https://www.sportscasting.com/ryan-leafs-troubled-past-returns-in-domestic-battery-arrest/

Davis, L.M.; Steele, J.L.; Bozick, R.; Williams, M.V.; Turner, S.; Miles, J.N.; Saunders, J.; and Steinberg, P.S. (2014). *How effective is correctional education, and where do we go from here? The results of a comprehensive evaluation.* Santa Monica, CA: RAND Corporation. Retrieved from https://www.rand.org/pubs/research_reports/RR564.html

Ferry, J. (2019, October 3). Ryan Leaf shares story at Penn Foundation Autumn event. *Buckscountyherald.com* [Web Blog]. Bucks County Herald. Retrieved from http://buckscountyherald.com/ryan-leaf-shares-story-at-penn-foundation-autumn-event-p2792-175.htm

Gladwell, M. (2008). Outliers: The story of success. New York: Little, Brown and Company.

Griffith, E. (2017, July 1). On message, off target. Fortune Magazine, 176(1), p 44. Article retrieved electronically July 14, 2017, from http://fortune.com/2017/06/27/startup-advice-data-failure/

Hartley, S. (2016). Surprising facts about business success rates [Blog post]. West Tisbury, MA: Enlightened Marketing Blog. Retrieved December 10, 2016 from http://www.enlightenedmarketing.com/2012/07/surprising-facts-about-business-success-rates/

Horowitz, B. (2014). The hard thing about hard things. New York: Harper Business

Jorden, R. (2014). What are the real small business survival rates? [Blog post]. Retrieved December 10, 2016 from https://www.linkedin.com/pulse/20140915223641-170128193-what-are-the-real-small-business-survival-rates

Laboy, J. (1998, March 11). Here's a businessman who knows the value of a second chance. The Wall Street Journal. Retrieved from http://www.rhinotek.com/wsj-secondchance.aspx .

Leaf, R. (2020). Ryan D. Leaf [Website]. Retrieved from https://www.theryandleaf.com/

Marchetti, M. (1999). Selling saved their lives. Sales and Marketing Management, 151(2), 36–42. Retrieved from http://0-search.proquest.com.library.regent. edu/docview/211864990

Marchetti, M. (2005, June 27). Selling Saved Their Lives. Fortune, 151.

Meszaros, G. (2016, April 21). What percentage of businesses fail: The real number. SuccessHarbor blog. Retrieved April 6, 2017 from http://www.successharbor.com/percentage-businesses-fail-09092015/

Myers, C. (2017, August 27). Debunking the myth of the overnight success. Forbes.com: Entrepreneurs [Web Blog]. Retrieved from https://www.forbes.com/sites/chrismyers/2017/08/27/debunking-the-myth-of-the-overnight-success/?sh=afc328db640b

Neuman, F. (2017a). Dr. Neuman's Psychiatric Practice. www.Fredricneumanmd.com. Retrieved from http://www.fredricneumanmd.com/Psychiatry-Practice-for-Dr-Neuman.php

Neuman, F. (2017b). Why do some people do self-destructive things? *Psychology Today* [Web Blog]. New York: Sussex Publishers, LLC. Retrieved from https://www.psychologytoday.com/us/blog/fighting-fear/201701/why-do-some-people-do-self-destructive-things

NFL (2019). Former NFL quarterback Ryan Leaf shares life-changing decision to help prison inmates learn to read. (2019, June 28). *NFL.com* [Website]. National Football League. Retrieved from https://www.nfl.com/videos/former-nfl-quarterback-ryan-leaf-shares-life-changing-decision-to-help-prison-in

Patel, N. (2015). 90% of startups fail: Here's what you need to know about the 10%. [Blog post]. New York: Forbes Magazine, Entrepreneurs Blog. Retrieved December 10, 2016 from http://www.forbes.com/sites/neilpatel/2015/01/16/90-of-startups-will-fail-heres-what-you-need-to-know-about-the-10/#1ed40eaf55e1

Pennington, A. Y. (2002, August). Snapshot: Gerald W. Chamales. Entrepreneur, 30(8), 21.

Peter, J. (2017, April 25). Former QB Ryan Leaf has found his calling, and it's definitely not football. *USA Today: Sports* [Web Blog]. USA Today. Retrieved from https://www.usatoday.com/story/sports/nfl/2017/04/25/nfl-draft-bust-ryan-leaf-san-diego-chargers-peyton-manning/100849980/

Raley, D. (2020, May 24). Turning over an old Leaf: WSU QB great faces legal issues again. *Sports Illustrated : Washington Huskies News* [Web Blog]. Sports Illustrated. Retrieved from https://www.si.com/college/washington/football/ryan-leaf-finds-himself-in-trouble-again

Ritchie, P. (2018, May 18). A Real-Life Comeback: Former NFL QB Ryan Leaf to Share Story of Addiction, Recovery at Free Event on May 24th. NY State Senate. https://www.nysenate.gov/newsroom/articles/patty-ritchie/real-life-comeback-former-nfl-qb-ryan-leaf-share-story-addiction

Rexrode, J. (2019, May 14). Ryan Leaf can stand next to Peyton Manning now and be proud. *The Tennessean* [Web Blog]. USA Today Network. Retrieved from https://www.tennessean.com/story/sports/columnist/joe-rexrode/2019/05/13/rexrode-ryan-leaf-nfl-bust-and-convicted-felon-has-finally-earned-peyton-manning-comparison/1186183001/

Rodriguez, M.N., & Emsellem, M. (2011, March). *65 million "need not apply:" The case for reforming criminal background checks for employment.* New York, NY: National Employment Law Project.

Romero, L.E. (2016, August 8). Overnight success is a myth–here is why. Forbes.com: Leadership Strategy [Web Blog]. Retrieved from https://www.forbes.com/sites/luisromero/2016/08/08/overnight-success-is-bs-here-is-why/?sh=7294f0915e2c

Schrager, A. (2014, July 28). Failed entrepreneurs find more success the second time. Bloomberg Business Week: Bloomberg.com. Retrieved March 15, 2017 from https://www.bloomberg.com/news/articles/2014-07-28/study-failed-entrepreneurs-find-success-the-second-time-around

Sivers, D. (2018). Hell yeah or no. New York: Hit Media.

SOC Telemed. (2018, April 6). The Ryan Leaf story: From failure to future. *SOC Telemed* [Web Blog]. SOC Telemed. Retrieved from https://www.soctelemed.com/blog/from-failure-to-future-the-ryan-leaf-story-on-addiction-recovery/

Willis, Z. (2019, August 2). Former NFL bust Ryan Leaf goes from prison to the broadcast booth. *Sportscasting: Pure Sports* [Web Blog]. Endgame360 Inc. Retrieved from https://www.sportscasting.com/former-nfl-bust-ryan-leaf-goes-from-prison-to-the-broadcast-booth/

Chapter 11 | It is God Who Makes Things Grow

Bucci, J.J. (2016). *Redemptive leadership: Offering second chances as a value-added management practice.* New York: Palgrave Macmillan.

Cialdini, R.B. (2006). *Influence: The psychology of persuasion.* New York: William Morrow and Company.

Dilkes, C. (2018, May 18). Personal interview.

Korisko, G. (2013). *How the law of reciprocity can make or break your business.* Retrieved from http://rebootauthentic.com/law-of-reciprocity/.

Nickels, W., McHugh, J., & McHugh, S. (2016). *Understanding Business, 11th Edition.* Boston: McGraw-Hill Irwin.

Pearcey, N. (2004). *Total truth: Liberating Christianity from Its cultural captivity.* Wheaton, Ill.: Crossway Books.

Spears, S. (2013, August 14). *The importance of business reciprocity.* Retrieved from https://spearsmarketing.com/1399/business-reciprocity/.

Taylor, C. (2021, August 10). Personal interview.

Taylor, C. (2018, May 16). Personal interview.

Taylor, C. (2017, August 11). Personal interview.

Chapter 12 | The Elephant in the Room

Anderson, J.Q.; & Rainie, L. (2008). The future of the internet III. *Pew Internet & American Life Project*. Retrieved from https://www.elon.edu/u/imagining/surveys/iii-2008/

Borrelli, C. (2010, October 13). Horror, shock, redemption, repeat: Exploring a society stuck in scandal's loop. Chicago Tribune. Retrieved from http://articles.chicagotribune.com/2010-10-13/entertainment/ct-live-1013-laura-kipnis-20101013_1_scandal-laura-kipnis-eliot-spitzer

Bucci, J.J. (2016). Redemptive Leadership.

Cincinnati Enquirer Editorial Board (2020, August 28). Brennaman should be fired; our role is to forgive. Cincinnati Enquirer: Cincinnati.com [Web Blog]. Retrieved from https://www.cincinnati.com/story/opinion/2020/08/28/editorial-brennaman-should-fired-our-role-forgive/5629513002/

Daugherty, P. (2020, August 20). Words matter. Words create perceptions. Too often, perception is reality. Cincinnati Enquirer: Cincinnati.com [Web Blog]. Retrieved from https://www.cincinnati.com/story/sports/columnists/paul-daugherty/2020/08/19/doc-thom-brennaman-slur-words-matter-words-create-perceptions/5614164002/

Giegerich, S. (2011). JobWatch: Teacher won't get second chance to escape porn-star past. *St. Louis Post-Dispatch*. Retrieved from http://www.stltoday.com/business/columns/job-watch/article_844d1e34-52f9-51f1-9034-577343e3011e.html

Holland, E. (2011, March 9). Teacher who once made porn films steps down. *St. Louis Post-Dispatch*. Retrieved from https://www.stltoday.com/news/local/education/teacher-who-once-made-porn-films-steps-down/article_cb46fea8-f3df-5605-a4f9-60ed3ec7737b.html

Kalaf, S. (2020, August 21). Baseball Announcer Thom Brennaman found a new, surreal way to ruin a public apology. Slate.com [Web Blog]. Retrieved from https://slate.com/culture/2020/08/reds-announcer-thom-brennaman-found-a-new-surreal-way-to-ruin-a-public-apology.html

Keller, T. (2013). Encounters with Jesus: Unexpected answers to life's biggest questions. New York, NY.: Penguin Books

Know Your Phrase (2021). An elephant never forgets. *Know Your Phrase*. Retrieved from https://knowyourphrase.com/an-elephant-never-forgets

Martin, J. (2020, August 20). Cincinnati Reds suspend broadcaster Thom Brennaman after he uttered anti-gay slur on air. CNN [Web Blog]. Retrieved from https://www.cnn.com/2020/08/19/us/cincinnati-reds-broadcaster-thom-brennaman-anti-gay-slur-spt-trnd/index.html

Mushnick, P. (2020, August 20). Thom Brennaman's slur was wrong but so is selective justice. New Yory Post [Web Blog]. Retrieved from https://nypost.com/2020/08/20/thom-brennamans-slur-was-wrong-but-so-is-selective-justice/

Odovitch, M. (2003, October 19). The Sobering Life of Robert Downey, Jr. *New York Times*. Retrieved from https://www.nytimes.com/2003/10/19/magazine/the-sobering-life-of-robert-downey-jr.html

Padecky, B. (2020, August 24). In a world of 2nd chances, using a slur is one-strike-and-you're-out. Santa Rosa, CA: The Press Democrat. Retrieved from https://www.pressdemocrat.com/article/sports/padecky-in-a-world-of-second-chances-using-a-slur-is-one-strike-and-your/.

ProCon.org (2020, August 5). Is cancel culture (or "Callout Culture") good for society? Chicago, IL.: Encyclopedia Britannica. Retrieved from https://www.procon.org/headlines/is-cancel-culture-or-callout-culture-good-for-society/

Ritchie, J. (2009, January 12). Fact or Fiction?: Elephants Never Forget. Scientific American. Retrieved from https://www.scientificamerican.com/article/elephants-never-forget/

Sheehy, K. (2011, March 9). Hot for Teacher. NY Post. Retrieved from https://nypost.com/2011/03/09/hot-for-teacher/

Trennert, J.D. (2020, August 27). Why cancel culture is anti-Christian. American Greatness [Web Blog]. Retrieved from https://amgreatness.com/2020/08/27/why-cancel-culture-is-anti-christian

Whiteside, K. (2012, May 04). Can Bobby Petrino, Jim Tressel travel road to redemption? USA Today. Retrieved from http://www.usatoday.com/sports/college/football/story/2012-05-03/Bobby-Petrino-Jim-Tresell-redemption-infidelity/54738610/1

Chapter 13 | The Scarlet Thread

Conradt, S.; Mills, L. & Green, J. (2007, December 14). 8 Fairy Tales and Their Not-So-Happy Endings. MentalFloss [Web Blog]. (JB–Sleeping Beauty, Little Mermaid, Cinderella, Snow White & others). Retrieved from https://www.mentalfloss.com/article/17601/8-fairy-tales-and-their-not-so-happy-endings

Devine, P. (2016, June 14). Fairy Tales Without Happy Endings. The People's Movies {Web Blog]. (JB–Sleeping Beauty, Little Mermaid, others). Retrieved from https://thepeoplesmovies.com/2016/06/fairytales-without-happy-endings/

Fleming, R. (2018, July 16). Why Can't We Redeem the Sex Offender? National Incarceration Association (NIA). Retrieved from https://joinnia.com/why-cant-we-redeem-the-sex-offender/

GotQuestions Ministries (2022). What is the significance of a scarlet thread? GotQuestions.org [Web Blog]. Retrieved from https://www.gotquestions.org/scarlet-thread.html

Jones. P.A. (2016, October 10). The Original Unhappy Endings of 3 Famous Fairy Tales. MentalFloss [Web Blog]. (JB–Little Mermaid, Cinderella, Pinocchio). Retrieved from https://www.mentalfloss.com/article/86818/original-unhappy-endings-3-famous-fairy-tales

K. Williams, personal communication, January 30, 2015.

Law Office of George Gedulin (2017, April 19). Surprising Things That Could Make You a Sex Offender. Law Office of George Gedulin [Web Blog]. Retrieved from https://www.gedulinlaw.com/blog/2017/april/surprising-things-that-could-make-you-a-sex-offe/

Lowenstein. L. (2010, March 12). The sorry truth is that sex offenders CAN"T be rehabilitated. Daily Mail.com [Web Blog]. Retrieved from http://www.dailymail.co.uk/debate/article-1256779/Some-offenders-like-Jon-Venables-Peter-Chapman-CANT-rehabilitated.html

Meyers, C. (2021). Rahab: Bible. AN entry in the Shalvi/Hyman Encyclopedia of Jewish Women. Retrieved from https://jwa.org/encyclopedia/article/rahab-bible

Chapter 14 | A Second Chance is the Best Choice

American Enterprise Institute (2017, February 7). To Whom is Given: Business for the Common Good. AEI Values and Capitalism Project. Retrieved from https://www.aei.org/multimedia/to-whom-is-given-business-for-the-common-good/

APF (2012, May 27). Salvadoran ex-gangsters seek redemption in work. Agence France-Presse (AFP.com). Retrieved December 27, 2015 from http://www.taipeitimes.com/News/world/archives/2012/05/27/2003533874

APF (2012, May 25). Salvadoran ex-gang members seek redemption in work. *The Kuwait Times*, p.16. Retrieved May 25, 2012, from http://issuu.com/kuwaitnews/docs/25may2012

Aquino, K., Lewis, M.U., & Bradfield, M. (1999). Justice Constructs, Negative Affectivity, and Employee Deviance: A Proposed Model and Empirical Test. *Journal of Organizational Behavior, 20*, 1073-1091

Barret, V. (2010, July 19). Salvation at the Call Center. *Forbes*. Retrieved October 11, 2015 from http://www.forbes.com/global/2010/0719/ideas-prison-televerde-james-hooker-salvation-at-call-center.html

Beelove (2015). Retrieved from www.sweetbeginningsllc.com/

Belay Enterprises (2015). Retrieved November 14, 2015 from www.belay.org/

Blanchard, K. H., Zigarmi, P., & Zigarmi, D. (1985). *Leadership and the one minute manager increasing effectiveness through situational leadership.* New York: Morrow.

Boschee, J., & Jones, S. (2000). *The Mimi Silbert story: Recycling ex-cons, addicts and prostitutes.* San Francisco, CA: The Institute for Social Entrepreneurs.

Brown, E. (2008, April 21). Rehab, Reuse, Recycle. *Forbes,* 70-72.

Bucci, J. J. (2011). *Evidence of redemptive manager behaviors in successfully reinstating terminated workers.* Doctoral dissertation, Anderson University. ProQuest, UMI Dissertations Publishing, 3476151.

Bucci, J. J. (2011). An examination of redemptive manager behaviors in reinstating terminated workers: An organizational case study. In *Christian Business Faculty Association Annual Conference.* Mount Vernon, OH: Mount Vernon Nazarene University.

Bucci, J.J., & Bruce, M.L. (2013). Manager tendencies to offer second-chance opportunities: Follow-up research comparing faith-oriented managers with a general manager population. In proceedings of the *Christian Business Faculty Association Annual Conference.* Bourbonnais, IL: Olivet Nazarene University.

Central City Concern (2014). About Central City Concern. *Central City Concern.* Retrieved August 24, 2014, from http://www.centralcityconcern.org/

Danovich, T.K. (2018, February 27). Against the Grain. *The Ringer.com* [Web Blog]. Retrieved from https://www.theringer.com/2018/2/27/17055800/daves-killer-bread-dave-dahl-feature

Dave's Killer Bread (2015). Retrieved November 14, 2015 from www.daveskillerbread.com

Davis, L.M.; Steele, J.L.; Bozick, R.; Williams, M.V.; Turner, S.; Miles, J.N.; Saunders, J.; and Steinberg, P.S. (2014). *How effective is correctional education, and where do we go from here? The results of a comprehensive evaluation.* Santa Monica, CA: RAND Corporation. Retrieved from https://www.rand.org/pubs/research_reports/RR564.html

Delancey Street - How We Work. (2007). *Delancey Street Foundation.* Retrieved May 30, 2014, from http://www.delanceystreetfoundation.org/hww.php

Equity Value Group (2021). Retrieved from http://www.equityvaluegroup.com/Home_Page.html

Felony Franks (2015). Retrieved November 14, 2015 from www.felonyfranks.com/

Fowler, G.A. (2011, September 8). For 40 years, an advocate for the underclass. Wall Street Journal. Retrieved May 17, 2014, from http://online.wsj.com/news/articles/SB10001424053111904537404576554790064918716

Gang Rehabilitation Program. (n.d.). League Collegiate Outfitters. Retrieved May 30, 2014, from http://www.league91.com/blog/?page_id=90

Giang, V. (2012, December 4). Why Criminals Might Make Better Employees. Business Insider. Retrieved May 30, 2014, from http://www.businessinsider.com/a-criminal-record-might-increase-productivity-2012-12

Goodwill Industries International (2014). About Us. *Goodwill Industries International.* Retrieved August 23, 2014, from http://www.goodwill.org/about-us/

Goger, A.; Harding, D. & Henderson, H. (2021, April). A better path forward for criminal justice: Prisoner reentry. *Brookings Institute.* Retrieved from https://www.brookings.edu/research/a-better-path-forward-for-criminal-justice-prisoner-reentry/

Grisales, C. (2021, May 20). Congress Wants to Set Up One-Stop Shops to Help Ex-Inmates Stay Out of Prison. *National Public Radio (NPR).* Retrieved from https://www.npr.org/2021/05/20/998497401/an-effort-to-help-ex-prisoners-gains-momentum-with-bipartisan-lawmakers-support

Grow Ensemble (2021). Entrepreneurship as Second Chance. *Grow Ensemble: Bthechange.com* [Web Blog]. Retrieved from https://bthechange.com/entrepreneurship-as-a-second-chance-4b9dbcc5dfae

Harper, D. (1990). Spotlight abuse-save profits. Industrial Distribution, 79, 47- 51.

Hayes, R. (2008). *Strategies to detect and prevent workplace dishonesty.* Alexandria, VA: ASIS Foundation.

Hoke, C. (2017). *A second chance: For you, for me, and for the rest of us*. New York, NY.: Do You Zoom, Inc. for Defy Ventures.

Holodny, E. (2017, July 30). 'It still haunts me': What it's like to get a job after prison in America. *Business Insider*. Retrieved March 21, 2018 from http://www.businessinsider.com/finding-job-after-prison-2017-7

I Have a Bean Coffee Store (2015). Retrieved November 14, 2015 from www.ihaveabean.com/

Iqbal, M. (2012, May 26). Ex-gang members seek redemption in work. *The Business Recorder*. Retrieved May 28, 2012, from http://www.brecorder.com/world/south-america/59057-ex-gang-members-seek-redemption-in-work.html

James, E. (2011, November 15). Richard Branson champions employment of ex-offenders. *The Guardian*. Retrieved November 15, 2015, from http://www.theguardian.com/society/2011/nov/15/richard-branson-champions-employment-ex-offenders

JPMorgan Chase (2021, April 26). *JPMorgan Chase expands second chance hiring efforts in Columbus.* [Press Release]. Retrieved from https://www.jpmorganchase.com/news-stories/jpmc-expands-second-chance-hiring-efforts-in-columbus

Kent, D. (2010, July 9). Televerde Featured in Forbes. Retrieved October 11, 2015, from http://www.televerde.com/televerde-featured-in-forbes/

League Collegiate Outfitters (2014). LCA in the News. *League Collegiate Outfitters: Our Company*. Retrieved August 24, 2014, from http://www.league91.com/blog/

L2 Brands (2021). Retrieved from https://league-legacy.com/pages/our-story

Malkin, E. (2015, September 21). At Salvadoran factory, helping troubled youth makes business sense. *The New York Times: Americas Section. El Salvador Journal*. Retrieved December 27, 2015 from http://www.nytimes.com/2015/09/22/world/americas/at-salvadoran-factory-helping-troubled-youth-makes-business-sense.html?r=0

Marchetti, M. (2005, June 27). Selling Saved Their Lives. *Fortune, 151*.

McGray, D. (2012, May). House of second chances. *Fast Company* 165, 116. Retrieved May 30, 2014, from http://www.fastcompany.com/1826868/house-second-chances

Our History: Dave's Killer Bread (2018). Retrieved from http://www.daveskillerbread.com/our-history#our-history-1

Nothstine, R. (2015a, Spring). Molding men, shaping futures: An interview with Bert Smith. Religion and Liberty, 25(2).

Nothstine, R. (2015b, Spring). Prison entrepreneurs: From Shark Tank to redemption. Religion and Liberty, 25(2).

Patterson, K., Grenny, J., Maxfield, D., McMillan, R., and Switzler, A. (2007). Influencer: The power to change anything. New York, NY: McGraw-Hill.

Petroff, A. (2016, July 20). Richard Branson wants you to hire an ex-con. CNN Money [Web Blog]. Retrieved from https://money.cnn.com/2016/07/20/news/richard-branson-virgin-jobs-prison-offenders-convicts/index.html

Pierce, S. (n.d.). Building a business one felon at a time. *All Business*. Retrieved from http://www.allbusiness.com/labor-employment/human-resources-personnel-management/14562122-1.html

Prisoner Re-Entry - Goodwill Industries of the Valleys. (n.d.). Goodwill Industries. Retrieved May 30, 2014, from http://www.goodwillvalleys.com/work-and-training-services/adult-services/prisoner-re-entry/

Rodrigues, M. (2015, May 26). Ban the box: U.S. Cities, Counties, and States Adopt Fair Hiring Policies. *National Employment Law Project*. Retrieved June 8, 2015, from http://www.nelp.org/publication/ban-the-box-fair-chance-hiring-state-and-local-guide/

Rodriguez, M. N., & Emsellem, M. (2011). 65 million "need not apply": The case for reforming criminal background checks for employment. New York: National Employment Law Project.

Scott, D. (2012, June 10). Café offers ex-cons chance at redemption. http://www.journalgazette.net/ Retrieved May 30, 2014, from http://www.journalgazette.net/article/20120610/LOCAL/306109892/1002/local

Shegerian, J. (2021). Entrepreneur John Shegerian. Retrieved from https://johnshegerian.com/about/

Society for Human Resource Management (2010, January 22). *Background Checking: General Background Checks SHRM Poll.* SHRM Online - Society for Human Resource Management. Retrieved January 19, 2012, from http://www.shrm.org/Research/SurveyFindings/Articles/Pages/BackgroundCheckingGeneral.aspx

Stout, J. (2015). Ban the Box Campaign. Retrieved June 8, 2015 from http://bantheboxcampaign.org/

Treon, R. & Behr, F. (2021, March 31). The reason Dave Dahl of Dave's Killer Bread went to jail. *Mashed.com* [Web Blog]. Retrieved from https://www.mashed.com/370544/the-reason-dave-dahl-of-daves-killer-bread-went-to-jail/

Weifield Group (2021). Karla Nugent a panelist at 2021 Denver Institute for Faith & Work 'Business for the Common Good' conference. *Weifield Group* [Press Release]. Retrieved from https://www.weifieldcontracting.com/news-posts/karla-nugent-a-panelist-at-2021-denver-institute-for-faith-work-business-for-the-common-good-conference/

Wellman, J. (2014, December 25). What Does Redemption Mean In The Bible? *Patheos.com*. Retrieved June 12, 2015, from http://www.patheos.com/blogs/christiancrier/2014/12/25/what-does-redemption-mean-in-the-bible-christian-definition-of-redemption/

Yukl, G. A. (2002). *Leadership in organizations* (5th ed.). Upper Saddle River, NJ: Pearson/Prentice Hall.

Zablocki, E. (2011). Work as sharing in God's redemptive activity. *Work Commission Resources - Secular Franciscan Order*. Retrieved from http://www.nafra-sfo.org/work_commission_resources/wrkart8.html

Zaimont, R.H. (2014, April). From addicts to ad execs. *Fast Company 184*, 60-62.

Conclusion | The Beauty of a Restored Live

Blank, S. (2013). Why the lean start-up changes everything. *Harvard Business Review, 91*(5), 63-72.

Blank, S. (2012). *The startup owner's manual: The step-by-step guide for building a great company*. BookBaby.

Bloom, J. (2015) *Fueled by Failure*. Irvine, CA: Entrepreneur Media.

Bryant, S. (2020, November 9). How many startups fail and why? *Investopedia: Personal Finance* [Web Blog]. Retrieved from https://www.investopedia.com/articles/personal-finance/040915/how-many-startups-fail-and-why.asp

Buckingham, M., and Coffman, C. (1999). First break all the rules: What the world's greatest managers do differently. New York, NY.: Gallup Press.

Burchell, B.; & Hughes, A. (2006). The stigma of failure: An international comparison of failure tolerance and second chancing. Cambridge, UK: University of Cambridge, Centre for Business Research. Retrieved from http://citeseerx.ist.psu.edu/viewdoc/download?rep=rep1&type=pdf&doi=10.1.1.167.6149

DeGraaf, L. (2013). *Edison and the rise of innovation*. New York: Sterling Pub Co Inc.

Ellis, J. (2017, February 22). Never giving up: Nine successful entrepreneurs who failed at least once. *Business.com Blog*. Retrieved June 10, 2017 from https://www.business.com/articles/never-giving-up-9-entrepreneurs-and-millionaires-who-failed-at-least-once/

George, K. (n.d.). 10 famous entrepreneurs that failed in business before becoming successful. http://small-bizsense.com/10-famous-entrepreneurs-who-failed-in-business-before- Small Business Sense Blog [Web Blog]. Retrieved June 10, 2017 from becoming-successful/

Gerber, M.E. (2001). The E-myth revisited. New York, NY.: HarperCollins.

Gompers, P.A.; Kovner, A.; Lerner, J.; and Scharfstein, D.S. (2006, October). Skill vs. luck in entrepreneurship and venture capital: Evidence from serial entrepreneurs. Working paper 12592. *National Bureau of Economic Research*. Retrieved April 6, 2017 from http://papers.ssrn.com/sol3/papers.cfm?abstract_id=933932

Griffith, E. (2014, September 25). Why startups fail, according to their founders. *Fortune Magazine: Leadership Blog.* Retrieved from http://fortune.com/2014/09/25/why-startups-fail-according-to-their-founders/

Grow Ensemble (2021). Entrepreneurship as Second Chance. *Grow Ensemble: Bthechange.com* [Web Blog]. Retrieved from https://bthechange.com/entrepreneurship-as-a-second-chance-4b9dbcc5dfae

Hartley, S. (2016). Surprising facts about business success rates [Blog post]. West Tisbury, MA: *Enlightened Marketing Blog.* Retrieved December 10, 2016 from http://www.enlightenedmarketing.com/2012/07/surprising-facts-about-business-success-rates/

Hegarty, C.; Gallagher, P.; Cunningham, I. & Stephens, S. (2020, January). ReSTART: Developing entrepreneurial competencies for second chance entrepreneurs. In (Sebestova, J., Ed) *Developing Entrepreneurial Competencies for Start-Ups and Small Business.* Hershey, PA: IGI Global, pp.253-270.

Hoke, C. (2017). *A second chance: For you, for me, and for the rest of us.* New York, NY.: Do You Zoom, Inc. for Defy Ventures.

Jorden, R. (2014). What are the real small business survival rates? [Blog post]. Retrieved December 10, 2016 from https://www.linkedin.com/pulse/20140915223641-170128193-what-are-the-real-small-business-survival-rates

Laymon, K. (2021). Paul and Barnabas split: The progression of John Mark. *Glory Books: Year One* [Web Blog]. Also found at *KevinLaymon.Com.* Retrieved from http://glorybooks.org/paul-barnabas-split-progression-john-mark/

Lafontaine, F., and Shaw, K. (2014). Serial entrepreneurship: Learning by doing? *Journal of Labor Economics, 34*(S2), pages. Also found at the National Bureau for Economic Research, July 2014. Retrieved March 26, 2017 from http://www.ncpa.org/sub/dpd/index.php?Article_ID=24677#sthash.8spBZCTa.dpuf

Macfarlan, L. (2013, August 27). John Mark: A lesson on second chances. Cross My Heart Ministry [Web Blog]. Retrieved from https://www.crossmyheartministry.com/2013/08/27/john-mark-a-lesson-on-second-chances/

Menefee, C. (2016). *Losing isn't everything.* Dey Street Books, an imprint of HarperCollins.

Meszaros, G. (2016, April 21). What percentage of businesses fail: The real number. *SuccessHarbor* blog. Retrieved April 6, 2017 from http://www.successharbor.com/percentage-businesses-fail-09092015/

Nelson, R. (2019). Who Was John Mark? The Beginner's Guide. OverviewBible.com [Web Blog]. Retrieved from https://overviewbible.com/john-mark/

Patel, N. (2015). 90% of startups fail: Here's what you need to know about the 10%. [Blog post]. New York: Forbes Magazine, Entrepreneurs Blog. Retrieved December 10, 2016 from http://www.forbes.com/sites/neilpatel/2015/01/16/90-of-startups-will-fail-heres-what-you-need-to-know-about-the-10/#1ed40eaf55e1

Report of the Expert Group (2011). *A second chance for entrepreneurs: Prevention of bankruptcy, simplification of bankruptcy procedures and support for a fresh start.* Enterprise and Industry Directorate General, European Commission. Retrieved from http://ec.europa.eu/sme2chance

Richards, K. (2015, September 4). 4 Characteristics of trailblazing entrepreneurs. INC: Innovate Blog [Web Blog]. Retrieved from https://www.inc.com/kelli-richards/4-characteristics-of-trailblazing-entrepreneurs.html

Ries, E. (2011). *The lean startup: How today's entrepreneurs use continuous innovation to create radically successful businesses.* Crown Business.

Schrager, A. (2014, July 28). Failed entrepreneurs find more success the second time. *Bloomberg Business Week: Bloomberg.com.* Retrieved March 15, 2017 from https://www.bloomberg.com/news/articles/2014-07-28/study-failed-entrepreneurs-find-success-the-second-time-around

Shepherd, D. A. (2004). Educating entrepreneurship students about emotion and learning from failure. *Academy of Management Learning & Education, 3*(3), 274-287.

Smith, D. (2019, April 19) What everyone gets wrong about this Steve Jobs quote, according to Lyft's design boss. *Business Insider: Tech* [Web Blog]. Retrieved from https://www.businessinsider.com/steve-jobs-quote-misunderstood-katie-dill-2019-4

Stolze, H. (2021). *Wisdom-based business: Applying Biblical principles and evidence-based research for a purposeful and profitable business.* Grand Rapids, MI.: Zondervan.

Wissman, B. (2017, November 27). 10 Strategies for Entrepreneurs Dealing with Failure. *Entrepreneurship Magazine* [Web Blog]. Retrieved from https://www.entrepreneur.com/article/304948

Cowper, W. (1772). *There is a Fountain Filled with Blood.* Retrieved from http://www.cyberhymnal.org/htm/t/f/tfountfb.htm.

Johnson, V. (2013). Biography of William Cowper. *Proclaim & Defend* [Web Blog]. Foundations Baptist Fellowship International. Retrieved from https://www.proclaimanddefend.org/2013/03/25/there-is-a-fountain-filled-with-blood-william-cowper-17311800/.

APPENDIX I

Comparative Models of Redemptive Leadership: Scripture & Other Sources (Bucci, 2022)

Exodus 6:2-9 God speaks of His process of redemption & restoration	Steps in the Redemptive Intervention Process Based on Key Scripture Passages (Bucci, 2019)	Romans 5: 1-11 A similar description of God's redemptive process through Christ
[2] God spoke to Moses and said to him, "I am the LORD. [3] I appeared to Abraham, to Isaac, and to Jacob, as God Almighty, but by my name the LORD I did not make myself known to them. [4] I also (1) established my covenant with them (2) to give them the land of Canaan, the land in which they lived as sojourners. [5] Moreover, (3) I have heard the groaning of the people of Israel (4) whom the Egyptians hold as slaves, and I have remembered my covenant. [6] Say therefore to the people of Israel, 'I am the LORD, and (5) I will bring you out from under the burdens of the Egyptians, and I will deliver you from slavery to them, and I will redeem you with an outstretched arm and with great acts of judgment. [7] I will (6) take you to be my people, and I will be your God, and you shall know that I am the LORD your God, who has brought you out from under the burdens of the Egyptians. [8] I (7) will bring you into the land that I swore to give to Abraham, to Isaac, and to Jacob. (8) I will give it to you for a possession. I am the LORD.'" [9] Moses spoke thus to the people of Israel, but they did not listen to Moses, because of their broken spirit and harsh slavery.	(1) A leadership commitment. Not by rule or law but covenant (contract: mutually beneficial; covenant: pledge). There is a covenant or commitment (of a leader) to faithfully support a person and give them an opportunity to change. (2) There was is a plan for an inheritance, permanence. The confidence that this person would become established as a full contributor. (3) Groaning. Not fulfilling plan. The "groaning" piece represents that point in time when after being disciplined by a leader or through a "last chance" agreement an individual is confronted with behaviors which could results in loss (their job, their family). (4) Bondage of old habits. There is a reflection time to understand one's condition, the issues and the potential consequences. Insight and clarity may come as a result of being removed or stepping back from the situation. This is the teachable moment where the subordinate recognizes that change needs to occur. But they may need help to accomplish this. (5) Leadership undertakes pledged action. Remove debt, remove guilt, start fresh. Opportunity and support for a change of behavior is provided. Outside counseling or EAP might be necessary for destructive habit patterns. (6) Leader's ownership of process, to mentor and disciple. Trust is built with and by the leader. The leader becomes coach, mentor, and friend. Through the building of trust there is intimate knowledge, and then confidence to follow through on the changes needed. No mention of disciple's response here; but the literature suggests that there is often humility and willingness on the part of the disciple to put oneself under authority through a process of re-learning new habit patterns. But as v9 here suggests, this is not always the case. (7) A commitment to follow through on this plan to help the disciple achieve success. This is a covenant pledge fulfilled. (8) The release of the disciple to own their own success, no strings attached. The employee is fully restored to a position of reliability as a contributing member of the community.	Therefore, since we have been justified by faith, (1) we have peace with God through our Lord Jesus Christ. [2] Through him we have also (2) obtained access by faith into this grace in which we stand, and we rejoice in hope of the glory of God. [3] Not only that, (3) but we rejoice in our sufferings, knowing that (4) suffering produces endurance, [4] and endurance produces character, and character produces hope, [5] and hope does not put us to shame, because (6) God's love has been poured into our hearts through the Holy Spirit who has been given to us. [6] For (5) while we were still weak, at the right time Christ died for the ungodly. [7] For one will scarcely die for a righteous person—though perhaps for a good person one would dare even to die— [8] but God shows his love for us in that while we were still sinners, Christ died for us. [9] Since, therefore, (7) we have now been justified by his blood, much more shall we be saved by him from the wrath of God. [10] For if while we were enemies we were reconciled to God by the death of his Son, much more, (8) now that we are reconciled, shall we be saved by his life. [11] More than that, we also rejoice in God through our Lord Jesus Christ, through whom we have now received reconciliation.

Steps in the Redemptive Intervention Process Based on Key Scripture Passages (Bucci, 2019)	Summary of the Key Principles from the Original Research (Bucci, 2011)
(1) A leadership commitment. Not by rule or law but covenant (contract: mutually beneficial; covenant: pledge). There is a covenant or commitment (of a leader) to faithfully support a person and give them an opportunity to change. (2) There was is a plan for an inheritance, permanence. The confidence that this person would become established as a full contributor. (3) Groaning. Not fulfilling plan. The "groaning" piece represents that point in time when after being disciplined by a leader or through a "last chance" agreement an individual is confronted with behaviors which could results in loss (their job, their family). (4) Bondage of old habits. There is a reflection time to understand one's condition, the issues and the potential consequences. Insight and clarity may come as a result of being removed or stepping back from the situation. This is the teachable moment where the subordinate recognizes that change needs to occur. But they may need help to accomplish this. (5) Leadership undertakes pledged action. Remove debt, remove guilt, start fresh. Opportunity and support for a change of behavior is provided. Outside counseling or EAP might be necessary for destructive habit patterns. (6) Leader's ownership of process, to mentor and disciple. Trust is built with and by the leader. The leader becomes coach, mentor, and friend. Through the building of trust there is intimate knowledge, and then confidence to follow through on the changes needed. No mention of disciple's response here; but the literature suggests that there is often humility and willingness on the part of the disciple to put oneself under authority through a process of re-learning new habit patterns. But as v9 here suggests, this is not always the case. (7) A commitment to follow through on this plan to help the disciple achieve success. This is a covenant pledge fulfilled. (8) The release of the disciple to own their own success, no strings attached. The employee is fully restored to a position of reliability as a contributing member of the community.	1. **Managers reflected on decision-making that led to the first termination; but then they reviewed the rationale for bringing someone back.** *(Steps in Redemptive Process: (1); (6))* **Key words -** [Process reflection; Decision review; assess risk of return (personal, corporate, employee, team). Which is the greater risk: brand new, background checks but seems OK; or renew, knowledge of their strengths and weaknesses.] Leaders reflected, inspected, fact-checked, decided and took ownership 2. **Managers sorted through organizational issues with stakeholder groups; but then they carefully considered the proper placement of the returning employee.** *(Steps in Redemptive Process: (2); (6))* **Key words -** [Stakeholder bias; Particular placement. Restorative justice, in community (are they ready?) Attribution as well (will they / can they forgive?)] Leaders anticipated, addressed issues head-on, acted 3. **Managers created structured agreements with conditional acceptance; then they communicated clearly and directly about conditions and consequences.** *(Steps in Redemptive Process: (4); (7))* **Key words -** [Conditional agreements; clear expectations. Clarity; if/then agreements – God loves unconditionally but He sets conditions (Matt 6:14-15). Worker accepts responsibility for past actions.] 4. **Managers were moved with compassion and empathy for the reinstated employee; but then they acted to ensure that the process for reinstatement demonstrated justice and fairness.** *(Steps in Redemptive Process: (5); (7))* **Key words -** [Empathetic action; just process. Christ-like justice with mercy.] 5. **Managers offered support and encouragement to the returning employee; but then they carefully scrutinized the reinstated employee's work, with greater follow-up frequency and continued consistent discipline.** *(Steps in Redemptive Process: (5); (6))* **Key words -** [Supportive reintegration; careful scrutiny. Re-train; renew; Matt 11:28-30 (the yoke of compassion vs the yoke of bondage [KJV]). Yoke of slavery (to the law) – Galatians 5:1.] 6. **Managers balanced the need (sometimes desperation) for good workers and their belief in second chances with the facts: this employee has displayed aberrant behavior, and they had previously failed at this opportunity.** *(Steps in Redemptive Process: (7); (8))* **Key words -** [Failed past; positive belief. Belief dictates behavior; failing forward. All those who failed early but given another opportunity took it: Abe Lincoln; Kurt Warner; Horatio Alger is hard work.

Steps in the Redemptive Intervention Process Based on Key Scripture Passages (Bucci, 2019)	Summary of the Key Principles from the Original Research (Bucci, 2011)	**Redemptive Leadership – Harv Powers Model**
(1) A leadership commitment. Not by rule or law but covenant (contract: mutually beneficial; covenant: pledge). There is a covenant or commitment (of a leader) to faithfully support a person and give them an opportunity to change. (2) There was is a plan for an inheritance, permanence. The confidence that this person would become established as a full contributor. (3) Groaning. Not fulfilling plan. The "groaning" piece represents that point in time when after being disciplined by a leader or through a "last chance" agreement an individual is confronted with behaviors which could results in loss (their job, their family). (4) Bondage of old habits. There is a reflection time to understand one's condition, the issues and the potential consequences. Insight and clarity may come as a result of being removed or stepping back from the situation. This is the teachable moment where the subordinate recognizes that change needs to occur. But they may need help to accomplish this. (5) Leadership undertakes pledged action. Remove debt, remove guilt, start fresh. Opportunity and support for a change of behavior is provided. Outside counseling or EAP might be necessary for destructive habit patterns. (6) Leader's ownership of process, to mentor and disciple. Trust is built with and by the leader. The leader becomes coach, mentor, and friend. Through the building of trust there is intimate knowledge, and then confidence to follow through on the changes needed. No mention of disciple's response here; but the literature suggests that there is often humility and willingness on the part of the disciple to put oneself under authority through a process of re-learning new habit patterns. But as v9 here suggests, this is not always the case.	1. **Managers reflected on decision-making that led to the first termination; but then they reviewed the rationale for bringing someone back.** *(Steps in Redemptive Process: (1); (6))* **Key words -** [Process reflection; Decision review; assess risk of return (personal, corporate, employee, team). Which is the greater risk: brand new, background checks but seems OK; or renew, knowledge of their strengths and weaknesses.] Leaders reflected, inspected, fact-checked, decided and took ownership 2. **Managers sorted through organizational issues with stakeholder groups; but then they carefully considered the proper placement of the returning employee.** *(Steps in Redemptive Process: (2); (6))* **Key words -** [Stakeholder bias; Particular placement. Restorative justice, in community (are they ready?) Attribution as well (will they / can they forgive?)] Leaders anticipated, addressed issues head-on, acted 3. **Managers created structured agreements with conditional acceptance; then they communicated clearly and directly about conditions and consequences.** *(Steps in Redemptive Process: (4); (7)* **Key words -** [Conditional agreements; clear expectations. Clarity; if/then agreements – God loves unconditionally but He sets conditions (Matt 6:14-15). Worker accepts responsibility for past actions.] 4. **Managers were moved with compassion and empathy for the reinstated employee; but then they acted to ensure that the process for reinstatement demonstrated justice and fairness.** *(Steps in Redemptive Process: (5); (7))* **Key words -** [Empathetic action; just process. Christ-like justice with mercy.] 5. **Managers offered support and encouragement to the returning employee; but then they carefully scrutinized the reinstated employee's work, with greater follow-up frequency and continued consistent discipline.** *(Steps in Redemptive Process: (5); (6))* **Key words -** [Supportive reintegration; careful scrutiny. Re-train; renew; Matt 11:28-30 (the yoke of compassion vs the yoke of bondage [KJV]). Yoke of slavery (to the law) – Galatians 5:1.] 6. **Managers balanced the need (sometimes desperation) for good workers and their belief in second chances with the facts: this employee**	1. Leadership is a development process occurring over the lifespan of a leader. Each stage built on previous stage incorporating past learning. 2. Pivotal transformation windows occur in the Crucible experiences. The Crucible may reveal the leader's dark side. 3. Counter-intuitively, the crisis of this revelation opens a portal to an inward journey of transformation. This process creates brokenness and results in humility that reshapes the leader's heart. 4. Redemptive influence emerges as leader discovers that deeper humility establishes a greater foundation of trust and the authority to speak into others' lives. 5. The ability to recognize the deeper redemptive narrative in others' lives allows the leader to support and guide individuals at Key inflection points. Leaders recognize and discern potential in the life of an individual going through crisis or failure. 6. The Redemptive Leadership Model is linear and cyclic. 7. Redemptive leadership must be understood as a framework a mindset and a value system.

(7) A commitment to follow through on this plan to help the disciple achieve success. This is a covenant pledge fulfilled. (8) The release of the disciple to own their own success, no strings attached. The employee is fully restored to a position of reliability as a contributing member of the community.	**has displayed aberrant behavior, and they had previously failed at this opportunity.** *(Steps in Redemptive Process: (7); (8))* **Key words -** [Failed past; positive belief. Belief dictates behavior; failing forward. All those who failed early but given another opportunity took it: Abe Lincoln; Kurt Warner; Horatio Alger is hard work,	Powers, H. (2019). *Redemptive leadership: Unleashing your greatest influence*. Littleton, CO.: Illumify Media Global.

APPENDIX II
Summary of the Original Research

Evidence of Redemptive Manager Behaviors in Successfully Reinstating Terminated Workers

Summary of the Project

Research on the successful reinstatement of employees terminated for cause had identified a series of variables as predictive of the future success of reinstated employees. In some eighteen studies reviewed for this research project, the focus of these studies was on the characteristics of the reinstated employee or the intentions of the adjudicator in directing that the employee be reinstated and the subsequent employment relationship. The initial research (Bamberger and Donahue, 1999) stated that these study findings are often inconsistent, and conclusions are often hard to draw due to sampling and study design problems (Bamberger and Donahue, 1999). No research had been conducted to assess the impact of the manager's leadership behaviors on post-reinstatement employees.

The Reformed view of the Christian faith is firmly in favor of redemption as it is expressed through restoration (Plantinga, 2002). In the Reformed viewpoint, God is not content to save souls, and God wants to save and restore individual activities, social systems, and economic structures (Plantinga, 2002). This includes restoring the management-labor relationship as well (Plantinga, 2002). With this core belief of the Reformed faith as the impetus, the researcher sought to identify where this practice of redemption leading to restoration might exist in the management literature. In this pursuit, consideration was given to those occasions where employees who had previously failed in their work performance in their first effort were given "second chances" through some remedy of reinstatement.

This research project aimed to identify those redemptive managerial behaviors that were most often observed in incidents of successful reinstatement and improved performance by employees previously discharged for cause. These shared behaviors are being called "redemptive behaviors" because they have been consistently present in the success of both the employee and the organization. Some measures of the success of the reinstatement were defined as employees who returned and remained with the firm for at least six months and demonstrated the same or an improved level of performance, as observed by the manager, such as higher work attendance rate, reduced or non-repeating absenteeism, lower turnover rates, and positive productivity.

It seemed from an overview of the data analysis that the findings represented a management balance between the execution of existing general management practices in hiring and managing the performance of all employees as noted in the traditional hiring process (forecasting and planning, candidate review, etc.) and a deepening personalized response to the unique variables present in the reinstatement process. The findings, therefore, represented a balancing of interests: the manager's own beliefs in the value of the individual with the pressing needs of the organization; similarly, a balance between the interests and objectives of the organization and its stakeholders for justice and performance with the fragile redemptive reinstatement of the failed employee.

A summary of the findings and their interpretation follows. Recommended actions were more wholly developed and presented in the author's book, *Redemptive Leadership: Offering Second Chances as a Value-Added Management Practice* (Bucci, 2016).

Finding and Interpretation:

1. **Managers reflected on the decision-making that led to the first termination, but they reviewed the rationale for bringing someone back.**

The managerial behaviors observed here centered on a self-reflection or thoughtful analysis of the reasons above for the worker's termination and a careful objective review of the circumstances leading up to the termination. Some of this reflected their empathy for the terminated worker, but it was also an expression of their role as an agent of the firm.

These managers checked on the facts leading up to the first termination to understand what occurred previously. This included looking into the previous work history of these employees; they also considered the investment made by the company in the employee's development. Employees with previous good work history were easier for managers to accept back and then "sell" back to the organization. This led to the willingness of the manager to take responsibility for the reinstatement of a terminated employee due to the consideration of the employee's past performance as a potential predictor of future success, as well as the financial investment made by the company in the employee's development.

Finding and Interpretation:

2. **Managers sorted through organizational issues with stakeholder groups, but then they carefully considered the proper placement of the returning employee.**

The managers' behaviors in this finding centered on managing the organizational environment into which the reinstated employee was re-entering. Before reinstatement, managers took the time to size up the workgroup and organizational environment. There were some concerns expressed by organizational stakeholders over the reinstated employee's return. Managers listened to the concerns of stakeholders and took the time to size up the workgroup and environment prior to reinstatement. The managers negotiated with stakeholders in the organizational environment into which the reinstated employee would be re-entering to ensure their concerns were addressed. In some cases, returning employees were reassigned to a smaller group and/or a different manager to help them adjust. It appeared prudent to the success of the reinstatement that managers anticipated these issues and addressed them head-on.

Eighty percent of the interviewed managers working in a union environment worked with the union to make this successful reinstatement happen. Managers acted as solid third-party facilitators (Kidder, 2005) in the successful reinstatement of the terminated employee, seeking to balance the concerns of the affected parties so that they would feel that justice was being served. Later in this chapter, there will be more on this facilitator role and restorative justice.

Finding and Interpretation:

3. **Managers created structured agreements with conditional acceptance; they communicated clearly and directly about conditions and consequences.**

Managers observed here carefully evaluated not only the circumstances leading to termination but also the worker's capabilities prior to reinstatement. Managers then created a structured and conditional plan for reinstating the terminated worker. In creating these conditional plans, managers acted in some cases to prevent a reoccurrence of the same behavior, which led to the original termination. However, in all cases, managers acted to protect the company in their role as an agent of the firm. Managers' behaviors at all times demonstrated decisions made to help the employee and the stakeholders through this process as a means of success.

Managers also pursued a directive approach to communication, pressing in to confront previous aberrant behaviors, questioning the employee about their motives for returning to the firm, and emphatically stressing this second chance opportunity. Managers challenged the returning employees to improve their performance, seeking to motivate them to be successful this time with this second chance. At times the manager's passion and directive communication elicited a verbal commitment from the employee to work harder to take advantage of this second chance opportunity. Due to this direct communication, workers expressed remorse for past mistakes and a commitment to work harder and regain trust.

Finding and Interpretation:

4. **Managers were moved with compassion and empathy for the reinstated employee, but then they acted to ensure that the process for reinstatement demonstrated justice and fairness.**

The managerial behaviors observed here included expressions by the manager of actions directed by a human sympathy for the reinstated worker. Many managers reflected on their own experiences with redemption or second chances; they also gave examples from their family history. In expressing their compassion, the managers considered what was best for the worker and the workgroup. If deemed necessary, they placed the employee in a different setting, on a different shift, or with a different workgroup. However, these expressions of support were balanced with careful monitoring of the reinstatement process to assure that this was done for the benefit to, and protection of, their organization, yet with justice towards the reinstated employee, to give the reinstated employee the opportunity for success the second time around.

Upon reinstatement, they sought to place employees in situations where they could succeed. They were perceived as being equitable and avoiding the perception that they were out to get the employee in this reinstatement agreement. Managers generally resisted the opportunity to form attributions towards their employees and demonstrate resentment (Williams and Taras, 2000) but instead offered support and a fair chance for the reinstated employees. In this finding, if the workgroup perceived the worker worth the investment, there were opportunities for support and re-engagement at the workgroup level to assist the manager in the reinstatement process.

Finding and Interpretation:

5. **Managers offered the returning employee support and encouragement, but then they carefully scrutinized the reinstated employee's work, with greater follow-up frequency and consistent discipline.**

The managers with successful reinstatements demonstrated an interest in all of their employees, getting to know them personally, but this was especially true with the reinstated employees due to the manager's careful due diligence and directive communication to the returning employee as a part of the reinstatement process.

Managers demonstrated active involvement with the terminated employees during this reinstatement process. Managers acted with fairness and justice in mind, but they were very up-front and outspoken with terminated employees in their reinstatement process, particularly about their approach to discipline. Managers were also very conscious of and attentive to the work and behaviors of the reinstated employees, more carefully monitoring the employee's behaviors and performance in this second opportunity. Therefore, the managers used a much more hands-on approach to restoring the employee, disciplining the employee, and indirectly evaluating the employee's performance. Managers demonstrated a greater oversight and closer evaluation of the restored employee's actions. Managers also seemed to take a more precise approach to employee discipline, following the company guidelines but with little room for flexibility.

Finding and Interpretation:

6. **Managers balanced the need (sometimes desperation) for good workers and their belief in second chances with the facts. This employee had displayed aberrant behavior, and they had previously failed at this opportunity.**

Each of the twelve managers interviewed expressed that they were willing or open to the reinstatement process. They were clear on the previous actions of the employee leading up to their termination. Ultimately, the managers recognized the risks and cost-benefits of reinstating an employee that had made mistakes and had to be terminated. However, these managers balanced this reality with two critical factors: their empathy and desire to offer a second chance; and the opportunity to not only assist an individual but meet the demands of their organization for good workers.

Managers were already known to have taken time to get some self-awareness on the issues related to this termination and examine their feelings towards the terminated workers. While balancing the demands of their business and the daily responsibilities and deadlines faced by managers, these managers seemed to make values-based decisions on reinstating workers. Their actions seemed more deliberate, focused, and time-consuming. These managers' actions could also have been described as missional because their efforts to reinstate these employees were more reflective of their values. These managers pursued a strategy that sought to meet the organization's demand for good workers and high performance by agreeing to reinstate a previously good worker who had failed in their behavior but had demonstrated some previous ability to perform. These managers all saw the organizational need, recognized a potential opportunity, and took the risk.

Conclusion

The reinstatement of an employee after termination was noted to be a rare occurrence (Darnay, Magee, and Hillstrom, 2007), and is still rare in many organizations. This is demonstrated by the fact that in these interviews, eight of the managers had never been involved in reinstatement in the past prior to working at their organization. As previously stated, among six of these eight managers, up to the point where the terminated employee was reinstated, there had never been an employee reinstatement at their organization in the past. As has been documented, there is undoubtedly a change in the employee-employer relationship, not simply in terms of rehiring and reinstating workers but also in interpersonal relationships. Some authors describe the worker's attitude reinstated through arbitration as untouchable now that they have been returned to work as if vindicated (Ponak, 1987; Ross, 1957). One manager in the interviews used the term "bulletproof." So the process of reinstatement for the manager, the workgroup, and the organization is not without complications.

Nevertheless, managers and organizations must also realize that all people are fallible, not perfect, and need training and nurturing to be successful. There is a significant disconnect in thinking that hiring involves drawing from a standard distribution curve (Blanchard, Zigarmi, and Zigarmi, 1985). Recruiting, training, and retaining "winners" are all three critical competencies necessary in organizations but are rarely a significant focus (Sullivan, 2002). This is not simply a function of the Human Resources department. Ultimately, managers must live with their efforts to develop a competent workforce (Yukl, 2002).

As noted in the study's limitations, the behaviors of the managers do not necessarily predict nor can they accurately determine the subordinate's reaction. Additional factors may affect employee commitment or disillusionment, such as cultural items, finances, or lack of opportunity elsewhere. Discipline by the managers, whether pre-termination or during post-termination reinstatement, must be seen by the employees and the workgroup as being directed at the employee's behaviors on the job rather than at the individual.

However, the manager deals with an effect and not a cause of the behavior. The managers know little about the personal and work-related factors (such as marital status and skill level) upon which the utility of such disciplinary practices may be contingent (Bamberger and Donahue, 1999). It is not recommended that a manager major in psychology, but it is recommended that managers know those they manage and their strengths, skills, and competencies (Blanchard, Zigarmi, and Zigarmi, 1985). The managers can control their behavior, and managers must demonstrate flexibility in implementing their leadership and reactions to these changing workplace challenges.

References to various citations can be found in the original Dissertation publication or the author's book based on the Dissertation Research:

References:

Bucci, J. J. (2011). *Evidence of redemptive manager behaviors in successfully reinstating terminated workers.* Doctoral dissertation, Anderson University. ProQuest, UMI Dissertations Publishing, 3476151.

Bucci, J. J. (2016). *Redemptive leadership: Offering second chances as a value-added management practice.* New York: Palgrave Macmillan

APPENDIX III

Comparative Behaviors of Managers: Traditional Hire vs. Reinstatement (Bucci, 2014)

The following table was originally created to contrast the difference between a traditional manager hiring process and what a manager would need to consider if they were reinstating an employee who had previously been terminated for cause. This was based on the original research and published in the author's first book on *Redemptive Leadership* (Bucci, 2016). The material is included here in this appendix as a guideline for an organization that might be considering either rehiring someone or was considering offering a second chance opportunity. The actions on the right were steps taken by managers who were successful at the reinstatement of a previously terminated employee (Bucci, 2016). These actions could be helpful in developing a process for offering a second chance opportunity.

Steps in the Employee Selection Process (Noe, 2011)	Traditional Managerial Actions in Hiring Process	Non-traditional Manager approach with Employee Reinstatement
A. Pre-hire: Forecasting and Planning for Staffing Positions	Consider new direction of firm, analyze job description	• Acted to reinstate worker because they saw value in the reinstatement. • Motivated to accept reinstatement efforts because they believed in workers and saw potential in them. Spoke of worker's potential. • Gained knowledge of worker. Familiar with them as a previously good performing worker. • Expressed sympathy for the worker; also empathy.
B. Screening of Applicants and Resumes	Review resumes/appl to screen out candidates, avoid discrimination.	• Conducted a self-reflective, introspective analysis of termination. What could the organization have done differently? • Checked the process and themselves prior to implementing the reinstatement. • Careful fact-checking and consideration of impact of re-hiring this person into the same situation. • They considered organizational issues. Weighed the impact of return. • Once they had reviewed the facts on previous termination, there was a willingness to take responsibility for reinstatement.
C. Testing and Reviewing Work Samples	Review samples of work; conduct tests of knowledge and aptitude. Looking for validity and reliability.	• Sought to find the right match or situation for the person before they were reinstated. • Conducted a performance assessment of the employee's previous work. Much more selective in taking them back.

		• Assessed workgroup's concerns and addressed justice issues head-on. • Talked to other leaders to get a sense if this would work.
D. Interviewing Candidates: Individually and with Committee	Ask job-related questions to determine capabilities and predictability of success.	• Pressed employee on motives for return. • Stressed with employee the significance of this opportunity. • Used a directive communication style. Employees challenged, often responding with remorse. • Gave strong warnings to employee: things could not be the same. • Clear expectations were given and parameters established. • Expressed that there would be more pressure on employees to perform this time.
E. Reference and Background Check	Seeking to confirm what has been seen in the interview and identify any potential discrepancies in stated job history.	• Acted to ensure that the reinstatement process would be perceived as fair and just to the workgroup and to protect company. • Acted with compassion, yet knew the process needed to be conducted with equity. • Could not be perceived as putting the employee into a situation where they would fail. • Had to lead people through this process (which for many was the first time this was done). • Demonstrated familiarity with competing organizational interests.
F. Employment Offer	Generally a manager or HR communicate an offer including the responsibilities; schedule; rate of pay; and starting date	• Sought to protect company from repeated bad behavior. • Used Last Chance Agreement or something similar to protect company. • Created a conditional reinstatement document or process. • Acted with business savvy in negotiating the employee's return. • Worked to get all of the groups to participate together.
G. Orientation and Integration to Workgroup	Integrate new employee into organization and workgroup.	• Created a process of reinstatement which was much more thorough and

		structured (more scrutiny and structure). • Acted with flexibility, sometimes changing their approach to break the work down into smaller pieces. • Had more persons observing work. More careful and frequent follow-up on performance. More hands-on in their approach. • Implemented a more precise approach to discipline with less flexibility. • Acted with zero tolerance towards any repeated aberrant behavior. • Sought to give the employee the opportunity to get the help they needed, in order to see them succeed. • Encouraged them to seek help if any problems, acquainted them with EAP.

AUTHOR BIOGRAPHY

Dr. Joseph J. Bucci, DBA

Business, Leadership and Management Department
College of Arts and Sciences, Regent University

Dr. Joseph Bucci is an Associate Professor of Business, and Chair of the Business, Leadership and Management Department in the College of Arts and Sciences at Regent University. Dr. Bucci has over 20 years' experience in various Human Resources, Consulting and Training roles, including five years as Director of the Learning Department of a large corporation in Philadelphia, PA. He received his Doctor of Business Administration degree from Anderson University in Anderson, IN.

Dr. Bucci is currently in his eleventh year as an Associate Professor of Business and Chair of the Business, Leadership and Management Department in the College of Arts and Sciences at Regent University in Virginia Beach, VA. Dr. Bucci previously taught for 6 years in the Business, Accounting and Management Department at Geneva College in Western Pennsylvania. Dr Bucci is also an Ordained Minister with Vanguard Ministries.

Dr. Bucci has a blog for which he writes at www.rediscoveringredemption.com. Dr. Bucci also promotes redemptive managerial behavior following a number of news feeds to his followers using his Twitter account @ Redemption. He has presented an extensive number papers on redemptive leadership behaviors and other research on the influence of faith on managerial decision-making at various conferences. His research has been published in the proceedings of the Christian Business Faculty Association.

His first book, "Redemptive Leadership: Offering Second Chances as a Value-Added Management Practice" was published by Palgrave MacMillan in 2016.

Education

- Anderson University, Anderson, IN
- Doctor of Business Administration, concentration Management–July 2011
- West Chester University, West Chester, PA
- Master of Business Administration, December 2000–GPA 3.80
- William Paterson University, Wayne, NJ
- Master of Education, May 1981–GPA 3.30
- Bachelor of Arts: Political Science, May 1979–GPA 3.73
- Berean University, Springfield, MO
- Ministerial Diploma, June 1986–GPA 4.00

Association Memberships:

- Past Member, American Society for Training & Development (ASTD)
- Past Member, Society of Human Resources Management (SHRM)
- Member, Christian Business Faculty Association
- Ordained Minister, Vanguard Ministries

Honors and Awards

- Chancellor's Award for Excellence, received May 2017
- The Dean's Award for Teaching Excellence, received May 2016
- Presidential Citation, CARDONE Industries (Highest award given by organization).
- Achieved Advanced Toastmaster status (Bronze level), Toastmasters International
- Permanent Teacher Certification, State of New Jersey
- Certified Trainer: Situational Leadership (SLII), Leadership Training for Supervisors (LTS), The Ken Blanchard Companies

Selected Papers and Book Chapters Presented or Published

Bucci, J.J., & Lewis, P. (2021). Servant Leadership grounded in redemption: The example of Jesus serving others by "redemptive actions." In: Dhiman, S. (Ed.) *The Palgrave Handbook of Servant Leadership.* Cham, Switzerland: Palgrave Macmillan. Chapters available for download as of Spring 2022.

Bucci, J.J. (2021, April). Revising Entrepreneurial Instruction to Consider the Impact of Devastating Failure on the Businessperson's Future Endeavors. To be published in the anthology entitled, *Handbook of Entrepreneurship and Small Business Management*, **estimated target date Fall 2021.**

Bucci, J.J. (2020, January 11). Renewing the Soul: A Workplace Wellness Strategy Grounded in Redemption. In: Dhiman, S. (Ed.) *The Palgrave Handbook of Workplace Well-Being.* Cham, Switzerland: Palgrave Macmillan. Chapters available for download as of January 2020 - https://link.springer.com/referenceworkentry/10.1007/978-3-030-02470-3_23-1.

Bucci, J.J. (2019, November). *Leading others into Redemption.* Published in Renew: Operation Mobilization's Leadership Journal, Volume 3.4, November 2019.

Bucci, J.J. (2018). *Kingdom Entrepreneurship: Obeying the God Who Makes Things Grow.* Approved for poster presentation at the Christian Business Faculty Association (CBFA) Annual meeting at Covenant College, Chattanooga, TN in October 2018.

Bucci, J.J. (2018). Change Management: Considering a Peniel Approach for Managing Change In Organizations. In: **Dhiman, S.; Roberts, G.; & Crossman,** J. (Eds.) *Handbook of Workplace Spirituality and Fulfillment.* Cham, Switzerland: Palgrave Macmillan. Chapters available for download as of January 2018 - https://www.palgrave.com/us/book/9783319621623.

Bucci, J.J. (2017). *Revising Entrepreneurial Instruction to Consider the Impact of Devastating Failure on the Businessperson's Future Endeavors.* Approved for poster presentation at the Christian Business Faculty Association (CBFA) Annual meeting at Point Loma Nazarene University, San Diego, CA October 2017.

Presented a paper entitled, "*Revisiting the pedagogy for teaching entrepreneurship: The impact of devastating failure and the support of faith*" at the first annual College of Arts & Sciences Faculty-Student Research Conference, April 2017.

Bucci, J.J. (2016). *Redemptive Leadership: Offering Second Chances as a Value-Added Management Practice*. New York: Palgrave Macmillan.

Bucci, J.J., & Lewis, P. (2016). The Case for Inclusion of Redemptive Managerial Dimensions in Servant Leadership Theory. *Journal of Biblical Integration in Business 19*(1), 444-453. Retrieved from http://cbfa-jbib.org/index.php/jbib/article/view/444/453.

Bucci, J.J. (2014). *People Matters: Aligning Company Values and Expressions of Faith*. Published in the August 2014 newsletter of the Christian Business Chamber of Hampton Roads. Retrieved August 14, 2014, from http://www.chamberorganizer.com/cbcgate/v_newsletters/article_247988693.htm.

Bucci, J.J. (2014). The Case for Inclusion of Redemptive Managerial Dimensions in Servant Leadership Theory. Research Paper submitted to Christian Business Faculty Association (CBFA) for its annual meeting, 2014. Presented at the Christian Business Faculty Association Annual Conference 2014. Awarded "Best of Conference Award."

Bucci, J.J. (2014). Talent Acquisition: Developing Untapped Talent Utilizing Redemptive Manager Behaviors." Research Paper submitted to Christian Business Faculty Association (CBFA) presented at the Christian Business Faculty Association Annual Conference 2014.

"Manager Tendencies to Offer Second-Chance Opportunities: Follow-Up Research Comparing Faith-Oriented Managers with a General Manager Population." Presented at the Christian Business Faculty Association Annual Conference 2013.

"Evidence of Redemptive Manager Behaviors in Successfully Reinstating Terminated Workers" Published Doctoral Dissertation 2011. A summary of this dissertation was presented at the Christian Business Faculty Association Annual Conference 2012

Contributed two topical devotionals which were published as a part of a compilation edition, "*Solomon Was a Businessperson*." This book was published in the fall of 2008.

"An Examination of Redemptive Manager Behaviors in Reinstating Terminated Workers: An Organizational Case Study" presented at the Christian Business Faculty Association Annual Conference 2011. Awarded "Best of Conference Award."

Excellence in College Teaching: Entrepreneurship and Ethics Courses." Programs presented at the Christian Business Faculty Association Annual Conference 2009.

"Faith Influenced Managers and Terminal Worker Behavior." Presented at the Christian Business Faculty Association Annual Conference 2008.

"A Theology of Business: Leading like Jesus in the Workplace." Program presented at the monthly meeting of Leaders Serving Beaver County, Beaver, PA, April 2008.

"Empowering Business Students to Create Their Own Ethical Decision-Making Model." Presented at the Christian Business Faculty Association Annual Conference 2007.

See more at: https://www.regent.edu/faculty/d-b-a-joseph-j-bucci/.

You can reach Dr. Joseph J. Bucci via his contact information below:

Email: Joe@JosephJBucci.com

Website: www.JosephJBucci.com

Mailing Address: Joseph J. Bucci, DBA

c/o Regent University
1000 Regent University Drive
Virginia Beach VA 23464

Office Phone: (757) 352-4553

CPSIA information can be obtained
at www.ICGtesting.com
Printed in the USA
LVHW021236210523
747602LV00007B/314

9 781735 748337